# Phras

# and

# Idioms

## A Practical Guide
## to American English
## Expressions

Richard A. Spears, Ph.D.

New York  Chicago  San Francisco  Lisbon  London  Madrid  Mexico City
Milan  New Delhi  San Juan  Seoul  Singapore  Sydney  Toronto

The *McGraw-Hill* Companies

**Library of Congress Cataloging-in-Publication Data**

Spears, Richard A.
  Phrases and idioms : a practical guide to American English expressions /
Richard A. Spears.
      p.    cm. — (NTC reference)
  Includes index.
  ISBN 0-8442-0342-4
      1. English language—Terms and phrases.    2. English language—Idioms.
  3. Americanisms.    I. Title.    II. Series.
  PE1689.S73    1998
  423'.1—dc21                                                98-05735
                                                                CIP

15 16 17 18 19 20 21 22 23 24 25  QVS/QVS 1 5

ISBN 978-0-8442-0342-3
MHID    0-8442-0342-4

Cover design by Nick Panos
Interior design by Terry Stone

McGraw-Hill books are available at special quantity discounts to use as
premiums and sales promotions or for use in corporate training programs. To
contact a representative, please visit the Contact Us pages at
www.mhprofessional.com.

This book is printed on acid-free paper.

# Contents

# To the User

All languages have phrases and sentences that cannot be understood literally. Even if you know all the words in a phrase and understand all the grammar of the phrase completely, the meaning may still be confusing. Many proverbs, informal phrases, and common sayings offer this kind of problem. A phrase or sentence of this type is said to be idiomatic. This dictionary is a collection of basic and useful idiomatic phrases that occur frequently in standard American English.

The dictionary is designed for easy use by lifelong speakers of English as well as by those who are new to the language. Many special features, including sample sentences and dialogues that show the use of each phrase in context, make this dictionary uniquely effective for language learners.

# How to Use
# This Dictionary

First, try looking up the complete phrase in the dictionary. The entries are in absolute alphabetical order—that is, phrases are alphabetized letter by letter, disregarding spaces, hyphens, and punctuation—except that if the first word is an article (*a, an,* or *the*), the article is not counted. This means that **a bull in a china shop** will be found under the letter *B*. Entry phrases are never inverted or reordered; for example, **in full swing** is listed under **in**, not as **full swing, in** or **swing, in full**.

In entry phrases and definitions that refer to one or more persons or things, the word *someone* or *one* stands for persons, and *something* stands for things.

If you do not find the phrase you want, or if you cannot decide exactly what the phrase is, look up any of its major words in the Phrase-Finder Index, which begins on page 231. There you will find listed, under the key word you have looked up, all the phrases in the dictionary that contain that word. Pick out the phrase you want, and look it up in the main body of the dictionary.

# Terms and Symbols

□ (a box) marks the beginning of an example.

Ⓣ (a box containing a T) marks the beginning of an example in which the word order is different from that used in the entry head.

ALSO: introduces additional forms within an entry that are related to the main entry head.

AND indicates that an entry head has variant forms that are the same as, or similar to, the entry head in meaning. One or more variant forms may be preceded by AND.

**cliché** is a phrase that is overused and sounds trite.

**entry head** is the first word or phrase, in boldface type, of an entry; the word or phrase that the definition explains.

**see** means to turn to the entry head indicated.

**see also** means to consult the entry indicated, where you will find additional information or expressions similar in form or meaning to the entry head where the "see also" instruction appeared.

**see under** means to search within the text of the entry indicated for a phrase that is in boldface type and is introduced by ALSO.

**according to Hoyle** according to the rules; in keeping with the way it is normally done. (Refers to the rules for playing games. Edmond Hoyle wrote a book about games. This expression is usually used for something other than games.) □ *That's wrong. According to Hoyle, this is the way to do it.* □ *The carpenter said, "This is the way to drive a nail, according to Hoyle."*

**Achilles' heel** a weak point or fault in someone or something otherwise perfect or excellent. (From the Greek hero Achilles, who had only one vulnerable part of his body, his heel. According to the legend, his mother had held him by the heel and dipped him in the River Styx to make him invulnerable.) □ *He was very brave, but fear of spiders was his Achilles' heel.* □ *Bill is an excellent manager, but his Achilles' heel is that he trusts people too much. His employees take advantage of him.*

the **acid test** a final test whose findings are beyond doubt or dispute. □ *Her new husband seems generous, but the acid test will be whether he lets her mother stay with them.* □ *The mayor isn't very popular just now, but the acid test will be whether he gets reelected next year.*

**act high-and-mighty** to act proud and powerful; to act haughty. □ *Why does the doctor always have to act so high-and-mighty?* □ *If Sally stopped acting high-and-mighty, she'd have more friends.*

**Actions speak louder than words.** a proverb meaning that it is better to do something about a problem than just talk about it. □ *Mary kept promising to get a job. John finally looked her in the eye and said, "Actions speak louder than words!"* □ *After listening to the senator promising to cut federal spending, Ann wrote a simple note saying, "Actions speak louder than words."*

**act of God** an occurrence (usually an accident) for which no human is responsible; an act of nature such as a storm, an earthquake, or a windstorm. □ *My insurance company wouldn't pay for the damage* because it was an act of God. □ *The thief tried to convince the judge that the diamonds were in his pocket due to an act of God.*

**act one's age** to behave more maturely; to act as grown up as one really is. (This is frequently said to a child or a teenager.) □ *Come on, John, act your age. Stop throwing rocks.* □ *Mary! Stop picking on your little brother. Act your age!*

**add fuel to the fire** AND **add fuel to the flame** to make a problem worse; to say or do something that makes a bad situation worse; to make an angry person get even more angry. □ *To spank a crying child just adds fuel to the fire.* □ *Bill was shouting angrily, and Bob tried to get him to stop by laughing at him. Of course, that was just adding fuel to the flame.*

**add fuel to the flame** See add fuel to the fire.

**add insult to injury** to make a bad situation worse; to hurt the feelings of a person who has already been hurt. (A cliché.) □ *First, the basement flooded, and then, to add insult to injury, a pipe burst in the kitchen.* □ *My car barely started this morning, and to add insult to injury, I got a flat tire in the driveway.*

**afraid of one's own shadow** easily frightened; always frightened, timid, or suspicious. □ *After Tom was robbed, he was even afraid of his own shadow.* □ *Jane has always been a shy child. She has been afraid of her own shadow since she was three.*

**against the clock** in a race with time; in a great hurry to get something done before a particular time. □ *Don't bother me. I'm working against the clock to finish this project by noon.* □ *In a race against the clock, they rushed the special medicine to the hospital.*

**ahead of one's time** having ideas or attitudes that are too advanced to be acceptable to or appreciated by the society in which one is living. □ *People buy that artist's work now, but his paintings were laughed at when he was alive. He was ahead of his time.* □ *Mary's grandmother was ahead of her time in wanting to study medicine. Women were expected to stay at home.*

**air one's dirty linen in public** to discuss private or embarrassing matters in public, especially when quarreling. (This *linen* refers to problems as if they were sheets and tablecloths or other soiled cloth. See also wash one's dirty linen in public.) □ *John's mother had asked him repeatedly not to air the family's dirty linen in public.* □ *Mr. and Mrs. Johnson are arguing again. Why must they always air their dirty linen in public?*

**all in a day's work** part of what is expected; typical or normal. □ *I don't particularly like to cook, but it's all in a day's work.* □ *Putting up with rude customers isn't pleasant, but it's all in a day's work.*

**all joking aside** being serious for a moment; in all seriousness. □ *I know I laugh at him, but all joking aside, he's a very clever scientist.* □ *I know I threatened to leave and go round the world, but all joking aside, I do need a vacation.*

**all over but the shouting** decided and concluded; finished except for a celebration. (An elaboration of *all over*, which means "finished.") □ *The last goal was made just as the final whistle sounded. Tom said, "Well, it's all over but the shouting." □ John worked hard in college and graduated last month. When he got his diploma, he said, "It's all over but the shouting."*

**All roads lead to Rome.** a proverb meaning that there are many different routes to the same goal. □ *Mary was criticizing the way Jane was planting the flowers. John said, "Never mind, Mary, all roads lead to Rome." □ Some people learn by doing. Others have to be taught. In the long run, all roads lead to Rome.*

**all skin and bones** See nothing but skin and bones.

**All's well that ends well.** a proverb meaning that an event that has a good ending is good even if some things went wrong along the way. (This is the name of a play by Shakespeare. It is now used as a cliché.) □ *I'm glad you finally got here, even though your car had a flat tire on the way. Oh, well. All's well that ends well. □ The groom was late for the wedding, but everything worked out all right. All's well that ends well.*

**All that glitters is not gold.** a proverb meaning that many attractive and alluring things actually have little or no value. □ *The used car looked fine but didn't run well at all. "Ah, yes," thought Bill, "all that glitters is not gold." □ When Mary was disappointed because the handsome man had not noticed her, Jane reminded her, "All that glitters is not gold."*

**all thumbs** very awkward and clumsy, especially with one's hands. (It implies that one's hands have only thumbs.) □ *Poor Bob can't play the piano at all. He's all thumbs. □ Mary is all thumbs when it comes to sewing.*

**all walks of life** all social, economic, and ethnic groups. (Does not occur in the singular or without *all*.) □ *We saw people there from all* *walks of life.* □ *The people who came to the art exhibit represented all walks of life.*

**All work and no play makes Jack a dull boy.** a proverb meaning that one should have recreation as well as work. (*Jack* does not refer to anyone in particular, and the phrase can be used for persons of either sex.) □ *Stop reading that book, and go out and play! All work and no play makes Jack a dull boy.* □ *The doctor told Mr. Jones to stop working on weekends and start playing golf, because all work and no play makes Jack a dull boy.*

**any port in a storm** a phrase indicating that when one is having trouble, one must accept any way out, whether one likes the solution or not. □ *I didn't want to live with my parents, but it was a case of any port in a storm. I couldn't find an apartment.* □ *He hates his new job, but it's better than having no job at all. Any port in a storm, you know.*

the **apple of someone's eye** someone's favorite person or thing; a boyfriend or a girlfriend; a person or a thing that someone wants. (A person or a thing that has caught someone's eye or attracted someone's attention.) □ *Tom is the apple of Mary's eye. She thinks he's great.* □ *John's new car is the apple of his eye.*

**armed to the teeth** heavily armed with deadly weapons. (As if all types of armaments were used, up to and including weapons held in one's teeth.) □ *The bank robber was armed to the teeth when he was caught.* □ *There are too many guns around. The entire country is armed to the teeth.*

**arm-in-arm** [of persons] linked or hooked together by the arms. □ *The two lovers walked arm-in-arm down the street.* □ *Arm-in-arm, the line of dancers kicked high, and the audience roared its approval.*

**as a duck takes to water** easily and naturally. (Refers to baby ducks, who seem to be able to swim the first time they enter the water.) □ *She took to singing, just as a duck takes to water.* □ *The baby adapted to bottle-feeding as a duck takes to water.*

**as an aside** as a comment; as a comment that is not supposed to be heard by everyone. □ *At the wedding, Tom said as an aside, "The bride doesn't look well."* □ *At the ballet, Billy said as an aside to his mother, "I hope the dancers fall off the stage!"*

**(as) bad as all that** as bad as reported; as bad as it seems. (Usually expressed in the negative.) ☐ *Come on! Nothing could be as bad as all that.* ☐ *Stop crying. It can't be bad as all that.*

**(as) blind as a bat** with imperfect sight; blind. (Typically, bats are not blind, but the phrase survives because of the alliteration.) ☐ *My grandmother is as blind as a bat.* ☐ *I'm getting blind as a bat. I can hardly read this page.*

**(as) busy as a beaver** AND **(as) busy as a bee** very busy. (Survives because of the alliteration.) ☐ *I don't have time to talk to you. I'm as busy as a beaver.* ☐ *You don't look busy as a beaver to me.* ☐ *Whenever there is a holiday, we are all as busy as bees.*

**(as) busy as a bee** See (as) busy as a beaver.

**(as) busy as Grand Central Station** very busy; crowded with customers or other people. (Grand Central Station is a large railroad station in New York City.) ☐ *This house is as busy as Grand Central Station.* ☐ *When the tourist season starts, this hotel is busy as Grand Central Station.*

**(as) clear as mud** not understandable. (Informal or joking.) ☐ *Your directions are as clear as mud.* ☐ *This doesn't make sense. It's clear as mud.*

**(as) comfortable as an old shoe** very comfortable; very comforting and familiar. (Refers to a shoe that has been worn awhile and is comfortable.) ☐ *This old house is fine. It's as comfortable as an old shoe.* ☐ *That's a great tradition—comfortable as an old shoe.*

**(as) cool as a cucumber** calm and not agitated; with one's wits about one. (Cucumbers are not necessarily cool, but the phrase survives because of the alliteration.) ☐ *The captain remained as cool as a cucumber as the passengers boarded the lifeboats.* ☐ *During the fire the homeowner was cool as a cucumber.*

**(as) crazy as a loon** very silly; completely insane. (A loon is a waterfowl whose call sounds like a silly laugh.) ☐ *If you think you can get away with that, you're as crazy as a loon.* ☐ *Poor old John is crazy as a loon.*

**(as) dead as a dodo** dead; obsolete; outmoded; no longer in existence. (The dodo, an ancient bird of Mauritius, is extinct. The phrase survives because of the alliteration.) ☐ *Yes, the cruel dictatorship is really dead—as dead as a dodo.* ☐ *That silly old idea is dead as a dodo.*

**(as) dead as a doornail** dead; totally lifeless. (Survives because of the alliteration.) □ *This fish is as dead as a doornail.* □ *John kept twisting the chicken's neck even though it was dead as a doornail.*

**(as) different as night and day** completely different. □ *Although Bobby and Billy are twins, they are as different as night and day.* □ *Birds and bats appear to be similar, but they are different as night and day.*

**(as) easy as (apple) pie** very easy. (Making pies is assumed to be easy.) □ *Mountain climbing is as easy as pie.* □ *Making a simple dress out of cotton cloth is easy as apple pie.*

**(as) easy as duck soup** very easy; requiring no effort. (When a duck is cooked, it releases a lot of fat and juices, making a "soup" without effort.) □ *Finding your way to the shopping center is easy as duck soup.* □ *Passing the test was as easy as duck soup for the clever child.*

**as far as it goes** as much as something does, covers, or accomplishes. (Usually said of something that is inadequate.) □ *Your plan is fine as far as it goes. It doesn't seem to take care of everything, though.* □ *As far as it goes, this law is a good one. It should require stiffer penalties, however.*

**(as) fast as one's feet would carry one** as fast as possible. □ *I left there as fast as my feet would carry me.* □ *Billy ran home fast as his feet would carry him.*

**(as) fit as a fiddle** healthy and physically fit. (Survives because of the alliteration.) □ *Mary is as fit as a fiddle.* □ *Tom used to be fit as a fiddle. Look at him now!*

**(as) flat as a pancake** very flat. □ *The punctured tire was as flat as a pancake.* □ *Bobby squashed the bug flat as a pancake.*

**(as) free as a bird** carefree; completely free. □ *Jane is always happy and free as a bird.* □ *The convict escaped from jail and was as free as a bird for two days.* □ *In the summer I feel free as a bird.*

**(as) full as a tick** AND **(as) tight as a tick** very full of food or drink. (Refers to a tick that has filled itself full of blood.) □ *Little Billy ate and ate until he was as full as a tick.* □ *Our cat drank the cream until he became full as a tick.*

**(as) funny as a crutch** not funny at all. □ *Your trick was about as funny as a crutch. Nobody laughed.* □ *The well-dressed lady slipped and fell in the gutter, which was funny as a crutch.*

**as good as done** the same as being done; almost done. (Many different past participles can replace *done* in this phrase: *dead, finished, painted, typed,* etc.) ☐ *This job is as good as done. It'll just take another second.* ☐ *Yes, sir, if you hire me to paint your house, it's as good as painted.* ☐ *When I hand my secretary a letter to be typed, I know that it's as good as typed right then and there.*

**(as) good as gold** genuine; authentic. (A cliché. Survives because of the alliteration.) ☐ *Mary's promise is as good as gold.* ☐ *Yes, this antique vase is genuine—good as gold.*

**(as) happy as a clam** happy and content. (Note the variations in the examples.) ☐ *Tom sat there smiling, as happy as a clam.* ☐ *There they all sat, eating corn on the cob and looking happy as clams.*

**(as) happy as a lark** visibly happy and cheerful. (Note the variations in the examples.) ☐ *Sally walked along whistling, as happy as a lark.* ☐ *The children danced and sang, happy as larks.*

**(as) hard as nails** very hard; cold and cruel. (Refers to the nails that are used with a hammer.) ☐ *The old loaf of bread was dried out and became as hard as nails.* ☐ *Ann was unpleasant and hard as nails.*

**(as) high as a kite** AND **(as) high as the sky 1.** very high. ☐ *The tree grew as high as the sky.* ☐ *Our pet bird got outside and flew up high as a kite.* **2.** drunk or drugged. ☐ *Bill drank beer until he got as high as a kite.* ☐ *The thieves were high as the sky on drugs.*

**(as) high as the sky** See (as) high as a kite.

**(as) hungry as a bear** very hungry. ☐ *I'm as hungry as a bear. I could eat anything!* ☐ *Whenever I jog, I get hungry as a bear.*

**(as) innocent as a lamb** guiltless; naive. (A cliché.) ☐ *"Hey! You can't throw me in jail," cried the robber. "I'm innocent as a lamb."* ☐ *Look at the baby, as innocent as a lamb.*

**as it were** as one might say; in a way. (Sometimes used to qualify an assertion that may not sound reasonable or that is technically not true.) ☐ *John likes to tell everyone in his household what to do. He's the king of the castle, as it were.* ☐ *Bill has a new job, as it were. He volunteers at the local school.*

**ask for the moon** to ask for too much; to make great demands; to ask for something that is difficult or impossible to obtain. ☐ *When* *you're trying to get a job, it's unwise to ask for the moon.* □ *Please lend me the money. I'm not asking for the moon!*

**ask for trouble** to do or say something that will cause trouble. □ *Stop talking to me that way, John. You're just asking for trouble.* □ *Anybody who threatens a police officer is just asking for trouble.*

**asleep at the switch** not attending to one's job; failing to do one's duty at the proper time. (Need not have anything to do with an actual electrical or mechanical switch.) □ *The guard was asleep at the switch when the robber broke in.* □ *If I hadn't been asleep at the switch, I'd have seen the stolen car.*

**(as) light as a feather** of little weight. □ *Sally dieted until she was as light as a feather.* □ *Of course I can lift the box. It's light as a feather.*

**(as) likely as not** probably; with an even chance either way. □ *He will as likely as not arrive without warning.* □ *Likely as not, the game will be canceled.*

**as luck would have it** by good or bad luck; as it turned out; by chance. □ *As luck would have it, we had a flat tire.* □ *As luck would have it, the check came in the mail today.*

**(as) mad as a hatter** **1.** crazy. (Often associated with a character called the Mad Hatter in Lewis Carroll's *Alice's Adventures in Wonderland*, though the phrase is actually older.) □ *Poor old John is as mad as a hatter.* □ *All these screaming children are driving me mad as a hatter.* **2.** angry. (This is a misunderstanding of *mad* in the first sense.) □ *You make me so angry! I'm as mad as a hatter.* □ *John can't control his temper. He's always mad as a hatter.*

**(as) mad as a hornet** angry. (Hornets are known to attack aggressively, as if they were very angry.) □ *You make me so angry. I'm as mad as a hornet.* □ *Jane can get mad as a hornet when somebody criticizes her.*

**(as) mad as a March hare** crazy. (Often associated with a character in Lewis Carroll's *Alice's Adventures in Wonderland*, though the phrase is actually older.) □ *Sally is getting as mad as a March hare.* □ *My Uncle Bill is mad as a March hare.*

**(as) mad as a wet hen** angry. (One can assume that a fussy hen would become angry if wet.) □ *Bob was screaming and shouting—as mad as a wet hen.* □ *What you said made Mary mad as a wet hen.*

**as one** as if a group were one person. (Especially with *act, move,* or *speak.*) □ *All the dancers moved as one.* □ *The chorus spoke as one.*

**(as) plain as day 1.** very plain and simple. □ *Although his face was as plain as day, his smile made him look interesting and friendly.* □ *Our house is plain as day, but it's comfortable.* **2.** clear and understandable. (As transparent as daylight.) □ *The lecture was as plain as day. No one had to ask questions.* □ *His statement was plain as day.*

**(as) plain as the nose on one's face** obvious; clearly evident. □ *What do you mean you don't understand? It's as plain as the nose on your face.* □ *Your guilt is plain as the nose on your face.*

**(as) poor as a church mouse** very poor. (A cliché. Assuming that those associated with churches are impoverished, the lowly mouse would be the poorest creature in a church. Note the variations in the examples.) □ *My aunt is as poor as a church mouse.* □ *The Browns are poor as church mice.*

**(as) pretty as a picture** very pretty. (A cliché. Survives because of the alliteration.) □ *Sweet little Mary is as pretty as a picture.* □ *Their new house is pretty as a picture.*

**(as) proud as a peacock** very proud; haughty. (A cliché. Refers to the beautiful tail feathers that the peacock displays. Survives because of the alliteration.) □ *John is so arrogant. He's as proud as a peacock.* □ *The new father was proud as a peacock.*

**(as) quick as a wink** very quickly. (A cliché. Refers to the wink of an eye.) □ *As quick as a wink, the thief took the lady's purse.* □ *I'll finish this work quick as a wink.*

**(as) quiet as a mouse** very quiet; shy and silent. (Often used with children.) □ *Don't yell; whisper. Be as quiet as a mouse.* □ *Mary hardly ever says anything. She's quiet as a mouse.*

**(as) regular as clockwork** dependably regular. □ *She comes into this store every day, as regular as clockwork.* □ *Our tulips come up every year, regular as clockwork.*

**(as) scarce as hens' teeth** AND **scarcer than hens' teeth** very scarce or nonexistent. (A cliché. Chickens don't have teeth.) □ *I've never seen one of those. They're as scarce as hens' teeth.* □ *I was told that the part needed for my car is scarcer than hens' teeth, and it would take a long time to find one.*

**(as) sick as a dog** very sick; sick and vomiting. (Refers to the agonized retching of a dog.) □ *We've never been so ill. We were all sick as dogs.* □ *Sally was as sick as a dog and couldn't go to the party.*

**(as) slippery as an eel** devious; undependable. (Also used literally.) □ *Tom can't be trusted. He's as slippery as an eel.* □ *It's hard to catch Joe in his office because he's slippery as an eel.*

**(as) smart as a fox** smart and clever. □ *My nephew is as smart as a fox.* □ *You have to be smart as a fox to outwit me.*

**(as) snug as a bug in a rug** cozy and snug. (The kind of thing said when putting a child to bed. Survives because of the rhyme.) □ *Let's pull up the covers. There you are, Bobby, as snug as a bug in a rug.* □ *What a lovely little house! I know I'll be snug as a bug in a rug.*

**(as) sober as a judge** (A cliché.) **1.** very formal, somber, or stuffy. □ *You certainly look gloomy, Bill. You're sober as a judge.* □ *Tom's as sober as a judge. I think he's angry.* **2.** not drunk; alert and completely sober. (This is a misunderstanding of the first sense.) □ *John's drunk? No, he's as sober as a judge.* □ *You should be sober as a judge when you drive a car.*

**(as) soft as a baby's bottom** very soft and smooth to the touch. □ *This cloth is as soft as a baby's bottom.* □ *No, Bob doesn't shave yet. His face is soft as a baby's bottom.*

**as soon as possible** at the earliest time. □ *I'm leaving now. I'll be there as soon as possible.* □ *Please pay me as soon as possible.*

**(as) strong as an ox** very strong. □ *Tom lifts weights and is as strong as an ox.* □ *Now that Ann has recovered from her illness, she's strong as an ox.*

**(as) stubborn as a mule** very stubborn. □ *My husband is as stubborn as a mule.* □ *Our cat is stubborn as a mule.*

**as the crow flies** straight across the land, as opposed to distances measured on a road, river, etc. (This assumes that crows fly in a straight line.) □ *It's twenty miles to town on the highway, but only ten miles as the crow flies.* □ *Our house is only a few miles from the lake as the crow flies.*

**(as) thick as pea soup** very thick. (Usually used in reference to fog.) □ *This fog is as thick as pea soup.* □ *Wow, this coffee is strong! It's thick as pea soup.*

**(as) thick as thieves** very close-knit; friendly; allied. (A cliché. Survives because of the alliteration.) □ *Mary, Tom, and Sally are as thick as thieves. They go everywhere together.* □ *Those two families are thick as thieves.*

**(as) tight as a tick** See **(as) full as a tick.**

**(as) tight as Dick's hatband** very tight. (Very old.) □ *I've got to lose some weight. My belt is as tight as Dick's hatband.* □ *This window is stuck tight as Dick's hatband.*

**(as) weak as a kitten** weak; weak and sickly. (Refers to a newborn kitten.) □ *John is as weak as a kitten because he doesn't eat well.* □ *Oh! Suddenly I feel weak as a kitten.*

**(as) white as the driven snow** very white. (A cliché.) □ *I like my bedsheets to be as white as the driven snow.* □ *We have a new kitten whose fur is white as the driven snow.*

**(as) wise as an owl** very wise. □ *Grandfather is as wise as an owl.* □ *My goal is to be wise as an owl.*

**at a premium** at a high price; priced high because of something special. □ *Sally bought the shoes at a premium because they were of very high quality.* □ *This model of car is selling at a premium because so many people want to buy it.*

**at a snail's pace** very slowly. □ *When you watch a clock, time seems to move at a snail's pace.* □ *You always eat at a snail's pace. I'm tired of waiting for you.*

**at a stretch** continuously; without stopping. □ *We all had to do eight hours of duty at a stretch.* □ *The baby doesn't sleep for more than three hours at a stretch.*

**at death's door** near death. (Euphemistic and literary.) □ *I was so ill that I was at death's door.* □ *The family dog was at death's door for three days, and then it finally died.*

**at half-mast** halfway up or down. (Primarily refers to flags. Can be used for things other than flags as a joke.) □ *The flag was flying at half-mast because the general had died.* □ *The little boy ran out of the house with his pants at half-mast.*

**at loggerheads** in opposition; at an impasse; in a quarrel. □ *Mr. and Mrs. Franklin have been at loggerheads for years.* □ *The two political parties were at loggerheads during the entire legislative session.*

**at loose ends** restless and unsettled; unemployed. □ *Just before school starts, all the children are at loose ends.* □ *Jane has been at loose ends ever since she lost her job.*

**at one fell swoop** AND **in one fell swoop** in a single incident; as a single event. (This phrase preserves the old word *fell*, meaning "terrible" or "deadly." Now a cliché, sometimes with humorous overtones.) □ *The party guests ate up all the snacks at one fell swoop.* □ *When the stock market crashed, many large fortunes were wiped out in one fell swoop.*

**at one's wit's end** at the limits of one's mental resources. □ *I'm at my wit's end with this problem. I cannot figure it out.* □ *Tom could do no more. He was at his wit's end.*

**at sea (about something)** confused; lost and bewildered. (As if one were lost at sea.) □ *Mary is all at sea about getting married.* □ *When it comes to higher math, John is totally at sea.*

**at sixes and sevens** disorderly; lost and bewildered. (Borrowed from gambling with dice.) □ *Mrs. Smith is at sixes and sevens since the death of her husband.* □ *Bill is always at sixes and sevens when he's home by himself.*

**at someone's doorstep** AND **on someone's doorstep** in someone's care; as someone's responsibility. □ *Why do you always have to lay your problems at my doorstep?* □ *I shall put this issue on someone else's doorstep.* □ *I don't want it on my doorstep.*

**at the bottom of the ladder** at the lowest level of pay and status. □ *Most people start work at the bottom of the ladder.* □ *When Ann got fired, she had to start all over again at the bottom of the ladder.*

**at the drop of a hat** immediately and without urging. □ *John was always ready to go fishing at the drop of a hat.* □ *If you need help, just call on me. I can come at the drop of a hat.*

**at the eleventh hour** at the last possible moment. □ *She always turned her term papers in at the eleventh hour.* □ *The workers were about to go on strike, but at the eleventh hour they reached an agreement with the company.*

**at the end of one's rope** AND **at the end of one's tether** at the limits of one's endurance. □ *I'm at the end of my rope! I just can't go on this way!* □ *These kids are driving me out of my mind. I'm at the end of my tether.*

**at the end of one's tether** See at the end of one's rope.

**at the last minute** at the last possible chance. □ *Please don't make reservations at the last minute.* □ *Why do you ask all your questions at the last minute?*

**at the outside** at the very most. □ *The car repairs will cost $300 at the outside.* □ *I'll be there in three weeks at the outside.*

**at the top of one's lungs** See at the top of one's voice.

**at the top of one's voice** AND **at the top of one's lungs** with a very loud voice; as loudly as is possible to speak or yell. □ *Bill called to Mary at the top of his voice.* □ *How can I work when you're all talking at the top of your lungs?*

**at this stage (of the game)** at the current point in some event or situation; currently. □ *We'll have to wait and see. There isn't much we can do at this stage of the game.* □ *At this stage, we are better off not calling the doctor.*

**away from one's desk** not available for a telephone conversation; not available to be seen. (Sometimes said by the person who answers a telephone in an office. It means that the person whom the caller wants is not immediately available due to personal or business reasons. Typically, the person has gone to the restroom.) □ *I'm sorry, but Ann is away from her desk just now. Can you come back later?* □ *Tom is away from his desk, but if you leave your number, he will call you right back.*

**babe in the woods** a naive or innocent person; an inexperienced person. □ *Bill is a babe in the woods when it comes to dealing with plumbers.* □ *As a painter, Mary is fine, but she's a babe in the woods as a musician.*

**back in circulation 1.** [for something to be] available to the public again. (Said especially of things that are said to circulate, such as money, library books, and magazines.) □ *I've heard that gold coins are back in circulation in Europe.* □ *I would like to read* War and Peace. *Is it back in circulation, or is it still checked out?* **2.** [for a person to be] socially active again; dating again after a divorce or breakup with one's lover. □ *Now that Bill is a free man, he's back in circulation.* □ *Tom was in the hospital for a month, but now he's back in circulation.*

**back-to-back 1.** adjacent and touching backs. □ *They started the duel by standing back-to-back.* □ *Two people who stand back-to-back can manage to see in all directions.* **2.** following immediately. (Said of things or events. In this case, the events may be pictured as figuratively back-to-front.) □ *The doctor had appointments set up back-to-back all day long.* □ *I have three lecture courses back-to-back every day of the week.*

**back to the drawing board** [it is] time to start over again; [it is] time to plan something over again. (Refers to a drafting board, where buildings or machines are designed.) □ *It didn't work. Back to the drawing board.* □ *The committee rejected my proposal. Well, back to the drawing board.*

**back to the salt mines** time to return to work, school, or something else that might be unpleasant. (The phrase implies that the speaker is a slave who works in the salt mines.) □ *It's eight o'clock. Time to go to work! Back to the salt mines.* □ *School starts again in the fall, and then it's back to the salt mines.*

**bag and baggage** with one's luggage; with all one's possessions. □ *Sally showed up at our door bag and baggage one Sunday morning.* □ *All right, if you won't pay the rent, out with you, bag and baggage!*

**bag of tricks** a collection of special techniques or methods. □ *What have you got in your bag of tricks that could help me with this problem?* □ *Here comes Mother with her bag of tricks. I'm sure she can help us.*

**ball someone or something up** to mess someone or something up; to make someone or something confused or muddled. □ *I hope I don't ball it up again!* ⊤ *You ball up another contract, and you are finished!*

**bang one's head against a brick wall** See beat one's head against the wall.

**bank on something** to count on something; to rely on something. (To trust in something the way one might trust in a bank.) □ *The weather service said it wouldn't rain, but I wouldn't bank on it.* □ *My word is to be trusted. You can bank on it.*

**bark up the wrong tree** to make the wrong choice; to ask the wrong person; to follow the wrong course. (Refers to a hunting dog that has chased a creature up a tree but stands barking or howling at the wrong tree.) □ *If you think I'm the guilty person, you're barking up the wrong tree.* □ *The baseball players blamed their bad record on the pitcher, but they were barking up the wrong tree.*

**be a copycat** to be a person who copies or mimics what someone else does. (Usually juvenile.) □ *Sally wore a pink dress just like Mary's. Mary called Sally a copycat.* □ *Bill is such a copycat. He bought a bike just like mine.*

**be a fan of someone** to be a follower of someone; to idolize someone. (This word *fan* is from *fanatic*, meaning a follower.) □ *My mother is still a fan of the Beatles.* □ *I'm a great fan of the mayor of the town.*

**be a marked man** to be in danger of harm by someone else. (Usually with males.) □ *Bob's a marked man. His tutor found out that he's missing lectures.* □ *Fred's a marked man, too. Jack is looking for him to get his money back from him.*

**beard the lion in his den** to face an adversary on the adversary's home ground. (To tease or threaten—as if grabbing the beard of—something frightening, such as a lion.) □ *I went to the bill collector's office to beard the lion in his den.* □ *He said he hadn't wanted to come to my home, but it was better to beard the lion in his den.*

**bear one's cross** AND **carry one's cross** to carry or bear one's burden; to endure one's difficulties. (This is a biblical theme. It is always used figuratively except in the biblical context.) □ *It's a very bad disease, but I'll bear my cross.* □ *I can't help you with it. You'll just have to carry your cross.*

**bear someone or something in mind** See keep someone or something in mind.

**bear the brunt (of something)** to withstand or endure the worst part or the strongest part of something, such as an attack. □ *I had to bear the brunt of her screaming and yelling.* □ *Why don't you talk with her the next time? I'm tired of bearing the brunt.*

**bear watching** to need watching; to deserve observation or monitoring. (This is the verb *to bear*.) □ *This problem will bear watching.* □ *This is a very serious disease, and it will bear watching for further developments.*

**beat about the bush** See beat around the bush.

**beat a dead horse** to continue fighting a battle that has been won; to continue to argue a point that is settled. (A phrase meaning that a dead horse will not run, no matter how hard it is beaten.) □ *Stop arguing! You have won your point. You are just beating a dead horse.* □ *Oh, be quiet. Stop beating a dead horse.*

**beat a path to someone's door** [for people] to come to someone in great numbers. (A phrase meaning that so many people wish to come and see you that they wear down a pathway leading to your door.) □ *I have a product so good that everyone is beating a path to my door.* □ *If you really become famous, people will beat a path to your door.*

**beat around the bush** AND **beat about the bush** to avoid answering a question; to stall; to waste time. □ *Stop beating around the bush and answer my question.* □ *Let's stop beating about the bush and discuss this matter.*

**be a thorn in someone's side** to be a constant bother or annoyance to someone. □ *This problem is a thorn in my side. I wish I had a solution to it.* □ *That neighbor was a thorn in my side for years, until he finally moved away.*

**beat one's head against the wall** AND **bang one's head against a brick wall** to waste one's time trying to accomplish something that is completely hopeless. □ *You're wasting your time trying to fix up this house. You're just beating your head against the wall.* □ *You're banging your head against a brick wall trying to get that dog to behave properly.*

16

**beat the gun** to manage to do something before the ending signal. (Originally from sports, referring to making a goal in the last seconds of a game.) □ *The ball beat the gun and dropped through the hoop just in time.* □ *Tom tried to beat the gun, but he was one second too slow.*

**Beauty is only skin deep.** a proverb meaning that looks are superficial. (Often implying that a beautiful person may not have a pleasing personality.) □ *BOB: Isn't Jane lovely? TOM: Yes, but beauty is only skin deep.* □ *I know that she looks gorgeous, but beauty is only skin deep.*

**be child's play** [for a task] to be easy to do; [for a task] to be effortless. □ *The exam was child's play to her.* □ *Finding the right street is child's play with a map.*

**been through the mill** been badly treated; exhausted. (Like grain that has been pulverized in a mill.) □ *This has been a rough day. I've really been through the mill.* □ *This old car is banged up, and it hardly runs. It's been through the mill.*

**before you can say Jack Robinson** almost immediately. (Often found in children's stories.) □ *And before you could say Jack Robinson, the bird flew away.* □ *I'll catch a plane and be there before you can say Jack Robinson.*

**be from Missouri** to require proof; to be skeptical; to have to be shown [something]. (This also has a longer form—*I'm from Missouri. Show me.*—and is related to the nickname of the state of Missouri, the Show Me State.) □ *You'll have to prove it to me. I'm from Missouri.* □ *She's from Missouri and has to be shown.*

**beggar description** to be impossible to describe well enough to give an accurate picture; to be impossible to do justice to in words. □ *Her cruelty to her child beggars description.* □ *The soprano's voice beggars description.*

**Beggars can't be choosers.** a proverb meaning that one should not criticize something one gets for free; if one asks or begs for something, one does not get a choice of things. □ *I don't like the old hat that you gave me, but beggars can't be choosers.* □ *It doesn't matter whether people like the free food or not. Beggars can't be choosers.*

**begin to see daylight** to begin to see the end of a long task. (As if facing dawn at the end of a long night of work.) □ *I've been working on my thesis for two years, and at last I'm beginning to see daylight.* □ *I've been so busy. Only in the last week have I begun to see daylight.*

**begin to see the light** to begin to understand (something). □ *My algebra class is hard for me, but I'm beginning to see the light.* □ *I was totally confused, but I began to see the light after your explanation.*

**be halfhearted (about someone or something)** to be unenthusiastic about someone or something. □ *Ann was halfhearted about the choice of Sally for president.* □ *She didn't look halfhearted to me. She looked enthusiastic.*

**believe it or not** one may choose to believe this or not believe it. (Used to indicate that something is true even though it may seem surprising or unlikely.) □ *Believe it or not, I just got home from work.* □ *I'm over fifty years old, believe it or not.*

**bend someone's ear** to talk to someone, perhaps annoyingly. □ *Tom is over there, bending Jane's ear about something.* □ *I'm sorry. I didn't mean to bend your ear for an hour.*

**be old hat** to be old-fashioned; to be outmoded. (Refers to anything—except a hat—that is out of style.) □ *That's a silly idea. It's old hat.* □ *Nobody does that anymore. That's just old hat.*

**be poles apart** to be very different; to be far from coming to an agreement. (These *poles* are the extreme points, like the North Pole and the South Pole of the earth.) □ *Mr. and Mrs. Jones don't get along well. They are poles apart.* □ *They'll never sign the contract because they are poles apart.*

**be putty in someone's hands** [for someone] to be easily influenced by someone else; excessively willing to do what someone else wishes. □ *Bob's wife is putty in his hands. She never thinks for herself.* □ *Jane is putty in her mother's hands. She always does exactly what her mother wants.*

**be the spit and image of someone** AND **be the spitting image of someone** to look very much like someone; to resemble someone very closely. □ *John is the spit and image of his father.* □ *I'm not the spit and image of anyone.* □ *At first, I thought you said I'm the spitting image of Mother.*

**be the spitting image of someone** See be the spit and image of someone.

**be the teacher's pet** to be the teacher's favorite student. (To be treated like a pet, such as a cat or a dog.) □ *Sally is the teacher's pet. She always gets special treatment.* □ *The other students don't like the teacher's pet.*

**between a rock and a hard place** AND **between the devil and the deep blue sea** in a very difficult position; facing a hard decision. □ *I couldn't make up my mind. I was caught between a rock and a hard place.* □ *He had a dilemma on his hands. He was clearly between the devil and the deep blue sea.*

**between the devil and the deep blue sea** See between a rock and a hard place.

**beyond one's depth 1.** [of someone] in water that is too deep; [of water] too deep for someone. (Literal.) □ *Sally swam out until she was beyond her depth.* □ *Jane swam out into deep water to get her little brother, even though it was beyond her depth, too.* **2.** [of someone] involved in something that is too difficult or advanced; [of something] beyond one's understanding or capabilities. □ *I'm beyond my depth in algebra class.* □ *Poor John was involved in a problem that was really beyond his depth.*

**beyond one's means** more than one can afford. □ *I'm sorry, but this house is beyond our means. Please show us a less expensive one.* □ *Mary wanted many things that were beyond her means.*

**beyond the pale** unacceptable; outlawed. □ *Your behavior is simply beyond the pale.* □ *Because of Tom's rudeness, he's considered beyond the pale and is never asked to parties anymore.*

**big frog in a small pond** to be a relatively important person in the midst of less important people. □ *I'd rather be a big frog in a small pond than the opposite.* □ *The trouble with Tom is that he's a big frog in a small pond. He needs more competition.*

**A bird in the hand is worth two in the bush.** a proverb meaning that something you already have is better than something you might get. □ *Bill has offered to buy my car for $3,000. Someone else might pay more, but Bill made a good offer, and a bird in the hand is worth two in the bush.* □ *I might be able to find a better coat at another store, but this one fits and looks fine, so I'll buy it. A bird in the hand is worth two in the bush.*

**the birds and the bees** human reproduction. (A euphemistic way of referring to human sex and reproduction.) □ *My father tried to teach* *me about the birds and the bees.* □ *He's twenty years old and doesn't understand about the birds and the bees.*

a **bird's-eye view 1.** a view seen from high above. (Refers to the height of a flying bird.) □ *We got a bird's-eye view of Chicago as the plane began its descent.* □ *From the top of the tower you get a splendid bird's-eye view of the village.* **2.** a brief survey of something; a hasty look at something. (Refers to the smallness of a bird's eye.) □ *The course provides a bird's-eye view of the works of Mozart, but it doesn't deal with them in enough detail for your purpose.* □ *All you need is a bird's-eye view of the events of World War II to pass the test.*

**Birds of a feather flock together.** a proverb meaning that people of the same type seem to attract one another and gather together. □ *Bob and Tom are just alike. They like each other's company because birds of a feather flock together.* □ *When Mary joined a club for redheaded people, she said, "Birds of a feather flock together."*

**bite off more than one can chew** to take (on) more than one can deal with; to be overconfident. (This is used literally for food and figuratively for other things, especially difficult projects.) □ *Billy, stop biting off more than you can chew. You're going to choke on your food some-day.* □ *Ann is exhausted again. She's always biting off more than she can chew.*

**bite one's nails** to be nervous or anxious; to bite one's nails from nervousness or anxiety. (Used both literally and figuratively.) □ *I spent all afternoon biting my nails, worrying about you.* □ *We've all been biting our nails from worry.*

**bite one's tongue** to struggle not to say something that one really wants to say. (Used literally only to refer to an accidental biting of one's tongue.) □ *I had to bite my tongue to keep from telling her what I really thought.* □ *I sat through that whole conversation biting my tongue.*

**bite the dust** to fall to defeat; to die. (Typically heard in movies about the U.S. western frontier.) □ *A bullet hit the sheriff in the chest, and he bit the dust.* □ *The team won several games before biting the dust in the final competition.*

**bite the hand that feeds one** to do harm to someone who does good things for one. (Refers to the act of a thankless dog.) □ *I'm your mother! How can you bite the hand that feeds you?* □ *She can hardly expect much when she bites the hand that feeds her.*

**black and blue** bruised; showing signs of having been physically harmed. □ *My knee is black and blue because I bumped into the side of my desk yesterday and hurt it.* □ *She was black and blue all over after falling out of the tree.*

**black sheep of the family** the worst member of the family. (A black sheep is an unwanted offspring in a herd of otherwise white sheep.) □ *Mary is the black sheep of the family. She's always in trouble with the police.* □ *He keeps making a nuisance of himself. What do you expect from the black sheep of the family?*

**blank check** freedom or permission to act as one wishes or thinks necessary. (From a signed bank check with the amount left blank.) □ *He's been given a blank check with regard to reorganizing the work force.* □ *The manager has been given no instructions about how to train the staff. He's just been given a blank check.*

the **blind leading the blind** having to do with a situation where people who don't know how to do something try to explain it to other people. □ *Tom doesn't know anything about cars, but he's trying to teach Sally how to change the oil. It's a case of the blind leading the blind.* □ *When I tried to show Mary how to use a computer, it was the blind leading the blind.*

**blow off steam** See let off steam.

**blow one's own horn** See toot one's own horn.

**blow someone's cover** to reveal someone's true identity or purpose. (Informal or slang.) □ *The spy was very careful not to blow her cover.* □ *I tried to disguise myself, but my dog recognized me and blew my cover.*

**blow something out of (all) proportion** See under out of (all) proportion.

**blow the whistle (on someone)** to report someone's wrongdoing to someone (such as the police) who can stop the wrongdoing. (As if one were blowing a police whistle.) □ *The citizens' group blew the whistle on the street gangs by calling the police.* □ *The gangs were getting very bad. It was definitely time to blow the whistle.* □ *An employee finally blew the whistle on the company's illegal practices.*

**blue blood** the blood (heredity) of a noble family; aristocratic ancestry. □ *The earl refuses to allow anyone who is not of blue blood to marry his son.* □ *Although Mary's family is poor, she has blue blood in her veins.*

**boggle someone's mind** to overwhelm someone; to mix up someone's thinking; to astound someone. □ *The size of the house boggles my mind.* □ *She said that his arrogance boggled her mind.*

**bone of contention** the subject or point of an argument; an unsettled point of disagreement. (Like a bone that dogs fight over.) □ *We've fought for so long that we've forgotten what the bone of contention is.* □ *The question of a fence between the houses has become quite a bone of contention.*

**born with a silver spoon in one's mouth** born with many advantages; born to a wealthy family; already showing the signs of great wealth at birth. □ *Sally was born with a silver spoon in her mouth.* □ *I'm glad I was not born with a silver spoon in my mouth.*

**bound hand and foot** with hands and feet tied up. □ *The robbers left us bound hand and foot.* □ *We remained bound hand and foot until the maid found us and untied us.*

**bow and scrape** to be very humble and subservient. (To bow low and touch the ground.) □ *Please don't bow and scrape. We are all equal here.* □ *The salesclerk came in, bowing and scraping, and asked if he could help us.*

**bread and butter** someone's livelihood or income. (The source of money that puts bread and butter, or other food, on the table.) □ *Selling cars is a lot of hard work, but it's my bread and butter.* □ *It was hard to give up my bread and butter, but I felt it was time to retire.*

**break camp** to close down a campsite; to pack up and move on. □ *Early this morning we broke camp and moved on northward.* □ *Okay, everyone. It's time to break camp. Take those tents down and fold them neatly.*

**break new ground** to begin to do something that no one else has done; to pioneer (in an enterprise). □ *Dr. Anderson was breaking new ground in cancer research.* □ *They were breaking new ground in consumer electronics.*

**break one's back (to do something)** See break one's neck (to do something).

**break one's neck (to do something)** AND **break one's back (to do something)** to work very hard to do something. □ *I broke my neck* to get here on time. □ *That's the last time I'll break my neck to help you.* □ *There is no point in breaking your back. Take your time.*

**break one's word** not to do what one said one would do; to fail to keep one's promise. □ *Don't say you'll visit your grandmother if you can't go. She hates for people to break their word.* □ *If you break your word, she won't trust you again.*

**break out in a cold sweat** to perspire from fever, fear, or anxiety; to begin to sweat profusely and suddenly. □ *I was so frightened I broke out in a cold sweat.* □ *The patient broke out in a cold sweat.*

**break (out) into tears** AND **break out in tears** to start crying suddenly. □ *I was so sad that I broke out into tears.* □ *I always break into tears at a funeral.* □ *It's hard not to break out in tears under those circumstances.*

**break someone's fall** to cushion a falling person; to lessen the impact of a falling person. □ *When the little boy fell out of the window, the bushes broke his fall.* □ *The old lady slipped on the ice, but a snowbank broke her fall.*

**break someone's heart** to cause someone emotional pain. □ *It just broke my heart when Tom ran away from home.* □ *Sally broke John's heart when she refused to marry him.*

**break the bank** to leave someone without any money. □ *It will hardly break the bank if we go out to dinner just once.* □ *Buying a new dress at that price won't break the bank.*

**break the ice** to initiate social interchanges and conversation; to get something started. (The *ice* sometimes refers to social coldness. Also used literally.) □ *Tom is so outgoing. He's always the first one to break the ice at parties.* □ *It's hard to break the ice at formal events.* □ *Sally broke the ice by bidding $500 for the painting.*

**break the news (to someone)** to tell someone some important news, usually bad news. □ *The doctor had to break the news to Jane about her husband's cancer.* □ *I hope that the doctor broke the news gently.*

**breathe down someone's neck 1.** to keep close watch on someone; to watch someone's activities. (Refers to standing very close behind a person. Can be used literally.) □ *I can't work with you breathing down my neck all the time. Go away.* □ *I will get through my life without your help. Stop breathing down my neck.* **2.** to try to hurry someone along;

to try to make someone get something done quickly. □ *I have to finish this project today. My boss is breathing down my neck.* □ *You must pay your loan on time, or the bank will start breathing down your neck.*

**breathe one's last** to die; to breathe one's last breath. □ *Mrs. Smith breathed her last this morning.* □ *I'll keep running every day until I breathe my last.*

**bring down the curtain (on something)** See ring down the curtain (on something).

**bring down the house** to excite a theatrical audience to laughter or applause or both. □ *Her performance didn't bring down the house. It emptied it.* Ⓣ *This is a great joke. The last time I told it, it brought the house down.*

**bring something to a head** to cause something to come to the point when a decision has to be made or action taken. □ *The latest disagreement between management and the union has brought matters to a head. There will be an all-out strike now.* □ *It's a relief that things have been brought to a head. The disputes have been going on for months.*

**bring something to light** to make something known; to discover something. (As if someone were bringing some hidden thing out into the light of day.) □ *The scientists brought their findings to light.* □ *We must bring this new evidence to light.*

**bring up the rear** to move along behind everyone else; to be at the end of a line. (Originally referred to marching soldiers.) □ *Here comes John, bringing up the rear.* □ *Hurry up, Tom! Why are you always bringing up the rear?*

**brush something under the carpet** See sweep something under the carpet.

**build castles in Spain** See build castles in the air.

**build castles in the air** AND **build castles in Spain** to daydream; to make plans that can never come true. □ *Ann spends most of her time building castles in Spain.* □ *I really like to sit on the porch in the evening, just building castles in the air.*

a **bull in a china shop** a very clumsy person around breakable things; a thoughtless or tactless person. (China is fine crockery.) □ *Look at Bill, as awkward as a bull in a china shop.* □ *Get that big dog out of my garden.*

*It's like a bull in a china shop.* □ *Bob is so rude, a regular bull in a china shop.*

**burn one's bridges (behind one) 1.** to make decisions that cannot be changed in the future. □ *If you drop out of school now, you'll be burning your bridges behind you.* □ *You're too young to burn your bridges that way.* **2.** to be unpleasant in a situation that one is leaving, ensuring that one will never be welcome to return. □ *If you get mad and quit your job, you'll be burning your bridges behind you.* □ *No sense burning your bridges. Be polite and leave quietly.* **3.** to cut off the way back to where one came from, making it impossible to retreat. □ *The army, which had burned its bridges behind it, couldn't go back.* □ *By blowing up the road, the spies had burned their bridges behind them.*

**burn someone at the stake 1.** to set fire to a person tied to a post (as a form of execution). □ *They used to burn witches at the stake.* □ *Look, officer, I only ran a stop sign. What are you going to do, burn me at the stake?* **2.** to chastise or denounce someone severely, but without violence. □ *Stop yelling. I made a simple mistake, and you're burning me at the stake for it.* □ *Sally only spilled her milk. There is no need to shout. Don't burn her at the stake for it.*

**burn someone or something to a crisp** to burn someone or something totally or very badly. □ *Stay in the shade, or the midday sun will burn you to a crisp.* □ *The cook burned the meat to a crisp.*

**burn the candle at both ends** to exhaust oneself by doing too much, for example by working very hard during the day and also staying up very late at night. □ *No wonder Mary is ill. She has been burning the candle at both ends for a long time.* □ *You can't keep on burning the candle at both ends.*

**burn the midnight oil** to stay up working, especially studying, late at night. (Refers to working by the light of an oil lamp in an earlier era.) □ *I have to go home and burn the midnight oil tonight.* □ *If you burn the midnight oil night after night, you'll probably become ill.*

**burn with a low blue flame** to be very angry, especially without displaying one's anger loudly. (Refers to the imaginary heat caused by extreme anger. A low blue flame is very hot despite its smallness and calmness.) □ *By the time she showed up three hours late, I was burning with a low blue flame.* □ *Whenever Ann gets mad, she just presses her lips together and burns with a low blue flame.*

**burst at the seams 1.** [for someone] to explode (figuratively) with pride or laughter. □ *Tom nearly burst at the seams with pride.* □ *We laughed so hard, we just about burst at the seams.* **2.** to explode from fullness. □ *The room was so crowded that it almost burst at the seams.* □ *I ate so much I almost burst at the seams.*

**burst with joy** to be full to the bursting point with happiness. □ *When I got my grades, I could have burst with joy.* □ *Joe was not exactly bursting with joy when he got the news.*

**bury one's head in the sand** AND **hide one's head in the sand** to ignore or hide from obvious signs of danger. (Refers to an ostrich, often pictured with its head stuck into the sand or the ground.) □ *Stop burying your head in the sand. Look at the statistics on smoking and cancer.* □ *And stop hiding your head in the sand. All of us will die somehow, whether we smoke or not.*

**bury the hatchet** to stop fighting or arguing; to end old resentments. (Burying a hatchet is symbolic of ending a war or a battle.) □ *All right, you two. Calm down and bury the hatchet.* □ *I wish Mr. and Mrs. Franklin would bury the hatchet. They argue all the time.*

the **business end of something** the part or end of something that actually does the work or carries out the procedure. □ *Keep away from the business end of the electric drill in case you get hurt.* □ *Don't point the business end of that gun at anyone. It might go off.*

**button one's lip** to get quiet and stay quiet. (Often used with children.) □ *All right now, let's button our lips and listen to the story.* □ *Button your lip, Tom! I'll tell you when you can talk.*

**buy a pig in a poke** to purchase or accept something without having seen or examined it. (*Poke* means "bag" or "sack.") □ *Buying a car without test-driving it is like buying a pig in a poke.* □ *He bought a pig in a poke when he ordered a wedding ring by mail.*

**buy something** to believe someone; to accept something to be a fact. (Also used literally.) □ *It may be true, but I don't buy it.* □ *I just don't buy the idea that you can swim that far.*

**buy something for a song** to buy something cheaply. □ *No one else wanted it, so I bought it for a song.* □ *I could buy this house for a song, because it's so ugly.*

**buy something sight unseen** to buy something without seeing it first. □ *I bought this land sight unseen. I didn't know it was so rocky.* □ *It isn't usually safe to buy something sight unseen.*

**by a hair's breadth** AND **by a whisker** just barely; by a very small distance. □ *I missed getting on the plane by a hair's breadth.* □ *The arrow missed the deer by a whisker.*

**by a show of hands** a vote expressed by people raising their hands. □ *We were asked to vote for the candidates for captain by a show of hands.* □ *Jack wanted us to vote on paper, not by a show of hands, so that we could have a secret ballot.*

**by a whisker** See by a hair's breadth.

**by leaps and bounds** rapidly; by large movements forward. (Not often used literally, but it could be.) □ *Our garden is growing by leaps and bounds.* □ *The profits of my company are increasing by leaps and bounds.*

**by return mail** by a subsequent mailing (back to the sender). (A phrase indicating that an answer is expected soon, by mail.) □ *Since this bill is overdue, would you kindly send us your check by return mail?* □ *I answered your request by return mail over a year ago. Please check your records.*

**by the nape of the neck** by the back of the neck. (Mostly found in real or mock threats. Grabbing in the way that one picks up a puppy.) □ *He grabbed me by the nape of the neck and told me not to turn around if I valued my life. I stood very still.* □ *If you do that again, I'll pick you up by the nape of the neck and throw you out the door.*

**by the same token** in the same way; reciprocally. □ *Tom must be good when he comes here, and by the same token, I expect you to behave properly when you go to his house.* □ *The mayor votes for his friend's causes. By the same token, the friend votes for the mayor's causes.*

**by the seat of one's pants** relying on one's instincts and experience, rather than on detailed plans and procedures or on complex machinery. (Especially with *fly*.) □ *The jungle pilot spent most of his days flying by the seat of his pants.* □ *Bob does everything by the seat of his pants, and he manages quite well.*

**by the skin of one's teeth** just barely; by an amount equal to the thickness of the (imaginary) skin on one's teeth. □ *I got through that* *class by the skin of my teeth.* □ *I got to the airport late and missed the plane by the skin of my teeth.*

**by the sweat of one's brow** by one's efforts; by one's hard work. □ *Tom raised these vegetables by the sweat of his brow.* □ *Sally polished the car by the sweat of her brow.*

**by virtue of something** because of something; due to something. □ *She's permitted to vote by virtue of her age.* □ *They are members of the club by virtue of their great wealth.*

**by word of mouth** by speaking rather than writing. □ *I learned about it by word of mouth.* □ *I need it in writing. I don't trust things I hear about by word of mouth.*

**call a spade a spade** to call something by its right name; to speak frankly about something, even if it is unpleasant. □ *Well, I believe it's time to call a spade a spade. We are just avoiding the issue.* □ *Let's call a spade a spade. The man is a liar.*

**call it a day** to quit work and go home; to say that the day's work has been completed. □ *I'm tired. Let's call it a day.* □ *The boss was mad because Tom called it a day at noon and went home.*

**call it quits** to quit; to resign from something; to announce that one is quitting. □ *Okay! I've had enough! I'm calling it quits.* □ *Time to go home, John. Let's call it quits.*

**call of nature** the need to go to the toilet. (Humorous.) □ *Stop the car here! I have to answer the call of nature.* □ *There was no interval in the meeting to take account of the call of nature.*

**call someone on the carpet** to reprimand a person. (The phrase presents images of a person called into the boss's carpeted office for a reprimand.) □ *One more error like that, and the boss will call you on the carpet.* □ *I'm sorry it went wrong. I really hope he doesn't call me on the carpet again.*

**call the dogs off** to stop threatening, chasing, or hounding (a person); (literally) to order dogs away from the chase. (Note the variations in the examples.) □ *All right, I surrender. You can call your dogs off.* ⊤ *Tell the sheriff to call off the dogs. We caught the robber.* ⊤ *Please call off your dogs!*

**can't carry a tune** unable to sing a simple melody; lacking musical ability. (Also with *cannot*.) □ *I wish that Tom wouldn't try to sing. He can't carry a tune.* □ *Listen to poor old John. He really cannot carry a tune.*

**can't hold a candle to someone** not equal to someone; not worthy to associate with someone; unable to measure up to someone. (Also with *cannot*. Refers to not being worthy enough even to hold a candle to light someone's way.) □ *Mary can't hold a candle to Ann when it comes to auto racing.* □ *As for singing, John can't hold a candle to Jane.*

**can't make heads or tails (out) of someone or something** unable to understand someone or something; unable to tell one end of someone or something from the other. (Because the thing or person is obscured or confusing. Also with *cannot*.) □ *John is so strange. I can't make heads or tails of him.* □ *Do this report again. I can't make heads or tails out of it.*

**can't see beyond the end of one's nose** unaware of the things that might happen in the future; not farsighted; self-centered. (Also with *cannot*.) □ *John is a very poor planner. He can't see beyond the end of his nose.* □ *Ann can't see beyond the end of her nose. She is very self-centered.*

**can't see one's hand in front of one's face** unable to see very far, usually due to darkness or fog. (Also with *cannot*.) □ *It was so dark that I couldn't see my hand in front of my face.* □ *Bob said that the fog was so thick he couldn't see his hand in front of his face.*

**carry a torch (for someone)** AND **carry the torch** to be in love with someone who does not love one in return; to brood over a hopeless love affair. □ *John is carrying a torch for Jane.* □ *Is John still carrying a torch?* □ *Yes, he'll carry the torch for months.*

**carry coals to Newcastle** to do something unnecessary; to do something that is redundant or duplicative. (An old proverb from England. Newcastle was a town from which coal was shipped to other parts of England. It would be senseless to bring coal into this town.) □ *Taking vegetables to a farmer is like carrying coals to Newcastle.* □ *Mr. Smith is so rich he doesn't need any more money. To give him money is carrying coals to Newcastle.*

**carry one's cross** See bear one's cross.

**carry the ball 1.** to be the player holding the ball, especially in football when a goal is made. □ *It was the fullback carrying the ball.* □ *Yes, Tom always carries the ball.* **2.** to be in charge; to make sure that a job gets done. □ *We need someone who knows how to get the job done. Hey, Sally! Why don't you carry the ball for us?* □ *John can't carry the ball. He isn't organized enough.*

**carry the torch** See carry a torch (for someone).

**carry the weight of the world on one's shoulders** to appear to be burdened by all the problems in the whole world. □ *Look at Tom. He appears to be carrying the weight of the world on his shoulders.* □ *Cheer up, Tom! You don't need to carry the weight of the world on your shoulders.*

**carry weight (with someone)** [for someone] to have influence with someone; [for something] to have significance for someone. (Often in the negative.) □ *Everything Mary says carries weight with me.* □ *Don't pay any attention to John. What he says carries no weight around here.* □ *Your proposal is quite good, but since you're not a member of the club, it carries no weight.*

**carte blanche** complete freedom to act or proceed as one pleases. (Literally, a white or blank card.) □ *We were given carte blanche to choose the color scheme.* □ *They were not instructed where to shop. It was a case of carte blanche.*

**case in point** an example of what one is talking about. □ *Now, as a case in point, let's look at nineteenth-century England.* □ *Fireworks can be dangerous. For a case in point, look what happened to Bob Smith last week.*

**cash-and-carry** having to do with a sale of goods or a way of selling that requires that the buyer pay for the goods and take them at the time of purchase. □ *I'm sorry. We don't deliver. It's strictly cash-and-carry.* □ *You cannot get credit at that drugstore. They only sell cash-and-carry.*

**cash in (on something)** to earn a lot of money at something; to make a profit from something. □ *This is a good year for farming, and you can cash in on it if you're smart.* □ *It's too late to cash in on that particular clothing fad.*

**cast in the same mold** very similar. □ *The two sisters are cast in the same mold—equally mean.* □ *All the members of that family are cast in the same mold, and all have ended up in prison.*

**cast (one's) pearls before swine** to waste something good on someone who doesn't care about it. (From a biblical quotation. As if throwing something of great value under the feet of pigs. It is considered insulting to refer to people as swine.) □ *To sing for them is to cast pearls before swine.* □ *To serve them French cuisine is like casting one's pearls before swine.*

**cast the first stone** to make the first criticism; to be the first to attack. (From a biblical quotation.) □ *Well, I don't want to be the one to cast* *the first stone, but she sang horribly.* □ *John always casts the first stone. Does he think he's perfect?*

**catch cold** AND **take cold** to contract a cold (the disease). □ *Please close the window, or we'll all catch cold.* □ *I take cold every year at this time.*

**catch one's death (of cold)** AND **take one's death (of cold)** to contract a cold; to catch a serious cold. □ *If I go out in this weather, I'll catch my death of cold.* □ *Dress warmly, or you'll catch your death of cold.* □ *Put on your raincoat, or you'll take your death.*

**catch someone napping** to find someone unprepared. (Informal. Literally, to discover someone asleep.) □ *The enemy caught our army napping.* □ *The thieves caught the security staff napping.*

**catch someone off balance** to encounter a person who is not prepared; to surprise someone. (Also used literally.) □ *Sorry I acted so flustered. You caught me off balance.* □ *The robbers caught Ann off balance and stole her purse.*

**catch someone's eye** AND **get someone's eye; have someone's eye** to establish eye contact with someone; to attract someone's attention. □ *The shiny red car caught Mary's eye.* □ *Tom got Mary's eye and waved to her.* □ *When Tom had her eye, he smiled at her.*

**caught in the cross fire** trapped between two fighting people or groups. (As if one were stranded between two opposing armies who are firing bullets at each other.) □ *In western movies, innocent people are always getting caught in the cross fire.* □ *In the war, Corporal Smith was killed when he got caught in the cross fire.*

**caught short** to be without something one needs, especially money. □ *I needed eggs for my cake, but I was caught short.* □ *Bob had to borrow money from John to pay for the meal. Bob is caught short quite often.*

**cause (some) eyebrows to raise** to shock people; to surprise and dismay people. □ *John caused eyebrows to raise when he married a poor girl from Toledo.* □ *If you want to cause some eyebrows to raise, just start dancing as you walk down the street.*

**cause (some) tongues to wag** to cause people to gossip; to give people something to gossip about. □ *The way John was looking at Mary will surely cause some tongues to wag.* □ *The way Mary was dressed will also cause tongues to wag.*

**champ at the bit** to be ready and anxious to do something. (Originally said about horses.) □ *The kids were champing at the bit to get into the swimming pool.* □ *The dogs were champing at the bit to begin the hunt.*

**change horses in midstream** to make major changes in an activity that has already begun; to choose someone or something else after it is too late. (Usually regarded as a bad idea.) □ *I'm already baking a cherry pie. I can't bake an apple pie instead. That would be changing horses in midstream.* □ *The house is half-built. It's too late to hire a different architect. You can't change horses in midstream.*

**a change of pace** a change of activity; a change. □ *I was bored and needed a change of pace.* □ *The trip to the seaside was a nice change of pace.*

**change the subject** to begin talking about something different. □ *They changed the subject suddenly when the person whom they had been discussing entered the room.* □ *We'll change the subject if we are embarrassing you.*

**Charity begins at home.** a proverb meaning that one should be kind to one's own family, friends, or fellow citizens before trying to help others. □ *"Mother, may I please have some pie?" asked Mary. "Remember, charity begins at home."* □ *At church, the minister reminded us that charity begins at home but we must remember others also.*

**chilled to the bone** very cold. □ *I was chilled to the bone in that snowstorm.* □ *The children were chilled to the bone in that unheated room.*

**a chip off the old block** a person (usually a male) who behaves in the same way as his father or resembles his father. (The father is the "old block.") □ *John looks like his father—a real chip off the old block.* □ *Bill Jones, Jr., is a chip off the old block. He's a banker just like his father.*

**clear the table** to remove the dishes and other eating utensils from the table after a meal. □ *Will you please help clear the table?* □ *After you clear the table, we'll play cards.*

**climb on the bandwagon** See get on the bandwagon.

**clip someone's wings** to restrain someone; to reduce or put an end to a teenager's privileges. (As with birds or fowl whose wings are clipped to keep them at home.) □ *You had better learn to get home on time, or I will clip your wings.* □ *My mother clipped my wings. I can't go out tonight.*

**cloak-and-dagger** involving secrecy and plotting. □ *A great deal of cloak-and-dagger stuff goes on in political circles.* □ *A lot of cloak-and-dagger activity was involved in the appointment of the director.*

**close at hand** within reach; handy. □ *I'm sorry, but your letter isn't close at hand. Please remind me what you said in it.* □ *When you're cooking, you should keep all the ingredients close at hand.*

**close ranks 1.** to move closer together in a military formation. □ *The soldiers closed ranks and marched on the enemy.* □ *All right! Stop that talking and close ranks.* **2.** to join (with someone). □ *We can fight this menace only if we close ranks.* □ *Let's all close ranks behind Ann and get her elected.*

The **coast is clear.** There is no visible danger. □ *I'm going to stay hidden here until the coast is clear.* □ *You can come out of your hiding place now. The coast is clear.*

**coast-to-coast** from the Atlantic Ocean to the Pacific Ocean (in North America); all the land between the Atlantic and Pacific oceans. □ *My voice was once heard on a coast-to-coast radio broadcast.* □ *Our car made the coast-to-coast trip in eighty hours.*

**cock-and-bull story** a silly, made-up story; a story that is a lie. □ *Don't give me that cock-and-bull story.* □ *I asked for an explanation, and all I got was your ridiculous cock-and-bull story!*

**cock of the walk** someone who acts more important than others in a group. □ *The deputy manager was cock of the walk until the new manager arrived.* □ *He loved acting cock of the walk and ordering everyone about.*

**cold comfort** no comfort or consolation at all. □ *She knows there are others worse off than she is, but that's cold comfort.* □ *It was cold comfort to the student to learn that others had failed the test also.*

**come a cropper** to have a misfortune; to fail. (Literally, to fall off one's horse.) □ *Bob invested all his money in the stock market just before it fell. Boy, did he come a cropper.* □ *Jane was out all night before she took her tests. She really came a cropper.*

**come apart at the seams** to lose one's emotional self-control suddenly. (From the literal sense, referring to a garment falling apart.) □ *Bill was so upset that he almost came apart at the seams.* □ *I couldn't take any more. I just came apart at the seams.*

**come away empty-handed** to return without anything. □ *All right, go gambling. Don't come away empty-handed, though.* □ *Go to the bank and ask for the loan again. This time don't come away empty-handed.*

**come by something 1.** to travel by a specific carrier, such as a plane, a boat, or a car. (The literal sense.) □ *We came by train. It's more relaxing.* □ *Next time, we'll come by plane. It's faster.* **2.** to find or get something. □ *How did you come by that haircut?* □ *Where did you come by that new shirt?*

**come down in the world** to lose one's social position or financial standing. □ *Mr. Jones has really come down in the world since he lost his job.* □ *If I became unemployed, I'm sure I'd come down in the world, too.*

**come full circle** to return to the original position or state of affairs. □ *The family sold the house generations ago, but things have come full circle and one of the family's descendants lives there now.* □ *The employer's power was reduced by the unions at one point, but now everything has come full circle.*

**come home (to roost)** to return to cause trouble (for someone). (As chickens or other birds return home to roost.) □ *Eventually, all his bad deeds will come home to roost, and he, too, will suffer.* □ *Yes, sooner or later troubles all come home.*

**come in out of the rain** to become alert and sensible. (Also used literally.) □ *Pay attention, Sally! Come in out of the rain!* □ *Bill will fail if he doesn't come in out of the rain and study.*

**come into one's or its own** [for someone or something] to achieve the proper recognition. □ *Video has only recently come into its own as an art medium.* □ *After years of trying, Sally finally came into her own.*

**come of age** to reach an age when one is old enough to own property, get married, vote, and sign legal contracts. □ *When Jane comes of age, she will buy her own car.* □ *Sally, who came of age last month, entered into an agreement to purchase a house.*

**come off second best** to win second place or worse; to lose out to someone else. □ *John came off second best in the race.* □ *Why do I always come off second best in an argument with you?*

**come out ahead** to end up with a profit; to improve one's situation. □ *I hope you come out ahead with your investments.* □ *It took a lot of money to buy the house, but I think I'll come out ahead.*

**come out in the wash** to work out all right. (This means that problems or difficulties will go away as dirt goes away in the process of washing.) □ *Don't worry about that problem. It'll all come out in the wash.* □ *This trouble will go away. It'll come out in the wash.*

**come out of the closet 1.** to reveal one's secret interests. □ *Tom Brown came out of the closet and admitted that he likes to knit.* □ *It's time that all of you lovers of chamber music came out of the closet and attended our concerts.* **2.** to reveal that one is a homosexual. □ *Tom surprised his parents when he came out of the closet.* □ *It was difficult for him to come out of the closet.*

**come to a bad end** to have a disaster, perhaps one that is deserved or expected; to die an unfortunate death. □ *My old car came to a bad end. Its engine burned up.* □ *The unscrupulous merchant came to a bad end.*

**come to a dead end** to arrive at an absolute stopping point. □ *The building project came to a dead end.* □ *The street came to a dead end.* □ *We were driving along and came to a dead end.*

**come to a head** to come to a crucial point; to reach a point where a problem must be solved. □ *Remember my problem with my neighbors? Well, last night the whole thing came to a head.* □ *The battle between the two factions of the city council came to a head yesterday.*

**come to an end** to stop; to finish. □ *The party came to an end at midnight.* □ *Her life came to an end late yesterday.*

**come to an untimely end** to die an early death; to die too soon, before one has lived the expected span of a lifetime. □ *Poor Mr. Jones came to an untimely end in a car accident.* □ *Cancer caused Mrs. Smith to come to an untimely end.*

**come to a standstill** to stop, temporarily or permanently. □ *The building project came to a standstill because the workers went on strike.* □ *The party came to a standstill until the lights were turned on again.*

**come to grief** to fail; to suffer trouble or bad luck. □ *I hope your marriage will not come to grief over such a silly argument!* □ *Bill moved to the city to improve his life, but he soon came to grief.*

**come to grips with something** to face something; to comprehend something. □ *He found it difficult to come to grips with his grandmother's death.* □ *Many students have a hard time coming to grips with algebra.*

**come to light** to become known. □ *Some interesting facts about your past have just come to light.* □ *If too many bad things come to light, you may lose your job.*

**come to one's senses** to wake up; to become conscious; to start thinking clearly. □ *John, come to your senses. You're being quite stupid.* □ *In the morning I don't come to my senses until I have had two cups of coffee.*

**come to pass** to happen. (Literary.) □ *When did all of this come to pass?* □ *When will this event come to pass?*

**come to the point** AND **get to the point** to get to the important part (of something). □ *He has been talking a long time. I wish he would come to the point.* □ *Quit wasting time! Get to the point!* □ *We are talking about money, Bob! Come on, get to the point.*

**come to think of it** I just remembered . . . ; now that I think about it . . . □ *Come to think of it, I know someone who can help.* □ *I have a screwdriver in the trunk of my car, come to think of it.*

**come true** to become real; [for a dream or a wish] actually to happen. □ *When I got married, all my dreams came true.* □ *Coming to the big city was like having my wish come true.*

**come up in the world** to improve one's status or situation in life. □ *Since Mary got her new job, she has really come up in the world.* □ *A good education helped my brother come up in the world.*

**come what may** no matter what might happen. □ *I'll be home for the holidays, come what may.* □ *Come what may, the mail will get delivered.*

**conspicuous by one's absence** to have one's absence (from an event) noticed. □ *We missed you last night. You were conspicuous by your absence.* □ *How could the bride's father miss the wedding party? He was certainly conspicuous by his absence.*

a **contradiction in terms** a phrase or statement containing a contradiction. □ *A "wealthy pauper" is a contradiction in terms.* □ *He's a straight-talking politician—though that may seem like a contradiction in terms.*

**control the purse strings** to be in charge of the money in a business or a household. □ *I control the purse strings at our house.* □ *Mr. Williams is the treasurer. He controls the purse strings.*

**cook someone's goose** to damage or ruin someone. (To do something that cannot be undone.) □ *I cooked my own goose by not showing up on time.* □ *Sally cooked Bob's goose for treating her the way he did.*

**cook the accounts** to cheat in bookkeeping; to make the accounts appear to balance when they do not. □ *Jane was sent to jail for cooking the accounts of her mother's store.* □ *It's hard to tell whether she really cooked the accounts or just didn't know how to add.*

**cool one's heels** to wait (for someone). □ *I spent all afternoon cooling my heels in the waiting room while the doctor talked on the telephone.* □ *All right. If you can't behave properly, just sit down here and cool your heels until I call you.*

**cost an arm and a leg** See under pay an arm and a leg (for something).

**cost a pretty penny** to cost a lot of money. □ *I'll bet that diamond cost a pretty penny.* □ *You can be sure that house cost a pretty penny. It has seven bathrooms.*

**count heads** See count noses.

**count noses** AND **count heads** to count people. (Because there is only one of these per person.) □ *I'll tell you how many people are here after I count noses.* □ *Everyone is here. Let's count heads so we can order hamburgers.*

**count one's chickens before they hatch** to plan how to utilize good results of something before those results have occurred. (Frequently used in the negative.) □ *You're way ahead of yourself. Don't count your chickens before they hatch.* □ *You may be disappointed if you count your chickens before they hatch.*

**cover a lot of ground 1.** to travel over a great distance; to investigate a wide expanse of land. □ *The prospectors covered a lot of ground looking for gold.* □ *My car can cover a lot of ground in one day.* **2.** to deal with much information and many facts. □ *The history lecture covered a lot of ground today.* □ *Mr. and Mrs. Franklin always cover a lot of ground when they argue.*

**cover for someone 1.** to make excuses for someone; to conceal someone's errors. □ *If I miss class, please cover for me.* □ *If you're late, I'll cover for you.* **2.** to handle someone else's work. □ *Dr. Johnson's partner agreed to cover for him during his vacation.* □ *I'm on duty this afternoon. Will you please cover for me? I have a doctor's appointment.*

**crack a joke** to tell a joke. □ *She's never serious. She's always cracking jokes.* □ *As long as she's cracking jokes, she's okay.*

**crack a smile** to smile a little, perhaps reluctantly. □ *She cracked a smile, so I knew she was kidding.* □ *The soldier cracked a smile at the wrong time and had to march for an hour as punishment.*

**cramp someone's style** to limit someone in some way. □ *I hope this doesn't cramp your style, but could you please not hum while you work?* □ *To ask him to keep regular hours would really be cramping his style.*

the **cream of the crop** the best of all. (A cliché.) □ *This particular car is the cream of the crop.* □ *The kids are very bright. They are the cream of the crop.*

**Crime doesn't pay.** a proverb meaning that crime will not benefit a person. □ *At the end of the radio program, a voice said, "Remember, crime doesn't pay."* □ *No matter how tempting it may appear, crime doesn't pay.*

**cross a bridge before one comes to it** to worry excessively about something before it happens. (Note the variations in the examples.) □ *There is no sense in crossing that bridge before you come to it.* □ *She's always crossing bridges before coming to them. She needs to learn to relax.*

**cross a bridge when one comes to it** to deal with a problem only when one is faced with the problem. (Note the variations in the examples.) □ *Please wait and cross that bridge when you come to it.* □ *He shouldn't worry about it now. He can cross that bridge when he comes to it.*

**cross-examine someone** to ask someone questions in great detail; to question a suspect or a witness closely. □ *The lawyer plans to cross-examine the witness tomorrow morning.* □ *Whenever I get home late, my parents cross-examine me about where I've been.*

**cross one's heart (and hope to die)** to make a pledge or vow that the truth is being told. □ *It's true, cross my heart and hope to die.* □ *It's really true—cross my heart.*

**cross swords (with someone)** to enter into an argument with someone. □ *I don't want to cross swords with Tom.* □ *The last time we crossed swords, we had a terrible time.*

the **crux of the matter** the central issue of the matter. (*Crux* is Latin for "cross.") □ *All right, this is the crux of the matter.* □ *It's about time that we looked at the crux of the matter.*

**cry before one is hurt** to cry or complain upon the threat of harm. □ *When he thinks there will be some change at work, Bill cries before he's hurt.* □ *There is no point in crying before you are hurt.*

**cry bloody murder** AND **scream bloody murder** to scream as if something very serious has happened. (As if one has found the result of a bloody act of murder.) □ *Now that Bill is really hurt, he's screaming bloody murder.* □ *There is no point in crying bloody murder about the bill if you aren't going to pay it.*

**cry one's eyes out** to cry very hard. □ *When we heard the news, we cried our eyes out with joy.* □ *She cried her eyes out after his death.*

**cry over spilled milk** to be unhappy about something that cannot be undone. (Usually viewed as a childish action. *Spilled* can also be spelled *spilt*.) □ *I'm sorry that you broke your bicycle, Tom. But there is nothing that can be done now. Don't cry over spilled milk.* □ *Ann is always crying over spilt milk. Why can't she just accept what's already happened?*

**cry wolf** to cry out for help or complain about something when nothing is really wrong. □ *Pay no attention. She's just crying wolf again.* □ *Don't cry wolf too often. No one will come.*

**Curiosity killed the cat.** a proverb meaning that it is dangerous or improper to be overly curious. □ *Don't ask so many questions, Billy. Curiosity killed the cat.* □ *Curiosity killed the cat. Mind your own business.*

**curl someone's hair** to frighten or alarm someone severely; to shock someone with sight, sound, or taste. (Also used literally.) □ *Don't ever sneak up on me like that again. You really curled my hair.* □ *The horror film curled my hair.*

**curl up and die** to retreat and die. □ *When I heard you say that, I could have curled up and died.* □ *No, it wasn't an illness. She just curled up and died.*

**cut both ways** to affect both sides of an issue equally. □ *The suggestion that costs should be shared cuts both ways. You will have to pay as well.* □ *If our side cannot take along fans to the game, then yours cannot either. The rule has to cut both ways.*

**cut class** to skip going to class. (Refers to high school or college classes.) □ *If Mary keeps cutting classes, she'll fail the course.* □ *I can't cut that class. I've missed too many already.*

**cut off one's nose to spite one's face** to harm oneself as a result of trying to punish another person. □ *Billy loves the zoo, but he refused to go with his mother because he was mad at her. He cut off his nose to spite his face.* □ *Find a better way to be angry. It is silly to cut off your nose to spite your face.*

**cut one's losses** to reduce one's losses of money, goods, or other things of value. □ *I sold the stock as it went down, thus cutting my losses.* □ *He cut his losses by putting better locks on the doors. There were fewer robberies.* □ *The mayor's reputation suffered because of the scandal. He finally resigned in order to cut his losses.*

**cut one's (own) throat** to cause certain failure for oneself; to do damage to oneself. (Also used literally.) □ *If I were to run for office, I'd just be cutting my throat.* □ *Judges who take bribes are cutting their own throats.*

**cut someone or something (off) short** to end something before it is finished; to end one's speaking before one is finished. □ *We cut the picnic short because of the storm.* □ *I'm sorry to cut you off short, but I must go now.*

**cut someone or something to the bone 1.** to slice deep to a bone. □ *The knife cut John to the bone. He had to be sewed up.* □ *Cut each slice of ham to the bone. Then each slice will be as big as possible.* **2.** [with something] to cut down severely (on something). □ *We cut our expenses to the bone and are still losing money.* □ *Congress had to cut the budget to the bone in order to balance it.*

**cut someone to the quick** to hurt someone's feelings very badly. (Can be used literally when *quick* refers to the tender flesh at the base of fingernails and toenails.) □ *Your criticism cut me to the quick.* □ *Tom's sharp words to Mary cut her to the quick.*

**cut something (too) fine** to allow scarcely enough time, money, etc., in order to accomplish something. □ *You're cutting it too fine if you want to catch the bus. It leaves in five minutes.* □ *Joan had to search her pockets for coins to use as bus fare. She really cut it fine.*

**cut the ground out from under someone** to destroy the foundation of someone's plans or argument. □ *The politician cut the ground out from under his opponent.* Ⓣ *Congress cut out the ground from under the president.*

**D**

**daily dozen** physical exercises done every day. (Informal.) □ *My brother always feels better after his daily dozen.* □ *She would rather do a daily dozen than go on a diet.*

**damn someone or something with faint praise** to criticize someone or something indirectly by not praising enthusiastically. □ *The critic did not say that he disliked the play, but he damned it with faint praise.* □ *Mrs. Brown is very proud of her son's achievements, but she damns her daughter's with faint praise.*

**dance to another tune** to shift quickly to different behavior; to change one's behavior or attitude. □ *After being yelled at, Ann danced to another tune.* □ *A stern talking-to will make her dance to another tune.*

**dark horse** someone whose abilities, plans, or feelings are little known to others. (From horse racing.) □ *It's difficult to predict who will win the prize—there are two or three dark horses in the tournament.* □ *The third candidate is a dark horse. She's new to politics and is just beginning her campaign.*

**dash cold water on something** See pour cold water on something.

**date back (to something)** to extend back to a particular time or event; to have been already alive or in existence at a particular time in the past. □ *The old house dates back to the Civil War.* □ *This record dates back to the sixties.* □ *My older brothers were born in the 1940s, but I don't date back that far.*

**Davy Jones's locker** the bottom of the sea, especially when it is a grave. (From the seamen's name for the spirit of the sea.) □ *They were going to sail around the world but ended up in Davy Jones's locker.* □ *Most of the gold from that trading ship is in Davy Jones's locker.*

**daylight robbery** the practice of blatantly or grossly overcharging. □ *It's daylight robbery to charge that amount of money for a hotel room!* □ *The cost of renting a car at that place is daylight robbery.*

**dead and buried** gone forever. (Refers literally to persons and figuratively to ideas and other things.) □ *Now that Uncle Bill is dead and buried, we can read his will.* □ *That kind of thinking is dead and buried.*

**dead to the world** tired; exhausted; sleeping soundly. (Asleep and oblivious to what is going on in the rest of the world.) □ *I've had such a hard day. I'm really dead to the world.* □ *Look at her sleep. She's dead to the world.*

**death on someone or something 1.** very effective in acting against someone or something. □ *This road is terribly bumpy. It's death on tires.* □ *The sergeant is death on lazy soldiers.* **2.** [with *something*] accurate or deadly at doing something requiring skill or great effort. □ *John is death on curve balls. He's our best pitcher.* □ *The boxing champ is really death on those fast punches.*

**desert a sinking ship** AND **leave a sinking ship** to leave a place, a person, or a situation when things become difficult or unpleasant. (Rats are said to be the first to leave a ship that is sinking.) □ *I hate to be the one to desert a sinking ship, but I can't stand it around here anymore.* □ *There goes Tom. Wouldn't you know he'd leave a sinking ship rather than stay around and try to help?*

a **diamond in the rough** a valuable or potentially excellent person or thing hidden by an unpolished or rough exterior. □ *Ann looks like a stupid woman, but she's a fine person—a real diamond in the rough.* □ *That piece of property is a diamond in the rough. Someday it will be valuable.*

**die of a broken heart 1.** to die of emotional distress. □ *I was not surprised to hear of her death. They say she died of a broken heart.* □ *In the movie, the heroine appeared to die of a broken heart, but the audience knew she was poisoned.* **2.** to suffer from emotional distress, especially from a failed romance. □ *Tom and Mary broke off their romance, and both died of broken hearts.* □ *Please don't leave me. I know I'll die of a broken heart.*

**die of boredom** to suffer from boredom; to be very bored. □ *I'll die of boredom if I have to stay home all day.* □ *We sat there and listened politely, even though we were dying of boredom.*

**die on the vine** See wither on the vine.

**dig in one's heels** to refuse to alter one's course of action or opinions; to be obstinate or determined. □ *I'm digging in my heels. I'm not going back.* Ⓣ *The student dug her heels in and refused to take the exam.*

**dig one's own grave** to be responsible for one's own downfall or ruin. □ *The manager tried to get rid of his assistant, but he dug his own grave. He was fired himself.* □ *The legislators have dug their own graves by passing that new taxation bill. They won't be reelected.*

**dig up some dirt on someone** to find out something bad about someone. (The *dirt* is gossip.) □ *The citizens' group dug up some dirt on the mayor and used it against her at election time.* Ⓣ *If you don't stop trying to dig some dirt up on me, I'll get a lawyer and sue you.*

**dirt cheap** extremely cheap. (Informal.) □ *Buy some more of those plums. They're dirt cheap.* □ *In Italy, the peaches are dirt cheap.*

**dirty one's hands** See get one's hands dirty.

**dirty work 1.** unpleasant or uninteresting work. □ *My boss does all the traveling. I get all the dirty work to do.* □ *She's tired of doing all the dirty work at the office.* **2.** dishonest or underhanded actions; treachery. □ *She knew there was some dirty work going on when she saw her opponents whispering together.* □ *The firm seems respectable enough, but there's a lot of dirty work that goes on.*

**do a land-office business** to do a large amount of business in a short period of time. (As if selling land during a land rush.) □ *The ice-cream shop always does a land-office business on a hot day.* □ *The accountant did a land-office business on the day that taxes were due.*

**dog eat dog** a situation in which one has to act ruthlessly in order to survive or succeed; ruthless competition. □ *It is dog eat dog in the world of business these days.* □ *Universities are not quiet, peaceful places. It's a case of dog eat dog for promotion.*

**dog in the manger** one who prevents others from enjoying something that one does not actually need or want for oneself. (From one of Aesop's fables in which a dog—which cannot eat hay—lay in the place where hay is kept, preventing the other animals from eating the hay.) □ *Jane is a real dog in the manger. She cannot drive, but she will not lend anyone her car.* □ *If Martin were not such a dog in the manger, he would let his brother have that evening suit he never wears.*

**dollar for dollar** considering the amount of money involved; considering the cost. (Often seen in advertising.) □ *Dollar for dollar, you cannot buy a better car.* □ *Dollar for dollar, this laundry detergent washes cleaner and brighter than any other product on the market.*

**Don't hold your breath.** Do not stop breathing (while waiting for something to happen), because the wait will be very long. □ *You think he'll get a job? Ha! Don't hold your breath.* □ *I'll finish building the fence as soon as I have time, but don't hold your breath.*

**Don't let someone or something get you down.** Do not allow yourself to be overcome by someone or something. □ *Don't let their constant teasing get you down.* □ *Don't let Tom get you down. He's not always unpleasant.*

**Don't look a gift horse in the mouth.** a proverb meaning that one should not expect perfect gifts. (*Don't* can be replaced with another negative word, such as *shouldn't* or *never*. See the examples. The age of a horse and, therefore, its usefulness can be determined by looking at its teeth. It would be acting ungrateful to inspect the teeth of a horse given as a gift to make sure the horse is of the best quality.) □ *Don't complain. You shouldn't look a gift horse in the mouth.* □ *John complained that the portable television set he got for his birthday was black-and-white rather than color. He was told, "Don't look a gift horse in the mouth."*

a **dose of one's own medicine** the same kind of treatment that one gives to other people. (Often with *give, get,* or *have.*) □ *Sally never is very friendly. Someone is going to give her a dose of her own medicine.* □ *He didn't like getting a dose of his own medicine.*

**do someone a good turn** to do something that is helpful to someone. □ *My neighbor did me a good turn by lending me his lawn mower.* □ *The teacher did me a good turn when he told me to work harder.*

**do someone's heart good** to make someone feel good emotionally. (Also used literally.) □ *It does my heart good to hear you talk that way.* □ *When she sent me a get-well card, it really did my heart good.*

**do something by hand** to do something with one's hands rather than using a machine. □ *The washing machine was broken, so I had to wash all of the clothes by hand.* □ *All this tiny stitching was done by hand. Machines cannot do this kind of work.*

**do the dishes** to wash the dishes; to wash and dry the dishes. □ *Bill, you cannot go out and play until you've done the dishes.* □ *Why am I always the one who has to do the dishes?*

**do the honors** to act as host or hostess and serve one's guests by pouring drinks, slicing meat, making (drinking) toasts, etc. □ *All the guests were seated, and a huge, juicy turkey sat on the table. Jane Jones turned to her husband and said, "Bob, will you do the honors?" Mr. Jones smiled and began carving thick slices of meat from the turkey.* □ *The mayor stood up and addressed the people, who were still eating their salads. "I'm delighted to do the honors this evening and propose a toast to your friend and mine, Bill Jones. Bill, good luck and best wishes in your new job in Washington." And everyone sipped a bit of wine.*

**doubting Thomas** someone who will not easily believe something without strong proof or evidence. (From the biblical account of the apostle Thomas, who would not believe that Jesus had risen from the grave until he had touched Him.) □ *Mary won't believe that I have a dog until she sees him. She's such a doubting Thomas.* □ *This school is full of doubting Thomases. They want to see Bob's new bike with their own eyes.*

**down and out** having no money or means of support. □ *There are many young people down and out in Los Angeles just now.* □ *John gambled away all his fortune and is now completely down and out.* ALSO: **down-and-out** someone who is very poor with no prospects of obtaining work or money. □ *New York City is filled with down-and-outs.* □ *Once wealthy, John is now counted among the down-and-outs.*

**down in the dumps** sad or depressed. □ *I've been down in the dumps for the past few days.* □ *Try to cheer Jane up. She's down in the dumps for some reason.*

**down in the mouth** sad-faced; depressed and unsmiling. (Refers to a frown or sagging mouth.) □ *Since her dog died, Barbara has been down in the mouth.* □ *Bob has been down in the mouth since the car wreck.*

**down the drain** lost forever; wasted. (Also used literally.) □ *I just hate to see all that money go down the drain.* □ *Well, there goes the whole project, right down the drain.*

**down the tube(s)** ruined; wasted. (Slang.) □ *His political career went down the tube after the scandal. He's lost his job.* □ *The business went down the tubes.*

**down-to-earth** practical; not fanciful; realistic. □ *Her ideas for the boutique are always very down-to-earth.* □ *The committee's plans for the village are anything but down-to-earth.*

**down to the wire** at the very last minute; up to the very last instant. (Refers to a wire that marks the end of a horse race.) □ *I have to turn this in tomorrow, and I'll be working down to the wire.* □ *When we get down to the wire, we'll know better what to do.*

**drag one's feet** to act very slowly, often deliberately. □ *The senators are dragging their feet on this bill because it will lose votes.* □ *If the planning department hadn't dragged their feet, the building would have been built by now.*

**draw a blank 1.** to get no response; to find nothing. □ *I asked Tom about the company's financial problems, and I just drew a blank.* □ *We looked in the files for an hour, but we drew a blank.* **2.** to fail to remember (something). □ *I tried to remember her telephone number, but I could only draw a blank.* □ *It was a very hard test with just one question to answer, and I drew a blank.*

**draw a line between something and something else** to separate two things; to distinguish or differentiate between two things. (The *a* can be replaced with *the.* Also used literally.) □ *It's necessary to draw a line between accidentally bumping into people and intentionally striking them.* □ *It's very hard to draw the line between slamming a door and just closing it loudly.*

**draw blood 1.** to hit or bite (a person or an animal) and make a wound that bleeds. □ *The dog chased me and bit me hard, but it didn't draw blood.* □ *The boxer landed just one punch and drew blood immediately.* **2.** to anger or insult a person. □ *Sally screamed out a terrible insult at Tom. Judging by the look on his face, she really drew blood.* □ *Tom started yelling and cursing, trying to insult Sally. He wouldn't be satisfied until he had drawn blood, too.*

a **dream come true** a wish or a dream that has become real. □ *Going to Hawaii was a dream come true for Bob.* □ *Having you for a friend is a dream come true.*

**dressing-down** a scolding. □ *After that dressing-down, I won't be late again.* □ *The boss gave Fred a real dressing-down for breaking the machine.*

**dribs and drabs** small, irregular quantities. (Especially with *in* and *by*.) □ *The checks for the charity are coming in dribs and drabs.* □ *The members of the orchestra arrived by dribs and drabs.*

**drink to excess** to drink too much alcohol; to drink alcohol continually. □ *Mr. Franklin drinks to excess.* □ *Some people drink to excess only at parties.*

**drive a hard bargain** to work hard to negotiate prices or agreements in one's own favor. □ *I saved $200 by driving a hard bargain when I bought my new car.* □ *All right, sir, you drive a hard bargain. I'll sell you this car for $12,450.* □ *You drive a hard bargain, Jane, but I'll sign the contract.*

**drive someone to the wall** See force someone to the wall.

**drop in one's tracks** to stop or collapse from exhaustion; to die suddenly. □ *If I keep working this way, I'll drop in my tracks.* □ *Uncle Bob was working in the garden and dropped in his tracks. We are all sorry that he's dead.*

**drop someone a few lines** See drop someone a line.

**drop someone a line** AND **drop someone a few lines** to write a letter or a note to someone. (The *line* refers to lines of writing.) □ *I dropped Aunt Jane a line last Thanksgiving.* □ *She usually drops me a few lines around the first of the year.*

**drop someone's name** AND **drop the name of someone** to mention the name of an important or famous person as if that person were a personal friend. (Also plural. See the examples.) □ *Mary always tries to impress people by dropping the names of well-known film stars.* □ *Joan's such a snob. Leave it to her to drop the names of all the local gentry.* ALSO: **name-dropping** □ *Mary always tries to impress people by name-dropping.* □ *Joan's such a snob. She's always name-dropping.*

**drop the ball** to make a blunder; to fail in some way. (Also literally, in sports, to drop a ball in error.) □ *Everything was going fine in the election until my campaign manager dropped the ball.* □ *You can't trust John to do the job right. He's always dropping the ball.*

**drop the name of someone** See drop someone's name.

**drown one's sorrows** See drown one's troubles.

**drown one's troubles** AND **drown one's sorrows** to try to forget one's problems by drinking a lot of alcohol. □ *Bill is in the bar, drowning his troubles.* □ *Jane is at home, drowning her sorrows.*

a **drug on the market** something that is for sale everywhere in great abundance; a glut on the market. □ *Right now, small computers are a drug on the market.* □ *Some years ago, small transistor radios were a drug on the market.*

**drum someone out of something** to expel or send someone away from something, especially in a formal or public fashion. (From the military use of drums on such occasions.) □ *The officer was drummed out of the regiment for misconduct.* □ *I heard that he was drummed out of the golf club for cheating.*

**drum something into someone('s head)** to make someone learn something through persistent repetition. □ *Yes, I know that. They drummed it into me as a child.* □ *I will drum it into their heads day and night.*

**drum up some business** to stimulate people to buy what one is selling. (As if someone were beating a drum to get the attention of customers.) □ *A little bit of advertising would drum up some business.* Ⓣ *I need to do something to drum some business up.*

**dry behind the ears** mature and grown up. (Usually expressed as a negative. See also **wet behind the ears**.) □ *Tom is going into business by himself? Why, he's hardly dry behind the ears.* □ *That kid isn't dry behind the ears. He'll go broke in a month.*

**dry run** an attempt; a rehearsal. □ *We had better have a dry run for the official ceremony tomorrow.* □ *The children will need a dry run before their procession in the pageant.*

**dry someone out** to cause someone to become sober; to cause someone to stop drinking alcohol to excess. (Informal.) □ *If the doctor at the clinic can't dry him out, no one can.* □ *Mary needs to be dried out. She's been drinking heavily since her divorce.*

**dry up** to become silent; to stop talking. (Informal.) □ *The young lecturer was so nervous that he forgot what he was going to say and dried up.* □ *Actors have a fear of drying up on stage.* □ *Oh, dry up! I'm sick of listening to you.*

**Dutch auction** an auction or sale that starts off with a high asking price, which is then reduced until a buyer is found. □ *Dutch auctions are rare—most auctioneers start with a lower price than they hope to obtain.* □ *My house agent advised me to ask a reasonable price for my house rather than get involved with a Dutch auction.*

**Dutch courage** unusual or artificial courage arising from the influence of alcohol. (Potentially offensive.) □ *It was Dutch courage that made the football fan attack the policeman.* □ *It will take a bit of Dutch courage for me to make an after-dinner speech.*

**Dutch treat** a social occasion where one pays for oneself. (See also go Dutch.) □ *"It's nice of you to ask me out to dinner," she said, "but could we make it a Dutch treat?"* □ *The office outing is always a Dutch treat.*

**Dutch uncle** a man who gives frank and direct advice to someone in the manner of a parent or relative. □ *I would not have to lecture you like a Dutch uncle if you were not so extravagant.* □ *He acts more like a Dutch uncle than a husband. He's forever telling her what to do in public.*

**eager beaver** someone who is very enthusiastic; someone who works very hard. □ *New volunteers are always eager beavers.* □ *The young assistant gets to work very early. She's a real eager beaver.*

**eagle eye** careful attention; an intently watchful gaze. (From the sharp eyesight of the eagle.) □ *The pupils wrote their essays under the eagle eye of the headmaster.* □ *The umpire kept his eagle eye on the tennis match.*

**early bird** someone who gets up or arrives early; someone who starts something very promptly, especially someone who gains an advantage of some kind by so doing. (See also the following entry.) □ *The Smiths are early birds. They caught the first ferry.* □ *I was an early bird and got the best selection of flowers.*

**The early bird gets the worm.** a proverb meaning that the person who is early will get the reward. (See also the previous entry.) □ *Don't be late again! Don't you know that the early bird gets the worm?* □ *I'll be there before the sun is up. After all, the early bird gets the worm.*

**Early to bed, early to rise(, makes a man healthy, wealthy, and wise).** a proverb that claims that going to bed early and getting up early is good for you. (Sometimes said to explain why a person is going to bed early. The last part of the saying is sometimes left out.) □ *Tom left the party at ten o'clock, saying "Early to bed, early to rise, makes a man healthy, wealthy, and wise."* □ *I always get up at six o'clock. After all, early to bed, early to rise.*

**earn one's keep** to help out with chores in return for food and a place to live; to earn one's pay by doing what is expected. □ *I earn my keep at college by shoveling snow in the winter.* □ *Tom hardly earns his keep around here. He should be fired.*

**easy come, easy go** said to explain the loss of something that required only a small amount of effort to get in the first place. □ *Ann found* *twenty dollars in the morning and spent it foolishly at noon. "Easy come, easy go," she said. □ John spends his money as fast as he can earn it. With John it's easy come, easy go.*

**Easy does it.** Act with care. □ *Be careful with that glass vase. Easy does it!* □ *Now, now, Tom. Don't get angry. Easy does it.*

**eat humble pie 1.** to act very humble when one is shown to be wrong. □ *I think I'm right, but if I'm wrong, I'll eat humble pie.* □ *You think you're so smart. I hope you have to eat humble pie.* **2.** to accept insults and humiliation. □ *John, stand up for your rights. You don't have to eat humble pie all the time.* □ *Beth seems quite happy to eat humble pie. She'll do anything to avoid a conflict.*

**eat like a bird** to eat only small amounts of food; to peck at one's food. □ *Jane is very slim because she eats like a bird.* □ *Bill is trying to lose weight by eating like a bird.*

**eat like a horse** to eat large amounts of food. □ *No wonder he's so fat. He eats like a horse.* □ *John eats like a horse, but he also works like a horse, so he never gets fat.*

**eat one's cake and have it too** See have one's cake and eat it too.

**eat one's hat** something that one says one will do if a certain very unlikely event were actually to happen. (Used to express the belief that the event will not occur. Always used with a phrase with *if.*) □ *If we get there on time, I'll eat my hat.* □ *I'll eat my hat if you get a raise.* □ *He said he'd eat his hat if she got elected.*

**eat one's heart out 1.** to be very sad (about someone or something). □ *Bill spent a lot of time eating his heart out after his divorce.* □ *Sally ate her heart out when she had to sell her house.* **2.** to be envious (of someone or something). □ *Do you like my new watch? Well, eat your heart out. It was the last one in the store.* □ *Don't eat your heart out about my new car. Go get one of your own.*

**eat one's words** to have to take back one's statements; to confess that one's predictions were wrong. □ *You shouldn't say that to me. I'll make you eat your words.* □ *John was wrong about the election and had to eat his words.*

**eat out of someone's hand(s)** to do what someone wants; to obey someone eagerly. (Often with *have.* See the examples.) □ *Just wait! I'll have everyone eating out of my hands. They'll do whatever I ask.* □ *The* *president has Congress eating out of his hand.* □ *A lot of people are eating out of his hand.*

**eat someone out of house and home** to eat a lot of food (in someone's home); to eat all the food in the house. □ *Billy has a huge appetite. He almost eats us out of house and home.* □ *When the kids come home from college, they always eat us out of house and home.*

an **end in itself** something done for its own sake; something that needs no additional purpose for it to be worthwhile. □ *For Bob, art is an end in itself. He doesn't hope to make any money from it.* □ *Learning is an end in itself. Knowledge does not have to have a practical application.*

the **end of the line** See end of the road.

the **end of the road** AND the **end of the line** 1. the end; the end of the whole process. (*Line* originally referred to railroad tracks.) □ *Our house is at the end of the road.* □ *We rode the train to the end of the line.* □ *When we reach the end of the road on this project, we'll get paid.* **2.** death. □ *When I reach the end of the road, bury me in a quiet place, near some trees.* □ *Bill was so sick that we thought he was approaching the end of the line.*

**end up with the short end of the stick** See get the short end of the stick.

**Enough is enough.** That is enough, and there should be no more. □ *Stop asking for money! Enough is enough!* □ *I've heard all the complaining from you that I can take. Stop! Enough is enough!*

**enter one's mind** to come to one's mind; [for an idea or memory] to come into one's consciousness; to be thought of. □ *Leave you behind? The thought never even entered my mind.* □ *A very interesting idea just entered my mind. What if I ran for Congress?*

**Every cloud has a silver lining.** a proverb meaning that there is something good in every bad situation. □ *Jane was upset when she saw that all her flowers had died from the frost. But when she saw that the weeds had died too, she said, "Every cloud has a silver lining."* □ *Sally had a sore throat and had to stay home from school. When she learned she missed a math test, she said, "Every cloud has a silver lining."*

**Every dog has his day.** See Every dog has its day.

**Every dog has its day.** AND **Every dog has his day.** a proverb meaning that everyone will get a chance, even the lowliest. □ *Don't worry,* *you'll get chosen for the team. Every dog has its day.* □ *You may become famous someday. Every dog has his day.*

**every inch a something** AND **every inch the something** completely [something]; in every way [something]. □ *Mary is every inch the schoolteacher.* □ *Her father is every inch a gentleman.*

**every inch the something** See every inch a something.

**every living soul** every person. □ *I expect every living soul to be there and be there on time.* □ *This is the kind of problem that affects every living soul.*

**every minute counts** AND **every moment counts** time is very important. □ *Doctor, please try to get here quickly. Every minute counts.* □ *When you take a test, you must work rapidly because every minute counts.* □ *When you're trying to meet a deadline, every moment counts.*

**every moment counts** See every minute counts.

**everything but the kitchen sink** almost everything one can think of. □ *When Sally went off to college, she took everything but the kitchen sink.* □ *John orders everything but the kitchen sink when he goes out to dinner, especially if someone else is paying for it.*

**everything from A to Z** See everything from soup to nuts.

**everything from soup to nuts** AND **everything from A to Z** almost everything one can think of. (The main entry is used especially when describing the many things served at a meal.) □ *For dinner we had everything from soup to nuts.* □ *In college I studied everything from soup to nuts.* □ *She mentioned everything from A to Z.*

**every Tom, Dick, and Harry** everyone, without discrimination; ordinary people. (Not necessarily males.) □ *That golf club is very exclusive. It won't let every Tom, Dick, and Harry join.* □ *Mary's sending out very few invitations. She doesn't want every Tom, Dick, and Harry turning up.*

**expecting (a child)** pregnant. (A euphemism.) □ *Tommy's mother is expecting a child.* □ *Oh, I didn't know she was expecting.*

**eyeball-to-eyeball** person-to-person; face-to-face. □ *The discussions will have to be eyeball-to-eyeball to be effective.* □ *Telephone conversations are a waste of time. We need to talk eyeball-to-eyeball.*

An **eye for an eye (and a tooth for a tooth).** a proverb indicating that a punishment or act of revenge should be of the same degree as the crime or offense committed. (Biblical.) □ *His mother told him to hit the boy who had hit him. An eye for an eye.* □ *I don't feel bad about reporting him for being late, because he did the same to me last week. After all—an eye for an eye and a tooth for a tooth.*

**face the music** to receive punishment; to accept the unpleasant results of one's actions. □ *Mary broke a dining room window and had to face the music when her father got home.* □ *After failing a math test, Tom had to go home and face the music.*

**fair game** someone or something that it is quite permissible to attack. □ *I don't like seeing articles exposing people's private lives, but politicians are fair game.* □ *Journalists always regard movie stars as fair game.*

**fair-weather friend** a person who is one's friend only when things are going well for one. (When things go badly, this person will desert one.) □ *Bill wouldn't help me when I needed him. He's just a fair-weather friend.* □ *A fair-weather friend isn't much help in an emergency.*

**fall between two stools** to come somewhere between two possibilities and so fail to meet the requirements of either. □ *The material is not suitable for an academic book, and it is not suitable for a popular one either. It falls between two stools.* □ *He tries to be both teacher and friend, but falls between two stools.*

**fall down on the job** to fail to do something properly; to fail to do one's job adequately. (Also used literally.) □ *The team kept losing because the coach was falling down on the job.* □ *Tom was fired because he fell down on the job.*

**fall flat (on one's or its face)** to be completely unsuccessful. □ *I fell flat on my face when I tried to give my speech.* □ *The play fell flat on its face.* □ *My jokes fall flat most of the time.*

**fall foul of someone or something** to do something that annoys or offends someone or something; to do something that is contrary to the rules. □ *He has fallen foul of the police more than once.* □ *The political activists fell foul of the authorities.*

**fall from grace** to cease to be held in favor, especially because of some wrong or foolish action. □ *He was the teacher's prize pupil until he fell* *from grace by failing the history exam.* □ *Mary was the favorite grandchild until she fell from grace by running away from home.*

**fall in(to) place** to fit together; to become organized. □ *After we heard the whole story, things began to fall in place.* □ *When you get older, the different parts of your life begin to fall into place.*

**fall short (of something) 1.** to lack something; to lack enough of something. □ *We fell short of money at the end of the month.* □ *When baking a cake, the cook fell short of eggs and had to go to the store for more.* **2.** to fail to achieve a goal. □ *We fell short of our goal of collecting a thousand dollars.* □ *Ann ran a fast race but fell short of the record.*

**Familiarity breeds contempt.** a proverb meaning that knowing a person closely for a long time leads to bad feelings. □ *Bill and his brothers are always fighting. As they say, "Familiarity breeds contempt."* □ *Mary and John were good friends for many years. Finally they got into a big argument and became enemies. That just shows that familiarity breeds contempt.*

**fan the flames (of something)** to make something more intense; to make a situation worse. □ *The riot fanned the flames of racial hatred even more.* □ *The hostility in the school is bad enough without anyone fanning the flames.*

**farm someone or something out 1.** [with *someone*] to send someone (somewhere) for care or development. □ *When my mother died, they farmed me out to my aunt and uncle.* T *The team manager farmed out the baseball player to the minor leagues until he improved.* **2.** [with *something*] to send something (elsewhere) to be dealt with. □ *Bill farmed his chores out to his brothers and sisters and went to a movie.* T *I farmed out various parts of the work to different people.*

**fat chance** very little likelihood. (Informal.) □ *Fat chance he has of getting the promotion.* □ *You think she'll lend you the money? Fat chance!*

**The fat is in the fire.** a proverb meaning that serious trouble has broken out. □ *Now that Mary is leaving, the fat is in the fire. How can we get along without her?* □ *The fat's in the fire! There's $3,000 missing from the office safe.*

**feast one's eyes (on someone or something)** to look at someone or something with pleasure, envy, or admiration. (As if such visions provided a feast of visual delight for one's eyes.) □ *Just feast your eyes* *on that beautiful juicy steak!* □ *Yes, feast your eyes. You won't see one like that again for a long time.*

a **feather in one's cap** an honor; a reward for something. □ *Getting a new client was really a feather in my cap.* □ *John earned a feather in his cap by getting an A in physics.*

**feather one's (own) nest 1.** to decorate and furnish one's home in style and comfort. (Birds line their nests with feathers to make them warm and comfortable.) □ *Mr. and Mrs. Simpson have feathered their nest quite comfortably.* □ *It costs a great deal of money to feather one's own nest these days.* **2.** to use power and prestige to provide for oneself selfishly. (Said especially of politicians who use their offices to make money for themselves.) □ *The mayor seemed to be helping people, but she was really feathering her own nest.* □ *The building contractor used a lot of public money to feather his nest.*

**feed the kitty** to contribute money. (The *kitty* is a name for a container into which money is put.) □ *Please feed the kitty. Make a contribution to help sick children.* □ *Come on, Bill. Feed the kitty. You can afford a dollar for a good cause.*

**feel like a million (dollars)** to feel well and healthy, both physically and mentally. (To feel like something unbelievably good.) □ *A quick swim in the morning makes me feel like a million dollars.* □ *What a beautiful day! It makes you feel like a million.*

**feel like a new person** to feel refreshed and renewed, especially after getting well or getting dressed up. □ *I bought a new suit, and now I feel like a new person.* □ *Bob felt like a new person when he got out of the hospital.*

**feel out of place** to feel that one does not belong in some place. □ *I feel out of place at formal dances.* □ *Bob and Ann felt out of place at the picnic, so they went home.*

**feel something in one's bones** AND **know something in one's bones** to sense something; to have an intuition about something. □ *The train will be late. I feel it in my bones.* □ *I failed the test. I know it in my bones.*

**feel the pinch** to have money problems; to experience hardship because of having too little money. (Informal.) □ *The Smiths used to go abroad every year, but they're feeling the pinch since he retired.* □ *You're bound to feel the pinch a bit when you're a student.*

**fiddle while Rome burns** to do something frivolous or trivial, or to do nothing at all, while something disastrous happens. (From a legend that the emperor Nero played the lyre while Rome was burning.) □ *The Senate doesn't seem to be doing anything to stop this terrible bill. They're fiddling while Rome burns.* □ *The doctor should have sent for an ambulance right away instead of examining her. In fact, he was just fiddling while Rome burned.*

**fighting chance** a good possibility of success, especially if every effort is made. □ *They have at least a fighting chance of winning the race.* □ *The patient could die, but he has a fighting chance since the operation.*

**fight someone or something hammer and tongs** AND **fight someone or something tooth and nail; go at it hammer and tongs; go at it tooth and nail** to fight against someone or something energetically and with great determination. (These phrases are old and refer to fighting with and without weapons.) □ *They fought against the robber tooth and nail.* □ *The dogs were going at it hammer and tongs.* □ *The mayor fought the new law hammer and tongs.* □ *We'll fight this zoning ordinance tooth and nail.*

**fight someone or something tooth and nail** See fight someone or something hammer and tongs.

**fill someone's shoes** to take the place of some other person and do that person's work satisfactorily. (As if one were wearing the other person's shoes, that is, filling the shoes with one's own feet.) □ *I don't know how we'll be able to do without you. No one can fill your shoes.* □ *It'll be difficult to fill Jane's shoes. She did her job very well.*

**fill the bill** to be exactly the thing that is needed. □ *Ah, this steak is great. It really fills the bill.* □ *This new pair of shoes fills the bill nicely.*

**final fling** the last act or period of enjoyment before a change in one's circumstances or lifestyle. □ *You might as well have a final fling before the baby's born.* □ *Mary's going out with her girlfriends for a final fling. She's getting married next week.*

**Finders keepers(, losers weepers).** a proverb meaning that the person who finds something gets to keep it, and the person who loses it can only weep. □ *John lost a quarter in the dining room yesterday. Ann found the quarter there today. Ann claimed that since she found it, it was hers. She said, "Finders keepers, losers weepers."* □ *John said, "I'll say finders keepers when I find something of yours!"*

**find it in one's heart (to do something)** to have the courage or compassion to do something. □ *She couldn't find it in her heart to refuse to come home to him.* □ *I can't do it! I can't find it in my heart.*

**find one's feet** to become used to a new situation or experience. □ *She was lonely when she first left home, but she is finding her feet now.* □ *It takes time to learn the office routine, but you will gradually find your feet.*

**find one's or its way somewhere 1.** [with *one's*; for someone] to discover the route to a place. □ *Mr. Smith found his way to the museum.* □ *Can you find your way home?* **2.** [with *its*; for something] to end up in a place. (This expression avoids accusing someone of moving the thing or things to the place. In the plural, *their way* is used.) □ *The money found its way into the mayor's pocket.* □ *The secret plans found their way into the enemy's hands.*

**find one's own level** to find the position or rank to which one is best suited. (As water "seeks its own level.") □ *You cannot force junior staff to be ambitious. They will all find their own level.* □ *The new pupil is happier in the lower class. It was just a question of letting her find her own level.*

a **fine kettle of fish** a real mess; an unsatisfactory situation. □ *The dog has eaten the steak we were going to have for dinner. This is a fine kettle of fish!* □ *This is a fine kettle of fish. It's below freezing outside, and the furnace won't work.*

**Fire away!** Begin to do something. (Often refers to speaking or asking questions.) □ *Fire away! I'm ready to take dictation.* □ *If you want me to hear your complaints, fire away!*

**firing on all cylinders** working at full strength; making every possible effort. (From an internal combustion engine.) □ *The team is firing on all cylinders under the new coach.* □ *The factory is firing on all cylinders to finish the orders on time.*

**first and foremost** first and most important. (A cliché.) □ *First and foremost, I think you should work harder on your biology.* □ *Have this in mind first and foremost: Keep smiling!*

**first come, first served** [of a situation in which] the first people to arrive will be served first. (A cliché.) □ *They ran out of tickets before we got there. It was first come, first served, but we didn't know that.* □ *Please line up and take your turn. It's first come, first served.*

**first of all** the very first thing; before anything else. □ *First of all, put your name on this piece of paper.* □ *First of all, we'll try to find a place to live.*

**first thing (in the morning)** before anything else in the morning. □ *Please call me first thing in the morning. I can't help you now.* □ *I'll do that first thing.*

**First things first.** The most important things must be taken care of first. □ *It's more important to get a job than to buy new clothes. First things first!* □ *Do your homework now. Go out and play later. First things first.*

**fish for a compliment** to try to get someone to pay one a compliment. (As if one were tempting someone to utter a compliment.) □ *When she showed me her new dress, I could tell that she was fishing for a compliment.* □ *Tom was certainly fishing for a compliment when he modeled his stylish haircut for his friends.*

**fish in troubled waters** to involve oneself in a difficult, confused, or dangerous situation, especially with a view to gaining an advantage. □ *Frank is fishing in troubled waters by buying more shares of that firm. They are supposed to be in financial difficulties.* □ *The firm could make more money by selling weapons abroad, but they would be fishing in troubled waters.*

**fish or cut bait** either do the job you are supposed to be doing or quit and let someone else do it; either participate fully in something or stop entirely. □ *Mary is doing much better on the job since her manager told her to fish or cut bait.* □ *The boss told Tom, "Quit wasting time! Fish or cut bait!"*

**fit for a king** totally suitable; suitable for royalty. (A cliché.) □ *What a delicious meal. It was fit for a king.* □ *Our room at the hotel was fit for a king.*

**fit like a glove** to fit very well; to fit tightly or snugly. □ *My new shoes fit like a glove.* □ *My new coat is a little tight. It fits like a glove.*

**fit someone to a T** See suit someone to a T.

**fix someone's wagon** to punish someone; to get even with someone; to plot against someone. □ *If you ever do that again, I'll fix your wagon!* □ *Tommy! You clean up your room this instant, or I'll fix your wagon!* □ *He reported me to the principal, but I fixed his wagon. I knocked his lunch on the floor.*

a **flash in the pan** someone or something that draws a lot of attention for a very brief time. □ *I'm afraid that my success as a painter was just a flash in the pan.* □ *Tom had hoped to be a singer, but his career was only a flash in the pan.*

**flat broke** completely broke; with no money at all. □ *I spent my last dollar, and I'm flat broke.* □ *The bank closed its doors to the public. It was flat broke!*

**flesh and blood 1.** a living human body, especially with reference to its natural limitations; a human being. □ *This cold weather is more than flesh and blood can stand.* □ *Carrying 300 pounds is beyond mere flesh and blood.* **2.** the quality of being alive. □ *The paintings of this artist are lifeless. They lack flesh and blood.* □ *These ideas have no flesh and blood.* **3.** one's own relatives; one's own kin. □ *That's no way to treat one's own flesh and blood.* □ *I want to leave my money to my own flesh and blood.* □ *Grandmother was happier living with her flesh and blood.*

**flight of fancy** an idea or suggestion that is out of touch with reality or possibility. □ *What is the point of indulging in flights of fancy about exotic vacations when you cannot even afford the rent?* □ *We are tired of her flights of fancy about marrying a millionaire.*

**float a loan** to get a loan; to arrange for a loan. □ *I couldn't afford to pay cash for the car, so I floated a loan.* □ *They needed money, so they had to float a loan.*

**fly in the face of someone or something** AND **fly in the teeth of someone or something** to disregard, defy, or show disrespect for someone or something. □ *John loves to fly in the face of tradition.* □ *Ann made it a practice to fly in the face of standard procedures.* □ *John finds great pleasure in flying in the teeth of his father.*

**fly in the ointment** a small, unpleasant matter that spoils something; a drawback. □ *We enjoyed the play, but the fly in the ointment was not being able to find our car afterward.* □ *It sounds like a good idea, but there must be a fly in the ointment somewhere.*

**fly in the teeth of someone or something** See fly in the face of someone or something.

**fly off the handle** to lose one's temper. □ *Every time anyone mentions taxes, Mrs. Brown flies off the handle.* □ *If she keeps flying off the handle like that, she'll have a heart attack.*

**foam at the mouth** to be very angry. (Related to a "mad dog"—a dog with rabies—that foams at the mouth.) □ *Bob was raving—foaming at the mouth. I've never seen anyone so angry.* □ *Bill foamed at the mouth in anger.*

**follow one's heart** to act according to one's feelings; to obey one's sympathetic or compassionate inclinations. □ *I couldn't decide what to do, so I just followed my heart.* □ *I trust that you will follow your heart in this matter.*

**food for thought** something to think about. □ *I don't like your idea very much, but it's food for thought.* □ *Your lecture was very good. It contained much food for thought.*

A **fool and his money are soon parted.** a proverb meaning that a person who acts unwisely with money soon loses it. (Often said about a person who has just lost a sum of money because of poor judgment.) □ *When Bill lost a $400 bet on a horse race, Mary said, "A fool and his money are soon parted."* □ *When John bought a cheap used car that fell apart the next day, he said, "Oh, well, a fool and his money are soon parted."*

a **fool's paradise** a condition of seeming happiness that is based on false assumptions and will not last. (Treated as a place grammatically.) □ *They think they can live on love alone, but they are living in a fool's paradise.* □ *The inhabitants of the island feel politically secure, but they are living in a fool's paradise. They could be invaded at any time.*

**Fools rush in (where angels fear to tread).** a proverb meaning that people with little experience or knowledge often get involved in difficult or delicate situations that wiser people would avoid. □ *I wouldn't ask Jean about her divorce, but Kate did. Fools rush in, as they say.* □ *Only the newest member of the committee questioned the chairman's decision. Fools rush in where angels fear to tread.*

**footloose and fancy free** without responsibilities or commitments. □ *All the rest of them have wives, but John is footloose and fancy free.* □ *Mary never stays long in any job. She likes being footloose and fancy free.*

**foot the bill** to pay the bill; to pay (for something). □ *Let's go out and eat. I'll foot the bill.* □ *If the bank goes broke, don't worry. The government will foot the bill.*

**forbidden fruit** someone or something that one finds attractive or desirable partly because the person or thing is unobtainable. (Biblical.

From the fruit in the Garden of Eden that was forbidden to Adam and Eve by God.) □ *Jim is in love with his sister-in-law only because she's forbidden fruit.* □ *The boy watches that program only when his parents are out. It's forbidden fruit.*

**force someone's hand** to force a person to reveal plans, strategies, or secrets. (Refers to a handful of cards in card playing.) □ *We didn't know what she was doing until Tom forced her hand.* □ *We couldn't plan our game until we forced the other team's hand in the last play.*

**force someone to the wall** AND **drive someone to the wall** to push someone to an extreme position; to put someone into an awkward position. □ *He wouldn't tell the truth until we forced him to the wall.* □ *They don't pay their bills until you drive them to the wall.*

**for fear of something** out of fear for something; because of fear of something. □ *He doesn't drive for fear of an accident.* □ *They lock their doors for fear of being robbed.*

**forgive and forget** to forgive someone (for something) and forget that it ever happened. (A cliché.) □ *I'm sorry, John. Let's forgive and forget. What do you say?* □ *It was nothing. We'll just have to forgive and forget.*

**fork money out (for something)** to pay (perhaps unwillingly) for something. (Often includes a mention of the amount of money.) □ *Do you think I'm going to fork thirty dollars out for that book?* Ⓣ *I hate having to fork out money day after day.*

**form an opinion** to think up or decide on an opinion. (Note the variations in the examples.) □ *I don't know enough about the issue to form an opinion.* □ *Don't tell me how to think! I can form my own opinion.* □ *I don't form opinions without careful consideration.*

**for the devil of it** AND **for the heck of it; for the hell of it** just for fun; because it is slightly evil; for no good reason. (Some people may object to the word *hell*. Often with *just*.) □ *We filled their garage with leaves just for the devil of it.* □ *Tom bought a motorcycle for the heck of it.* □ *John picked a fight with Tom just for the hell of it.*

**for the heck of it** See for the devil of it.

**for the hell of it** See for the devil of it.

**for the record** so that (one's own version of) the facts will be known; so there will be a record of a particular fact. (This often is said when reporters are present.) □ *I'd like to say—for the record—that at no time* *have I ever accepted a bribe from anyone.* □ *For the record, I've never been able to get anything done around city hall without bribing someone.*

**foul one's own nest** to harm one's own interests; to bring disadvantage upon oneself. □ *He tried to discredit a fellow worker but just succeeded in fouling his own nest.* □ *The boss really dislikes Mary. She certainly fouled her own nest when she spread those rumors about him.*

**foul play** illegal activity; bad practices. □ *The police investigating the death suspect foul play.* □ *Each student got an A on the test, and the teacher imagined it was the result of foul play.*

**free and easy** casual. □ *John is so free and easy. How can anyone be so relaxed?* □ *Now, calm down. Just act free and easy. No one will know you're nervous.*

**free-for-all** a disorganized fight or contest involving everyone; a brawl. □ *The picnic turned into a free-for-all after midnight.* □ *The race started out in an organized manner but ended up being a free-for-all.*

**fresh blood** AND **new blood** new personnel; new members brought into a group to revive it. □ *This firm needs some fresh blood on its board to bring new ideas.* □ *We're trying to get some new blood in the club. Our membership is falling.*

A **friend in need is a friend indeed.** a proverb meaning that a true friend is a person who will help you when you really need some help. □ *When Bill helped me with geometry, I really learned the meaning of "A friend in need is a friend indeed."* □ *"A friend in need is a friend indeed" sounds silly until you need someone very badly.*

**from hand to hand** from one person to a series of other persons; from one person's hand to another person's hand, and so forth. □ *The book traveled from hand to hand until it got back to its owner.* □ *By the time the baby had been passed from hand to hand, it was crying.*

**from pillar to post** from one place to a series of other places; (figuratively) from person to person, as with gossip. (A cliché.) □ *My father was in the army, and we moved from pillar to post year after year.* □ *After I told one person my secret, it went quickly from pillar to post.*

**from rags to riches** from poverty to wealth; from modesty to elegance. □ *The princess used to be quite poor. She certainly moved from rags to riches.* □ *When I inherited the money, I went from rags to riches.*

**from start to finish** from the beginning to the end; throughout. □ *I disliked the whole business from start to finish.* □ *Mary caused problems from start to finish.*

**from stem to stern** from one end to another. (Refers to the front and back ends of a ship. Also used literally in reference to ships.) □ *Now, I have to clean the house from stem to stern.* □ *I polished my car carefully from stem to stern.*

**from the bottom of one's heart** sincerely. □ *When I returned the lost kitten to Mrs. Brown, she thanked me from the bottom of her heart.* □ *Oh, thank you! I'm grateful from the bottom of my heart.*

**from the ground up** from the beginning; from start to finish. (Used literally in reference to building a house or other building.) □ *We must plan our sales campaign carefully from the ground up.* □ *Sorry, but you'll have to start all over again from the ground up.*

**from the old school** holding attitudes or ideas that were popular and important in the past, but that are no longer considered relevant or in line with modern trends. □ *Grammar is not much taught nowadays, but fortunately my son has a teacher from the old school, so he's learning all about it.* □ *Aunt Jane is from the old school. She never goes out without wearing a hat and gloves.*

**from the word go** from the beginning; from the very start of things. (Actually from the uttering of the word *go.*) □ *I knew about the problem from the word go.* □ *She was failing the class from the word go.*

**from top to bottom** from the highest point to the lowest point; throughout. □ *I have to clean the house from top to bottom today.* □ *We need to replace our elected officials from top to bottom.*

**full of beans** very lively and cheerful; healthy and energetic. □ *The children tire their granny out. They're always so full of beans.* □ *Joan was ill last year, but she's full of beans now.*

**full of oneself** conceited; self-important. □ *Mary's very unpopular because she's so full of herself.* □ *She doesn't care about other people's feelings. She's too full of herself.*

**full steam ahead** forward at the greatest speed possible; with as much energy and enthusiasm as possible. (From an instruction given on a steamship.) □ *It will have to be full steam ahead for everybody if the factory gets this order.* □ *It's going to be full steam ahead for me this week.*

**fun and games** playing around; doing worthless things; activities that are a waste of time. □ *All right, Bill, the fun and games are over. It's time to get down to work.* □ *This isn't a serious course. It's nothing but fun and games.*

**funny business** trickery or deception; illegal activity. (Informal.) □ *From the silence as she entered the room, the teacher knew there was some funny business going on.* □ *There's some funny business going on at the warehouse. Stock keeps disappearing.*

**gain ground** to make progress; to advance; to become more important or popular. □ *Our new product is gaining ground against that of our competitor.* □ *Since the government announced its new policies, the opposition is gaining ground.*

**get a black eye** (Note variations in the examples. *Get* usually means to become, to acquire, or to cause. *Have* usually means to possess, to be, or to have resulted in.) **1.** to get a bruise near the eye from being struck. □ *I got a black eye from walking into a door.* □ *I have a black eye where John hit me.* **2.** to have one's character or reputation harmed. □ *Mary got a black eye because of her complaining.* □ *The whole group now has a black eye.* ALSO: **give someone a black eye 1.** to hit someone near the eye so that a dark bruise appears. □ *John became angry and gave me a black eye.* **2.** to harm the character or reputation of someone. □ *The constant complaining gave the whole group a black eye.*

**get above oneself** to behave as though one is better or more important than one is. □ *John is getting a bit above himself since he was promoted. He never goes for a drink with his old colleagues.* □ *There was no need for her to get above herself just because she married a wealthy man.*

**get a clean bill of health** [for someone] to be pronounced healthy by a physician. (Also with *have*. See the note at **get a black eye**.) □ *Sally got a clean bill of health from the doctor.* □ *Now that Sally has a clean bill of health, she can go back to work.* ALSO: **give someone a clean bill of health** [for a doctor] to pronounce someone well and healthy. □ *The doctor gave Sally a clean bill of health.*

**get (all) dolled up** to dress (oneself) up. (Usually used for females, but not necessarily.) □ *I have to get all dolled up for the dance tonight.* □ *I just love to get dolled up in my best clothes.*

**get a load off one's feet** AND **take a load off one's feet** to sit down; to enjoy the results of sitting down. □ *Come in, John. Sit down and* *take a load off your feet.* □ *Yes, I need to get a load off my feet. I'm really tired.*

**get a load off one's mind** to say what one is thinking. □ *He sure talked a long time. I guess he had to get a load off his mind.* □ *You aren't going to like what I'm going to say, but I have to get a load off my mind.*

**get along (on a shoestring)** to be able to afford to live on very little money. □ *For the last two years, we have had to get along on a shoestring.* □ *With so little money, it's hard to get along.*

**get a lump in one's throat** to have the feeling of something in one's throat—as if one were going to cry. (Also with *have*. See the note at get a black eye.) □ *Whenever they play the national anthem, I get a lump in my throat.* □ *I have a lump in my throat because I'm frightened.*

**get a word in edgeways** See get a word in edgewise.

**get a word in edgewise** AND **get a word in edgeways** to manage to say something when other people are talking and ignoring one. (Often in the negative. As if one were trying to fit in or squeeze in one's contribution to a conversation.) □ *It was such an exciting conversation that I could hardly get a word in edgewise.* □ *Mary talks so fast that nobody can get a word in edgeways.*

**get cold feet** to become timid or frightened; to have one's feet seem to freeze with fear. (Also with *have*. See the note at get a black eye.) □ *I usually get cold feet when I have to speak in public.* □ *John got cold feet and wouldn't run in the race.* □ *I can't give my speech now. I have cold feet.*

**get down to brass tacks** to begin to talk about important things. □ *Let's get down to brass tacks. We've wasted too much time chatting.* □ *Don't you think that it's about time to get down to brass tacks?*

**get down to business** AND **get down to work** to begin to get serious; to begin to negotiate or conduct business. □ *All right, everyone. Let's get down to business. There has been enough playing around.* □ *When the president and vice president arrive, we can get down to business.* □ *They're here. Let's get down to work.*

**get down to work** See get down to business.

**get fresh (with someone)** to become overly bold or impertinent. □ *When I tried to kiss Mary, she slapped me and shouted, "Don't get fresh with me!"* □ *I can't stand people who get fresh.*

**get goose bumps** AND **get goose pimples** [for someone's skin] to feel prickly or become bumpy due to fear or excitement. (Also with *have*. See the note at get a black eye. For one's flesh to become like the flesh of a plucked goose. Very few Americans have ever seen a plucked goose.) □ *When he sings, I get goose bumps.* □ *I never get goose pimples.* □ *That really scared her. Now she's got goose pimples.*

**get goose pimples** See get goose bumps.

**get in someone's hair** to bother or irritate someone. □ *Billy is always getting in his mother's hair.* □ *I wish you'd stop getting in my hair.*

**get into the swing of things** to join into the routine or the activities. (Refers to the rhythm of routinized activity.) □ *Come on, Bill. Try to get into the swing of things.* □ *John just couldn't seem to get into the swing of things.*

**get off scot-free** See go scot-free.

**get off to a flying start** to have a very successful beginning. □ *The new business got off to a flying start with those export orders.* □ *We shall need a large donation if the charity is to get off to a flying start.*

**get one's back up** See get one's dander up.

**get one's dander up** AND **get one's back up; get one's hackles up; get one's Irish up** to become angry. (Also with *have*. See the note at get a black eye.) □ *Now, don't get your dander up. Calm down.* □ *Bob had his Irish up all day yesterday. I don't know what was wrong.* □ *She really got her back up when I asked her for money.* □ *Now, now, don't get your hackles up. I didn't mean any harm.*

**get one's ducks in a row** to put one's affairs in order; to get things ready. (Informal or slang. As if one were lining up wooden ducks to shoot them one by one, as in a carnival game.) □ *You can't hope to go into a company and sell something until you get your ducks in a row.* □ *As soon as you people get your ducks in a row, we'll leave.*

**get one's feet on the ground** to get firmly established or reestablished. (Also with *have*. See the note at get a black eye.) □ *He's new at the job, but soon he'll get his feet on the ground.* □ *Her productivity will improve after she gets her feet on the ground again.* □ *Don't worry about Sally. She has her feet on the ground.* ALSO: **keep one's feet on the ground** to remain firmly established. □ *Sally will have no trouble keeping her feet on the ground.*

**get one's feet wet** to begin something; to have one's first experience of something. (As if one were wading into water.) □ *Of course he can't do the job right. He's hardly got his feet wet yet.* □ *I'm looking forward to learning to drive. I can't wait to get behind the steering wheel and get my feet wet.*

**get one's fill of someone or something** to receive enough of someone or something. (Also with *have*. See the note at get a black eye.) □ *You'll soon get your fill of Tom. He can be quite a pest.* □ *I can never get my fill of fruit. I love it.* □ *Three weeks of visiting grandchildren is enough. I've had my fill of them.*

**get one's fingers burned** to have a bad experience. (Also used literally.) □ *I tried that once before and got my fingers burned. I won't try it again.* □ *Billy got his fingers burned the first time he rode a horse, and now he's afraid to try riding again.*

**get one's foot in the door** to achieve a favorable position (for further action); to take the first step in a process. (People selling things from door to door used to block the door with a foot, so it could not be closed on them. Also with *have*. See the note at get a black eye.) □ *I think I could get the job if I could only get my foot in the door.* □ *It pays to get your foot in the door. Try to get an appointment with the boss.* □ *I have a better chance now that I have my foot in the door.*

**get one's hackles up** See get one's dander up.

**get one's hands dirty** AND **dirty one's hands; soil one's hands** to become involved with something illegal; to do a shameful thing; to do something that is beneath one. □ *The mayor would never get his hands dirty by giving away political favors.* □ *I will not dirty my hands by breaking the law.* □ *Sally felt that to talk to the beggar was to soil her hands.*

**get one's head above water** to get ahead of one's problems; to catch up with one's work or responsibilities. (Also used literally. Also with *have*. See the note at get a black eye.) □ *I can't seem to get my head above water. Work just keeps piling up.* □ *I'll be glad when I have my head above water.* ALSO: **keep one's head above water** to stay ahead of one's responsibilities. □ *Now that I have more space to work in, I can easily keep my head above water.*

**get one's Irish up** See get one's dander up.

**get one's just deserts** to get what one deserves. □ *I felt better when Jane finally got her just deserts. She really insulted me.* □ *Bill got back exactly the treatment that he gave out. He got his just deserts.*

**get one's second wind** (Also with *have*. See the note at get a black eye.) **1.** [for someone] to achieve stability in breathing again after a period of exhaustion, when one has been continuously exerting oneself. □ *John was having a hard time running until he got his second wind.* □ *Bill had to quit the race because he never got his second wind.* □ *"At last," thought Ann, "I have my second wind. Now I can really swim fast."* **2.** [for someone] to become more active or productive again after a period of slowing down due to exhaustion. □ *I usually get my second wind early in the afternoon.* □ *Mary is a better worker now that she has her second wind.*

**get one's teeth into something** to start on something seriously, especially a difficult task. (Also used literally in reference to eating.) □ *Come on, Bill. You have to get your teeth into your biology.* □ *I can't wait to get my teeth into this problem.*

**get on someone's nerves** to irritate someone. □ *Please stop whistling. It's getting on my nerves.* □ *All this arguing is getting on their nerves.*

**get on the bandwagon** AND **climb on the bandwagon; jump on the bandwagon** to join the popular side (of an issue); to take a popular position. □ *You really should get on the bandwagon. Everyone else is.* □ *Come join us! Climb on the bandwagon and support Senator Smith!* □ *Jane has always had her own ideas about things. She's not the kind of person to jump on the bandwagon.*

**get out of the wrong side of the bed** See get up on the wrong side of the bed.

**get second thoughts about someone or something** to have doubts about someone or something. (Also with *have*. See the note at get a black eye.) □ *I'm beginning to get second thoughts about Tom.* □ *Tom is getting second thoughts about it, too.* □ *We now have second thoughts about going to Canada.*

**get (someone) off the hook** to free someone from an obligation; to help someone out of an awkward situation. □ *Thanks for getting me off the hook. I didn't want to attend that meeting.* □ *I couldn't get off the hook by myself.*

**get someone over a barrel** AND **get someone under one's thumb** to put someone at one's mercy; to get control over someone. (Also with *have*. See the note at get a black eye.) □ *He got me over a barrel, and I had to do what he said.* □ *Ann will do exactly what I say. I've got her over a barrel.* □ *All right, John. You've got me under your thumb. What do you want me to do?*

**get someone's ear** to get someone to listen (to one); to have someone's attention. (Also with *have*. See the note at get a black eye.) □ *He got my ear and talked for an hour.* □ *While I have your ear, I'd like to tell you about something I'm selling.*

**get someone's eye** See catch someone's eye.

**get someone under one's thumb** See get someone over a barrel.

**get something into someone's thick head** See get something through someone's thick skull.

**get something off one's chest** to tell something that has been bothering one. (Also with *have*. See the note at get a black eye.) □ *I have to get this off my chest. I broke your window with a stone.* □ *I knew I'd feel better when I had that off my chest.*

**get something off (the ground)** to get something started. □ *I can relax after I get this project off the ground.* □ *You'll have a lot of free time when you get the project off.*

**get something sewed up** (Also with *have*. See the note at get a black eye.) **1.** to have something stitched together (by someone). (Literal.) □ *I want to get this tear sewed up now.* □ *I'll have this hole sewed up tomorrow.* **2.** AND **get something wrapped up** to have something settled or finished. (Also with *have*.) □ *I'll take the contract to the mayor tomorrow morning. I'll get the whole deal wrapped up by noon.* □ *Don't worry about the car loan. I'll have it sewed up in time to make the purchase.* □ *I'll get the order wrapped up, and you'll have the car this week.*

**get something straight** to understand something clearly. (Also with *have*. See the note at get a black eye.) □ *Now, get this straight. You're going to fail history.* □ *Let me get this straight. I'm supposed to go there in the morning?* □ *Let me make sure I have this straight.*

**get something through someone's thick skull** AND **get something into someone's thick head** to make someone understand something; to get some information into someone's mind. (*Someone* includes *oneself.*) □ *He can't seem to get it through his thick skull.* □ *If I could just get this into my thick head once, I'd remember it.*

**get something under one's belt** (Also with *have*. See the note at get a black eye.) **1.** to eat or drink something. (This means the food goes into one's stomach and is under one's belt.) □ *I'd feel a lot better if I had a cool drink under my belt.* □ *Come in out of the cold and get a nice warm meal under your belt.* **2.** to learn something well; to assimilate some information. □ *I have to study tonight. I have to get a lot of algebra under my belt.* □ *Now that I have my lessons under my belt, I can rest easy.*

**get something under way** to get something started. (Also with *have*. See the note at get a black eye. Originally nautical.) □ *The time has come to get this meeting under way.* □ *Now that the president has the meeting under way, I can relax.*

**get something wrapped up** See get something sewed up.

**get stars in one's eyes** to be obsessed with show business; to be stagestruck. (Also with *have*. See the note at get a black eye. Refers to stardom, as in the stars of Hollywood or New York.) □ *Many young people get stars in their eyes at this age.* □ *Ann has stars in her eyes. She wants to go to Hollywood.*

**get the benefit of the doubt** to receive a judgment in one's favor when the evidence is neither for one nor against one. (Also with *have*. See the note at get a black eye.) □ *I was right between a B and an A. I got the benefit of the doubt—an A.* □ *I thought I should have had the benefit of the doubt, but the judge made me pay a fine.* ALSO: **give someone the benefit of the doubt** to decide in someone's favor when the evidence is unclear. □ *I'm glad the teacher gave me the benefit of the doubt.* □ *"Please, Your Honor," I said to the judge, "give me the benefit of the doubt."*

**get the blues** to become sad or depressed; to become melancholy. (Also with *have*. See the note at get a black eye.) □ *You'll have to excuse Bill. He has the blues tonight.* □ *I get the blues every time I hear that song.*

**get the final word** See get the last word.

**get the hang of something** to learn how to do something; to learn how something works. (Also with *have*. See the note at get a black eye.) □ *As soon as I get the hang of this computer, I'll be able to work faster.*

☐ *Now that I have the hang of starting the car in cold weather, I won't have to get up so early.*

**get the inside track** to get the advantage (over someone) because of special connections, special knowledge, or favoritism. (Also with *have*. See the note at **get a black eye**.) ☐ *If I could get the inside track, I could win the contract.* ☐ *The boss likes me. Since I have the inside track, I'll probably be the new office manager.*

**get the jump on someone** to do something before someone; to get ahead of someone. (Also with *have*. See the note at **get a black eye**.) ☐ *I got the jump on Tom and got a place in line ahead of him.* ☐ *We'll have to work hard to get the contract, because they have the jump on us.*

**get the last laugh** to laugh at or ridicule someone who has laughed at or ridiculed one; to put someone in the same bad position that one was once in. (Also with *have*. See the note at **get a black eye**.) ☐ *John laughed when I got a D on the final exam. I got the last laugh, though. He failed the course.* ☐ *Mr. Smith said I was foolish when I bought an old building. I had the last laugh when I sold it a month later for twice what I paid for it.*

**get the last word** AND **get the final word** to make the final point (in an argument); to make the final decision (in some matter). (Also with *have*. See the note at **get a black eye**.) ☐ *The boss gets the last word in hiring.* ☐ *Why do you always have to have the final word in an argument?*

**get the message** See **get the word**.

**get the nod** to be chosen. (Also with *have*. See the note at **get a black eye**.) ☐ *The boss is going to pick the new sales manager. I think Ann will get the nod.* ☐ *I had the nod for captain of the team, but I decided not to do it.*

**get the red-carpet treatment** to receive very special treatment; to receive royal treatment; to be treated like royalty. (This refers—sometimes literally—to the rolling out of a clean red carpet for someone to walk on.) ☐ *I love to go to fancy stores where I get the red-carpet treatment.* ☐ *The queen expects to get the red-carpet treatment wherever she goes.* ALSO: **give someone the red-carpet treatment** to give someone very special treatment; to treat someone like royalty. ☐ *We always give the queen the red-carpet treatment when she comes to visit.* ALSO: **roll out the red carpet for someone** to provide special treatment for someone. □ *There's no need to roll out the red carpet for me.* □ *We rolled out the red carpet for the visiting diplomats.*

**get the runaround** to receive a series of excuses, delays, and referrals. □ *You'll get the runaround if you ask to see the manager.* □ *I hate it when I get the runaround.* ALSO: **give someone the runaround** to give someone a series of excuses, delays, and referrals. □ *If you ask to see the manager, they'll give you the runaround.*

**get the shock of one's life** to receive a serious (emotional) shock. (Also with *have*. See the note at **get a black eye**.) □ *I opened the telegram and got the shock of my life.* □ *I had the shock of my life when I won $5,000.*

**get the short end of the stick** AND **end up with the short end of the stick** to get less (than someone else); to be cheated or deceived. (Also with *have*. See the note at **get a black eye**.) □ *Why do I always get the short end of the stick? I want my fair share!* □ *She's unhappy because she has the short end of the stick again.* □ *I hate to end up with the short end of the stick.*

**get the upper hand (on someone)** to get into a position superior to someone; to gain an advantage over someone. (Also with *have*. See the note at **get a black eye**.) □ *John is always trying to get the upper hand on me.* □ *He never ends up having the upper hand, though.*

**get the word** AND **get the message** to receive an explanation; to receive the final and authoritative explanation. (Also with *have*. See the note at **get a black eye**.) □ *I'm sorry, I didn't get the word. I didn't know the matter had been settled.* □ *Now that I have the message, I can be more effective in answering questions.*

**get time to catch one's breath** to find enough time to relax or behave normally. (Also with *have*. See the note at **get a black eye**.) □ *When things slow down around here, I'll get time to catch my breath.* □ *Sally was so busy she didn't even have time to catch her breath.*

**get to first base (with someone or something)** AND **reach first base (with someone or something)** to make a major advance with someone or something. (*First base* refers to baseball.) □ *I wish I could get to first base with this business deal.* □ *John adores Sally, but he can't reach first base with her. She won't even speak to him.* □ *He smiles and acts friendly, but he can't get to first base.*

**get to one's feet** to stand up. □ *On a signal from the director, the singers got to their feet.* □ *I was so weak, I could hardly get to my feet.*

**get to the bottom of something** to reach an understanding of the causes of something. □ *We must get to the bottom of this problem immediately.* □ *There is clearly something wrong here, and I want to get to the bottom of it.*

**get to the heart of the matter** to focus on the essentials of a matter. □ *We have to stop wasting time and get to the heart of the matter.* □ *You've been very helpful. You really seem to be able to get to the heart of the matter.*

**get to the point** See come to the point.

**get two strikes against one** to get several factors against one; to be at a disadvantage; to get into a position where success is unlikely. (From baseball, where a player is "out" after three strikes. Also with *have*. See the note at get a black eye.) □ *Poor Bob got two strikes against him when he tried to explain where he was last night.* □ *I can't win. I have two strikes against me, and I haven't even started yet.*

**get under someone's skin** to bother or irritate someone. (Refers to an irritant such as an insect or chemical that penetrates the skin.) □ *John is so annoying. He really gets under my skin.* □ *I know he's bothersome, but don't let him get under your skin.* □ *This kind of problem gets under my skin.*

**get up enough nerve (to do something)** to become brave enough to do something. □ *I could never get up enough nerve to sing in public.* □ *I'd do it if I could get up enough nerve, but I'm shy.*

**get up on the wrong side of the bed** AND **get out of the wrong side of the bed** to get up in the morning in a bad mood; to start the day in a bad mood. (As if the choice of the side of the bed makes a difference in one's humor.) □ *What's wrong with you? Did you get up on the wrong side of the bed today?* □ *Excuse me for being grouchy. I got out of the wrong side of the bed.*

**get wind of something** to hear about something; to receive information about something. (The *wind* may be someone's breath or words, but more likely it refers to catching the scent of something in the wind long before the thing itself appears.) □ *I just got wind of your marriage. Congratulations.* □ *Wait until the boss gets wind of this. Somebody is going to get in trouble.*

**get worked up about something** See get worked up (over something).

**get worked up (over something)** AND **get worked up about something** to become excited or emotionally distressed about something. □ *Please don't get worked up over this matter.* □ *They get worked up about these things very easily.* □ *I try not to get worked up.*

**gild the lily** to add ornament or decoration to something that is pleasing in its original state; to attempt to improve something that is already fine the way it is. (Often refers to flattery or exaggeration. The lily is considered beautiful enough as it is. Gilding it—covering it with gold—is overdoing it.) □ *Your house has lovely brickwork. Don't paint it. That would be gilding the lily.* □ *Oh, Sally. You're beautiful the way you are. You don't need makeup. That would be gilding the lily.*

**gird (up) one's loins** to get ready; to prepare oneself (for something). (A cliché. Means essentially to dress oneself in preparation for something. From biblical references.) □ *Well, I guess I had better gird up my loins and go to work.* □ *Somebody has to do something about the problem. Why don't you gird your loins and do something?*

**give a good account of oneself** to do something well or thoroughly. □ *John gave a good account of himself when he gave his speech last night.* □ *Mary was not hungry, and she didn't give a good account of herself at dinner.*

**give as good as one gets** to give as much as one receives; to pay someone back in kind. (Usually in the present tense.) □ *John can take care of himself in a fight. He can give as good as he gets.* □ *Sally usually wins a formal debate. She gives as good as she gets.*

**give credit where credit is due** to give credit to someone who deserves it; to acknowledge or thank someone who deserves it. (A cliché.) □ *We must give credit where credit is due. Thank you very much, Sally.* □ *Let's give credit where credit is due. Mary is the one who wrote the report, not Jane.*

**Give one an inch, and one will take a mile.** AND **If you give one an inch, one will take a mile.** a proverb meaning that a person who is granted a little of something (such as a reprieve or lenience) will want more. □ *I told John he could turn in his paper one day late, but he turned it in three days late. Give him an inch, and he'll take a mile.* □ *First we let John borrow our car for a day. Now he wants to go on a two-week vacation. If you give him an inch, he'll take a mile.*

**give one one's freedom** to set someone free; to divorce someone. (Usually euphemistic for divorce.) □ *Mrs. Brown wanted to give her husband his freedom.* □ *Well, Tom, I hate to break it to you this way, but I have decided to give you your freedom.*

**give oneself airs** to act conceited or superior. □ *Sally is always giving herself airs. You'd think she had royal blood.* □ *Come on, John. Don't act so haughty. Stop giving yourself airs.*

**give one's right arm (for someone or something)** to be willing to give something of great value for someone or something. □ *I'd give my right arm for a nice cool drink.* □ *I'd give my right arm to be there.* □ *Tom really admired John. Tom would give his right arm for John.*

**give someone a black eye** See under get a black eye.

**give someone a buzz** See give someone a ring.

**give someone a clean bill of health** See under get a clean bill of health.

**give someone a piece of one's mind** to bawl someone out; to scold someone; to tell someone off. (Actually to give someone a helping of what one is thinking about.) □ *I've had enough from John. I'm going to give him a piece of my mind.* □ *Sally, stop it, or I'll give you a piece of my mind.*

**give someone a ring** AND **give someone a buzz** to call someone on the telephone. (*Ring* and *buzz* refer to the bell in a telephone.) □ *Nice talking to you. Give me a ring sometime.* □ *Give me a buzz when you're in town.*

**give someone or something a wide berth** to keep a reasonable distance from someone or something; to steer clear of someone or something. (Originally referred to sailing ships.) □ *The dog we are approaching is very mean. Better give it a wide berth.* □ *Give Mary a wide berth. She's in a very bad mood.*

**give someone the benefit of the doubt** See under get the benefit of the doubt.

**give someone the eye** to look at someone in a way that communicates romantic interest. □ *Ann gave John the eye. It really surprised him.* □ *Tom kept giving Sally the eye. She finally left.*

**give someone the red-carpet treatment** See under get the red-carpet treatment.

**give someone the runaround** See under get the runaround.

**give someone the shirt off one's back** to be very generous or solicitous toward someone. □ *Tom really likes Bill. He'd give Bill the shirt off his back.* □ *John is so friendly that he'd give anyone the shirt off his back.*

**give someone tit for tat** to give someone something equal to what that person has given one; to exchange a series of things, one by one, with someone. □ *They gave me the same kind of difficulty that I gave them. They gave me tit for tat.* □ *He punched me, so I punched him. Every time he hit me, I hit him. I just gave him tit for tat.*

**give someone what for** to scold or rebuke someone strongly. (Informal.) □ *I really got what for from my boss when I was late.* □ *Jane got what for from her father for damaging his car.*

**give something a lick and a promise** to do something poorly—quickly and carelessly. □ *John! You didn't clean your room! You just gave it a lick and a promise.* □ *This time, Tom, comb your hair. It looks as if you just gave it a lick and a promise.*

**give the bride away** [for a bride's father] to accompany the bride to the groom in a wedding ceremony. □ *Mr. Brown is ill. Who'll give the bride away?* □ *In the traditional wedding ceremony, the bride's father gives the bride away.*

**give the devil her due** See give the devil his due.

**give the devil his due** AND **give the devil her due** to give one's foe proper credit (for something). (A cliché. This usually refers to a person who has acted in an evil manner—like the devil.) □ *She's generally impossible, but I have to give the devil her due. She cooks a terrific cherry pie.* □ *John may cheat on his taxes and yell at his wife, but he keeps his car polished. I'll give the devil his due.*

**give up the ghost** to die; to release one's spirit. (A cliché. Considered literary or humorous.) □ *The old man sighed, rolled over, and gave up the ghost.* □ *I'm too young to give up the ghost.*

a **glutton for punishment** someone who seems to like doing or seeking out difficult, unpleasant, or badly paid tasks. □ *If you work for this charity, you'll have to be a glutton for punishment and work long hours* *for nothing.* □ *Jane must be a real glutton for punishment. She's typing Bill's manuscript free of charge, and he won't even thank her.*

**go about one's business** to mind one's business; to move elsewhere and mind one's own business; to focus on one's own tasks. □ *Leave me alone! Just go about your business!* □ *I have no more to say. I would be pleased if you would go about your business.*

**go against the grain** to go against one's natural inclination; to be contrary to one's nature. (Refers to the lay of the grain of wood. Against the grain is perpendicular to the lay of the grain.) □ *Don't expect me to help you cheat. That goes against the grain.* □ *Would it go against the grain for you to call in sick for me?*

**go along for the ride** to accompany (someone) for the pleasure of riding along; to accompany someone for no special reason. (Also with *come*. See the examples.) □ *Bill and Tom are going. You can go along for the ride.* □ *I don't really need to go to the grocery store, but if you're driving, I'll go along for the ride.* □ *We're having a little party next weekend. Nothing fancy. Why don't you come along for the ride?*

**go and never darken one's door again** to go away and not come back. (A cliché.) □ *The heroine of the drama told the villain to go and never darken her door again.* □ *She touched the back of her hand to her forehead and said, "Go and never darken my door again!"*

**go (a)round in circles** to keep going over the same ideas or repeating the same actions, often resulting in confusion and without reaching a satisfactory decision or conclusion. □ *We're just going round in circles discussing the problems of the plan. We need to consult someone else to get a new point of view.* □ *Fred's trying to find out what happened, but he's going around in circles. No one will tell him anything useful.*

**go (a)round the bend 1.** to travel around a turn or a curve; to make a turn or a curve. □ *You'll see the house you're looking for as you go around the bend.* □ *John waved to his father until the car went round the bend.* **2.** to go crazy; to lose one's mind. □ *If I don't get some rest, I'll go round the bend.* □ *Poor Bob. He has been having trouble for a long time. He finally went around the bend.*

**go at it hammer and tongs** See fight someone or something hammer and tongs.

**go at it tooth and nail** See fight someone or something hammer and tongs.

**go away empty-handed** to depart with nothing. □ *I hate for you to go away empty-handed, but I cannot afford to contribute any money.* □ *They came hoping for some food, but they had to go away empty-handed.*

**go back on one's word** to break a promise that one has made. □ *I hate to go back on my word, but I won't pay you $100 after all.* □ *Going back on your word makes you a liar.*

**go down in history** to be remembered as historically important. (A cliché.) □ *Bill is so great. I'm sure that he'll go down in history.* □ *This is the greatest party of the century. I bet it'll go down in history.*

**go Dutch** to share the cost of a meal or some other event. (See also Dutch treat.) □ *JANE: Let's go out and eat. MARY: Okay, but let's go Dutch.* □ *It's getting expensive to have Sally for a friend. She never wants to go Dutch.*

**go in one ear and out the other** [for something] to be heard and then forgotten. □ *Everything I say to you seems to go in one ear and out the other. Why don't you pay attention?* □ *I can't concentrate. Things people say to me just go in one ear and out the other.*

**go into a nosedive** AND **take a nosedive** **1.** [for an airplane] to dive suddenly toward the ground, nose first. □ *It was a bad day for flying, and I was afraid we'd go into a nosedive.* □ *The small plane took a nosedive. The pilot was able to bring it out at the last minute, so the plane didn't crash.* **2.** [for one's health or one's emotional or financial situation] to decline rapidly. □ *Our profits took a nosedive last year.* □ *After he broke his hip, Mr. Brown's health went into a nosedive, and he never recovered.*

**go into a tailspin** **1.** [for an airplane] to lose control and spin to the earth, nose first. □ *The plane shook and then suddenly went into a tailspin.* □ *The pilot was not able to stop the plane from going into a tailspin, and it crashed into the sea.* **2.** [for someone] to become disoriented or panicked; [for someone's life] to fall apart. □ *Although John was a great success, his life went into a tailspin. It took him a year to get straightened out.* □ *After her father died, Mary's world fell apart, and she went into a tailspin.*

**go into one's song and dance about something** to start giving one's usual or typical explanations and excuses about something. (A cliché. One's can be replaced by *the same old.*) □ *Please don't go into your song and dance about how you always tried to do what was right.* □ *John went* *into his song and dance about how he was so busy all day that he couldn't phone me.* □ *He always goes into the same old song and dance every time he makes a mistake.*

**go like clockwork** to progress with regularity and dependability. (Refers more to processes or to mechanical works in general than to clocks.) □ *The building project is progressing nicely. Everything is going like clockwork.* □ *The elaborate pageant was a great success. It went like clockwork from start to finish.*

**go off on a tangent** suddenly to go in another direction; suddenly to change one's line of thought, course of action, etc. (A reference to geometry. The plural is *go off on tangents.*) □ *Please stick to one subject and don't go off on a tangent.* □ *If Mary would settle down and deal with one subject, she would be all right, but she keeps going off on tangents.*

**go off the deep end** AND **jump off the deep end** to become deeply involved (with someone or something) before one is ready; to follow one's emotions into a situation. (Refers to going into a swimming pool at the deep end—rather than the shallow end—and finding oneself in deep water. Applies especially to falling in love.) □ *Look at the way Bill is smiling at Sally. I think he's about to go off the deep end.* □ *Now, John, I know you really want to go to Australia, but don't go jumping off the deep end. It isn't all perfect there.*

**go on a fishing expedition** to attempt to discover information. (As if one were sending bait into the invisible depths of a body of water, trying to catch something, but nothing in particular. Also used literally.) □ *We are going to have to go on a fishing expedition to try to find the facts.* □ *One lawyer went on a fishing expedition in court, and the other lawyer objected.*

**go (out) on strike** [for a group of people] to quit working at their jobs until certain demands are met. □ *If we don't have a contract by noon tomorrow, we'll go out on strike.* □ *The entire work force went on strike at noon today.*

**go overboard 1.** to fall off or out of a boat or ship. □ *My fishing pole just went overboard. I'm afraid it's lost.* □ *That man just went overboard. I think he jumped.* **2.** to do too much; to be extravagant. □ *Look, Sally, let's have a nice party, but don't go overboard. It doesn't need to be fancy.* □ *Okay, you can buy a big, comfortable car, but don't go overboard.*

**go over someone's head** [for the intellectual content of something] to be too difficult for someone to understand. (As if it flew over one's head rather than entering into one's store of knowledge.) □ *All that talk about computers went over my head.* □ *I hope my lecture didn't go over the students' heads.*

**go over something with a fine-tooth comb** AND **search something with a fine-tooth comb** to search through something very carefully. (As if one were searching for something very tiny lost in some kind of fiber.) □ *I can't find my passport. I went over the whole house with a fine-tooth comb.* □ *I searched this place with a fine-tooth comb and still didn't find my ring.*

**go over with a bang** [for something] to be funny or entertaining. (Refers chiefly to jokes or stage performances.) □ *The play was a success. It really went over with a bang.* □ *That's a great joke. It went over with a bang.*

**go scot-free** AND **get off scot-free** to go unpunished; to be acquitted of a crime. (This *scot* is an old word meaning "tax" or "tax burden.") □ *The thief went scot-free.* □ *Jane cheated on the test and was caught, but she got off scot-free.*

**go stag** to go to an event (that is meant for couples) without a date. (Originally referred only to males.) □ *Is Tom going to take you, or are you going stag?* □ *Bob didn't want to go stag, so he took his sister to the party.*

**go the distance** to do the whole amount; to play the entire game; to run the whole race. (Originally sports use.) □ *That horse runs fast. I hope it can go the distance.* □ *This is going to be a long, hard project. I hope I can go the distance.*

**go the limit** to do or have as much as possible. □ *What do I want on my hamburger? Go the limit!* □ *Don't hold anything back. Go the limit.*

**go through channels** to proceed by consulting the proper persons or offices. (*Channels* refers to the route a piece of business must take through a hierarchy or a bureaucracy.) □ *If you want an answer to your questions, you'll have to go through channels.* □ *If you know the answers, why do I have to go through channels?*

**go through the motions** to make a feeble effort to do something; to do something insincerely. □ *Jane isn't doing her best. She's just going* *through the motions.* □ *Bill was supposed to be raking the yard, but he was just going through the motions.*

**go through the roof** to go very high; to reach a very high degree (of something). □ *It's so hot! The temperature is going through the roof.* □ *Mr. Brown got so angry he almost went through the roof.*

**go to bat for someone** to support or help someone. (From the use of a substitute batter in baseball.) □ *I tried to go to bat for Bill, but he said he didn't want any help.* □ *I heard them gossiping about Sally, so I went to bat for her.*

**go to Davy Jones's locker** to go to the bottom of the sea. (Thought of as a nautical expression.) □ *My camera fell overboard and went to Davy Jones's locker.* □ *My uncle was a sailor. He went to Davy Jones's locker during a terrible storm.*

**go to pot** AND **go to the dogs** to go to ruin; to become ruined; to deteriorate. □ *My whole life seems to be going to pot.* □ *My lawn is going to pot. I had better weed it.* □ *The government is going to the dogs.*

**go to rack and ruin** AND **go to wrack and ruin** to become ruined or destroyed, especially due to neglect. (The words *rack* and *wrack* mean "wreckage" and are found only in this expression.) □ *That lovely old house on the corner is going to go to rack and ruin.* □ *My lawn is going to wrack and ruin.*

**go to seed** See run to seed.

**go to someone's head** to make someone conceited; to make someone overly proud. □ *You did a fine job, but don't let it go to your head.* □ *He let his success go to his head, and soon he became a complete failure.*

**go to the dogs** See go to pot.

**go to the wall** to fail or be defeated after being pushed to the extreme. □ *We really went to the wall on that deal.* □ *The company went to the wall because of that contract. Now it's bankrupt.*

**go to town** to work hard or fast. (Also used literally.) □ *Look at all those ants working. They are really going to town.* □ *Come on, you guys! Let's go to town. We have to finish this job before noon.*

**go to wrack and ruin** See go to rack and ruin.

**go up in flames** AND **go up in smoke** to burn up; to be consumed in flames. □ *The whole museum went up in flames.* □ *My paintings—*

*my whole life's work—went up in flames.* □ *What a shame for all that to go up in smoke.*

**go up in smoke** See go up in flames.

**gray area** an area of a subject, etc., that is difficult to put into a particular category, as it is not clearly defined and may have connections or associations with more than one category. □ *The responsibility for social studies in the college is a gray area. Several departments are involved.* □ *Publicity is a gray area in that firm. It is shared between the marketing and design divisions.*

**gray matter** intelligence; brains; power of thought. (Informal.) □ *Use your gray matter and think what will happen if the committee resigns.* □ *Surely they'll come up with an acceptable solution if they use a bit of gray matter.*

**green with envy** envious; jealous. (A cliché.) □ *When Sally saw me with Tom, she turned green with envy. She likes him a lot.* □ *I feel green with envy whenever I see you in your new car.*

**grin and bear it** to endure something unpleasant in good humor. □ *There is nothing you can do but grin and bear it.* □ *I hate having to work for rude people. I guess I have to grin and bear it.*

**grind to a halt** to slow to a stop; to run down. □ *By the end of the day, the factory had ground to a halt.* □ *The car ground to a halt, and we got out to stretch our legs.*

**grit one's teeth** to grind one's teeth together in anger or determination. □ *I was so mad, all I could do was stand there and grit my teeth.* □ *All through the race, Sally was gritting her teeth. She was really determined.*

**gun for someone** to be looking for someone, presumably to harm that person, as with a gun. (Originally from western and gangster movies, where actual guns and shootings were involved.) □ *The coach is gunning for you. I think he's going to bawl you out.* □ *I've heard that the sheriff is gunning for me, so I'm getting out of town.*

**hail-fellow-well-met** friendly to everyone; falsely friendly to everyone. (Usually said of males.) □ *Yes, he's friendly, sort of hail-fellow-well-met.* □ *He's not a very sincere person. Hail-fellow-well-met—you know the type.* □ *What a pain he is! Good old Mr. Hail-fellow-well-met. What a phony!*

**hair of the dog (that bit one)** a drink of liquor taken when one has a hangover; a drink of liquor taken when one is recovering from drinking too much liquor. □ *Oh, I'm miserable. I need a hair of the dog.* □ *That's some hangover you've got there, Bob. Here, drink this. It's a hair of the dog that bit you.*

**hale and hearty** well and healthy. □ *Doesn't Ann look hale and hearty?* □ *I don't feel hale and hearty. I'm really tired.*

**Half a loaf is better than none.** a proverb meaning that having part of something is better than having nothing. □ *When my raise was smaller than I wanted, Sally said, "Half a loaf is better than none."* □ *People who keep saying "Half a loaf is better than none" usually have as much as they need.*

**hammer something home (to someone)** to try extremely hard to make someone understand or realize something. □ *The boss hopes to hammer the firm's precarious financial position home to the staff.* ⊤ *I tried to hammer home to Ann the fact that she would have to get a job.*

**hand in glove (with someone)** very close to someone. □ *John is really hand in glove with Sally.* □ *The teacher and the principal work hand in glove.*

**handle someone with kid gloves** to be very careful with a touchy person; to deal with someone who is very difficult. □ *Bill has become so sensitive. You really have to handle him with kid gloves.* □ *You don't have to handle me with kid gloves. I can take it.*

**hand over fist** [for money and merchandise to be exchanged] very rapidly. □ *What a busy day. We took in money hand over fist.* □ *They were buying things hand over fist.*

**hand over hand** [moving] one hand after the other (again and again). □ *Sally pulled in the rope hand over hand.* □ *The man climbed the rope hand over hand.*

**hands down** easily and without opposition; indisputably. □ *The mayor won the election hands down.* □ *She was the choice of the people hands down.*

**hang by a hair** AND **hang by a thread** to be in an uncertain position; to depend on something very insubstantial for support. (Also with *on*, as in the second example.) □ *Your whole argument is hanging by a thread.* □ *John isn't failing geometry, but he's just hanging on by a hair.*

**hang by a thread** See hang by a hair.

**hang fire** to delay or wait; to be delayed. □ *I think we should hang fire and wait for other information.* □ *Our plans have to hang fire until we get planning permission.*

**hang in the balance** to be in an undecided state; to be between two equal possibilities. □ *The prisoner stood before the judge with his life hanging in the balance.* □ *This whole issue will have to hang in the balance until Jane gets back from her vacation.*

**Hang on!** Be prepared for fast or rough movement. □ *Hang on! Here we go!* □ *The airplane passengers suddenly seemed weightless. Someone shouted, "Hang on!"*

**hang one's hat up somewhere** to take up residence somewhere. □ *George loves Dallas. He's decided to buy a house and hang his hat up there.* □ *Bill moves from place to place and never hangs his hat up anywhere.*

**hang on someone's every word** to listen carefully to everything someone says. □ *He gave a great lecture. We hung on his every word.* □ *Look at the way John hangs on Mary's every word. He must be in love with her.*

**Hang on to your hat!** AND **Hold on to your hat!** Prepare for a sudden surprise or shock. (Also literal. See the examples. Refers to the need to grasp one's hat so that it will not come off one's head.) □ *What a windy day. Hang on to your hat!* □ *Here we go! Hold on to your hat!* □

*Are you ready to hear the final score? Hang on to your hat! We won the game ten to nothing!*

**hang someone in effigy** to hang a dummy or some other figure of a hated person. □ *They hanged the dictator in effigy.* □ *The angry mob hanged the president in effigy.*

a **hard-and-fast rule** a strict rule. □ *It's a hard-and-fast rule that you must be home by midnight.* □ *You should have your project completed by the end of the month, but it's not a hard-and-fast rule.*

**hardly have time to breathe** to be very busy. □ *This was such a busy day. I hardly had time to breathe.* □ *They made him work so hard that he hardly had time to breathe.*

**hard on someone's heels** following someone very closely; following very closely to someone's heels. □ *I ran as fast as I could, but the dog was still hard on my heels.* □ *Here comes Sally, and John is hard on her heels.*

**Haste makes waste.** a proverb meaning that time gained in doing something rapidly and carelessly will be lost when one has to do the thing over again correctly. □ *Now, take your time. Haste makes waste.* □ *Haste makes waste, so be careful as you work.*

**hate someone's guts** to hate someone very much. (Informal and rude.) □ *Oh, Bob is terrible. I hate his guts!* □ *You may hate my guts for saying so, but I think you're getting gray hair.*

**haul someone over the coals** See rake someone over the coals.

**have a bee in one's bonnet** to have an idea or a thought remain in one's mind; to have an obsession. (The bee is a thought that is inside one's head, which is inside a bonnet.) □ *I have a bee in my bonnet that you'd be a good manager.* □ *I had a bee in my bonnet about swimming. I couldn't stop wanting to go swimming.* ALSO: **put a bee in someone's bonnet** to give someone an idea (about something). □ *Somebody put a bee in my bonnet that we should go to a movie.* □ *Who put a bee in your bonnet?*

**have a big mouth** to be a gossiper; to be a person who tells secrets. (The person's mouth is too loud or is heard by too many people.) □ *Mary has a big mouth. She told Bob what I was getting him for his birthday.* □ *You shouldn't say things like that about people all the time. Everyone will say you have a big mouth.*

**have a bone to pick (with someone)** to have a matter to discuss with someone; to have something to argue about with someone. □ *Hey, Bill. I have a bone to pick with you. Where is the money you owe me?* □ *I had a bone to pick with her, but she was so sweet that I forgot about it.* □ *You always have a bone to pick.*

**have a brush with something** to have a brief contact with something; to have an experience with something. (Especially with the law. Sometimes a *close brush.*) □ *Ann had a close brush with the law. She was nearly arrested for speeding.* □ *When I was younger, I had a brush with scarlet fever, but I got over it.*

**have a chip on one's shoulder** to be tempting someone to an argument or a fight. (An invitation to a fight can be expressed as an invitation to knock a chip off someone's shoulder, which would be sufficient provocation for a fight. A person who goes about seeming to have such a chip is always daring someone to fight or argue.) □ *Who are you mad at? You always seem to have a chip on your shoulder.* □ *John has had a chip on his shoulder ever since he lost the bet.*

**have a close call** See have a close shave.

**have a close shave** AND **have a close call** to have a narrow escape from something dangerous. (Also with *be.* See the examples.) □ *What a close shave I had! I nearly fell off the roof when I was working there.* □ *I almost got struck by a speeding car. It was a close call.*

**have a familiar ring** [for a story or an explanation] to sound familiar. □ *Your excuse has a familiar ring. Have you done this before?* □ *This term paper has a familiar ring. I think it has been copied.*

**have a foot in both camps** to have an interest in or to support each of two opposing groups of people. □ *The shop steward had been promised a promotion and so had a foot in both camps—workers and management—during the strike.* □ *Mr. Smith has a foot in both camps in the dispute between the parents and the teachers. He teaches math, but he has a son at the school.*

**have a frog in one's throat** to have a feeling of hoarseness. (Also with *get.*) □ *I cannot speak more clearly. I have a frog in my throat.* □ *When I get a frog in my throat, it's hard for me to talk.*

**have a good head on one's shoulders** to have common sense; to be sensible and intelligent. □ *Mary doesn't do well in school, but she has* a good head on her shoulders. □ *John has a good head on his shoulders and can be depended on to give good advice.*

**have a green thumb** to have the ability to grow plants well. □ *Just look at Mr. Simpson's garden. He has a green thumb.* □ *My mother has a green thumb when it comes to houseplants.*

**have a heart** to be compassionate; to be generous and forgiving. □ *Oh, have a heart! Give me some help!* □ *If Ann had a heart, she'd have made us feel more welcome.*

**have a heart of gold** to be generous, sincere, and friendly. □ *Mary is such a lovely person. She has a heart of gold.* □ *You think Tom stole your watch? Impossible! He has a heart of gold.*

**have a heart of stone** to be cold, unfeeling, and unfriendly. □ *Sally has a heart of stone. She never even smiles.* □ *The villain in the play had a heart of stone. He was an ideal villain.*

**have a lot going (for one)** to have many things working to one's benefit. □ *Jane is so lucky. She has a lot going for her.* □ *She has a good job and a nice family. She has a lot going.*

**have a low boiling point** to anger easily. □ *Be nice to John. He's upset and has a low boiling point.* □ *Mr. Jones sure has a low boiling point. I hardly said anything, and he got angry.*

**have an ax to grind** to have something to complain about. □ *Tom, I need to talk to you. I have an ax to grind.* □ *Bill and Bob went into the other room to argue. They had an ax to grind.*

**have an in (with someone)** to have a way to request a special favor from someone; to have influence with someone. (The *in* is a noun.) □ *Do you have an in with the mayor? I have to ask him a favor.* □ *Sorry, I don't have an in, but I know someone who does.*

**have an itching palm** See have an itchy palm.

**have an itchy palm** AND **have an itching palm** to be in need of a tip; to tend to ask for tips; to crave money. (As if placing money in the palm would stop the itching. Note the variations in the examples.) □ *All the waiters at that restaurant have itchy palms.* □ *The cab driver was troubled by an itching palm. Since he refused to carry my bags, I gave him nothing.*

**have a one-track mind** to have a mind that thinks entirely or almost entirely about one subject, often sex. □ *Adolescent boys often have one-track minds. All they're interested in is the opposite sex.* □ *Bob has a one-track mind. He can only talk about football.*

**have a price on one's head** to be wanted by the authorities, who have offered a reward for one's capture. (As if the presentation of one's head would produce payment or reward. Usually limited to western and gangster movies.) □ *We captured a thief who had a price on his head, and the sheriff gave us the reward.* □ *The crook was so mean, he turned in his own brother, who had a price on his head.*

**have a scrape (with someone or something)** to come into contact with someone or something; to have a small battle with someone or something. □ *I had a scrape with the county sheriff.* □ *John and Bill had a scrape, but now they are friends again.*

**have a soft spot in one's heart for someone or something** to be fond of someone or something. □ *John has a soft spot in his heart for Mary.* □ *I have a soft spot in my heart for chocolate cake.*

**have a sweet tooth** to desire to eat many sweet foods—especially candy and pastries. (As if a certain tooth had a craving for sweets.) □ *I have a sweet tooth, and if I don't watch it, I'll really get fat.* □ *John eats candy all the time. He must have a sweet tooth.*

**have a vested interest in something** to have a personal or biased interest, often financial, in something. □ *Ann has a vested interest in wanting her father to sell the family firm. She has shares in it and would make a large profit.* □ *Jack has a vested interest in keeping the village traffic-free. He has a summer home there.*

**have a weakness for someone or something** to be unable to resist someone or something; to be fond of someone or something; to be (figuratively) powerless against someone or something. □ *I have a weakness for chocolate.* □ *John has a weakness for Mary. I think he's in love.*

**have bats in one's belfry** to be slightly crazy. (The belfry—a bell tower—represents one's head or brains. The bats represent an infestation of confusion.) □ *Poor old Tom has bats in his belfry.* □ *Don't act so silly, John. People will think you have bats in your belfry.*

**have clean hands** to be guiltless. (As if the guilty person would have bloody hands.) □ *Don't look at me. I have clean hands.* □ *The police took him in, but they let him go again because he had clean hands.*

**have dibs on something** AND **put one's dibs on something** to reserve something for oneself; to claim something for oneself. □ *I have dibs on the last piece of cake.* □ *John put his dibs on the last piece again. It isn't fair.*

**have egg on one's face** to be embarrassed because of an error that is obvious to everyone. □ *Bob has egg on his face because he wore jeans to the party and everyone else wore formal clothing.* □ *John was completely wrong about the weather for the picnic. It snowed! Now he has egg on his face.*

**have eyes bigger than one's stomach** See under one's eyes are bigger than one's stomach.

**have eyes in the back of one's head** to seem to be able to sense what is going on outside of one's range of vision. (Not literal.) □ *My teacher seems to have eyes in the back of her head.* □ *Our coach doesn't need to have eyes in the back of his head. He watches us very carefully.*

**have feet of clay** [for a strong person] to have a defect of character. □ *All human beings have feet of clay. No one is perfect.* □ *Sally was popular and successful. She was nearly fifty before she learned that she, too, had feet of clay.*

**have foot-in-mouth disease** to embarrass oneself through a silly blunder; to put one's foot in one's mouth (not literally) a lot. (This is a parody on *foot-and-mouth disease* or *hoof-and-mouth disease*, which affects cattle and deer. See put one's foot in one's mouth.) □ *I'm sorry I keep saying stupid things. I guess I have foot-in-mouth disease.* □ *Yes, you really have foot-in-mouth disease tonight.*

**have had its day** to no longer be useful or successful. □ *Horse-drawn carriages have had their day in this country.* □ *Some people think that radio has had its day, but others prefer it to television.*

**have mixed feelings (about someone or something)** to be uncertain about someone or something. □ *I have mixed feelings about Bob. Sometimes I like him, and other times I don't.* □ *I have mixed feelings about my trip to England. I love the people, but the climate upsets me.* □ *Yes, I also have mixed feelings.*

**have money to burn** to have lots of money; to have more money than one needs; to have enough money that some can be wasted. □ *Look at the way Tom buys things. You'd think he had money to burn.* □ *If I had money to burn, I'd just put it in the bank.*

**have one's back to the wall** to be in a defensive position. (As if one has been forced toward a wall and can no longer run away.) □ *He'll have to give in. He has his back to the wall.* □ *How can I bargain when I have my back to the wall?* ALSO: **one's back is to the wall** one is in a defensive position. □ *I don't have much choice. My back is to the wall.*

**have one's cake and eat it too** AND **eat one's cake and have it too** to enjoy both having something and using it up. (Usually stated in the negative.) □ *Tom wants to have his cake and eat it too. It can't be done.* □ *Don't buy a car if you want to walk and stay healthy. You can't eat your cake and have it too.*

**have one's ear to the ground** AND **keep one's ear to the ground** to listen carefully, hoping to get warning of something. (As if one were listening for the sound of distant horses' hooves pounding on the ground.) □ *John had his ear to the ground, hoping to find out about new ideas in computers.* □ *His boss told him to keep his ear to the ground so that he'd be the first to know of a new idea.*

**have one's finger in the pie** to be involved in something. □ *I like to have my finger in the pie so I can make sure things go my way.* □ *As long as John has his finger in the pie, things will happen slowly.*

**have one's hand in the till** to be stealing money from a company or an organization. (The *till* is a cash box or drawer.) □ *Mr. Jones had his hand in the till for years before he was caught.* □ *I think that the new clerk has her hand in the till. There is cash missing every morning.*

**have one's hands full (with someone or something)** to be busy or totally occupied with someone or something. □ *I have my hands full with my three children.* □ *You have your hands full with the store.* □ *We both have our hands full.*

**have one's hands tied** to be prevented from doing something. □ *I can't help you. I was told not to, so I have my hands tied.* □ *John can help. He doesn't have his hands tied.* ALSO: **one's hands are tied** one is prevented from doing something. □ *I'd like to help you, but my hands are tied.*

**have one's head in the clouds** to be unaware of what is going on. □ *"Bob, do you have your head in the clouds?" said the teacher.* □ *She has her head in the clouds all day. She must be in love.*

**have one's heart in one's mouth** to feel strongly emotional about someone or something. □ *"Gosh, Mary," said John, "I have my heart in* *my mouth whenever I see you."* □ *I have my heart in my mouth whenever I hear the national anthem.* ALSO: **one's heart is in one's mouth** one feels strongly emotional. □ *It was a touching scene. My heart was in my mouth the whole time.*

**have one's heart set on something** to be desiring and expecting something. □ *Jane has her heart set on going to London.* □ *Bob will be disappointed. He had his heart set on going to college this year.* ALSO: **set one's heart on something** to become determined about something. □ *Jane set her heart on going to London.* ALSO: **one's heart is set on something** one desires or expects something. □ *Jane's heart is set on going to London.*

**have one's nose in a book** to be reading a book; to read books all the time. □ *Bob has his nose in a book every time I see him.* □ *He always has his nose in a book. He never gets any exercise.*

**have one's tail between one's legs** to be frightened or cowed. (Refers to a frightened dog. Also used literally with dogs.) □ *John seems to lack courage. Whenever there is an argument, he has his tail between his legs.* □ *You can tell that the dog is frightened because it has its tail between its legs.* ALSO: **one's tail is between one's legs** one is acting frightened or cowed. □ *He should have stood up and argued, but—as usual—his tail was between his legs.*

**have one's words stick in one's throat** to be so overcome by emotion that one can hardly speak. □ *I sometimes have my words stick in my throat.* □ *John said that he never had his words stick in his throat.* ALSO: **one's words stick in one's throat** one finds it difficult to speak because of emotion. □ *My words stick in my throat whenever I try to say something kind or tender.*

**have other fish to fry** to have other things to do; to have more important things to do. (*Other* can be replaced by *bigger* or *better*.) □ *I can't take time for your problem. I have other fish to fry.* □ *I won't waste time on your question. I have bigger fish to fry.*

**have someone dead to rights** to have proved someone unquestionably guilty. □ *The police burst in on the robbers while they were at work. They had the robbers dead to rights.* □ *All right, Tom! Now I have you dead to rights! Get your hands out of the cookie jar.*

**have someone in one's pocket** to have control over someone. □ *Don't worry about the mayor. She'll cooperate. I have her in my pocket.* □ *John will do just what Mary tells him. She has him in her pocket.*

**have someone or something in one's hands** to have control of or responsibility for someone or something. (*Have* can be replaced with *leave* or *put.*) □ *You have the whole project in your hands.* □ *The boss put the whole project in your hands.* □ *I have to leave the baby in your hands while I go to the doctor.*

**have someone's eye** See catch someone's eye.

**have something at hand** See have something at one's fingertips.

**have something at one's fingertips** AND **have something at hand** to have something within (one's) reach. (*Have* can be replaced with *keep.*) □ *I have a dictionary at my fingertips.* □ *I try to have everything I need at hand.* □ *I keep my medicine at my fingertips.*

**have something hanging over one's head** to have something bothering or worrying one; to have a deadline worrying one. □ *I keep worrying about getting drafted. I hate to have something like that hanging over my head.* □ *I have a history paper hanging over my head. It's due tomorrow.*

**have something in stock** to have merchandise available and ready for sale. □ *Do you have extra-large sizes in stock?* □ *Of course, we have all sizes and colors in stock.*

**have something to spare** to have more than enough of something. □ *Ask John for some firewood. He has firewood to spare.* □ *Do you have any candy to spare?*

**have the Midas touch** to have the ability to be successful, especially the ability to make money easily. (From the name of a legendary king whose touch turned everything to gold.) □ *Bob is a banker and really has the Midas touch.* □ *The poverty-stricken boy turned out to have the Midas touch and was a millionaire by the time he was twenty-five.*

**have the presence of mind to do something** to have the calmness and ability to act sensibly in an emergency or difficult situation. □ *Jane had the presence of mind to phone the police when the child disappeared.* □ *The child had the presence of mind to take a note of the car's license plate.*

**have the right-of-way** to possess the legal right to occupy a particular space or proceed before others on a public roadway. □ *I had a traffic accident yesterday, but it wasn't my fault. I had the right-of-way.* □ *Don't pull out onto a highway if you don't have the right-of-way.*

**have the time of one's life** to have a very good time; to have the most exciting time in one's life. □ *What a great party! I had the time of my life.* □ *We went to Florida last winter and had the time of our lives.*

**have too many irons in the fire** to be doing too many things at once. (A cliché. As if a blacksmith had more things get hot in the fire than could possibly be dealt with.) □ *Tom had too many irons in the fire and missed some important deadlines.* □ *It's better if you don't have too many irons in the fire.*

**head and shoulders above someone or something** clearly superior to someone or something. (Often with *stand*. See the examples.) □ *This wine is head and shoulders above that one.* □ *John stands head and shoulders above Bob.*

**heads will roll** some people will get into trouble. (Informal. From the use of the guillotine to execute people.) □ *When the company's end-of-year results become public, heads will roll.* □ *Heads will roll when the principal sees the damaged classroom.*

**He laughs best who laughs last.** See He who laughs last, laughs longest.

**hem and haw** [for someone] to make sounds expressing doubt or hesitation; to hesitate. (Informal.) □ *Stop hemming and hawing, and say whether you are coming or not.* □ *Jean hemmed and hawed for a long time before deciding to marry Henry.*

**Here's to someone or something.** an expression used as a toast to someone or something to wish someone or something well. □ *Here's to Jim and Mary! May they be very happy!* □ *Here's to your new job!*

**He who laughs last, laughs longest.** AND **He laughs best who laughs last.** a proverb meaning that whoever succeeds in making the last move or pulling the last trick has the most enjoyment. □ *Bill had pulled many silly tricks on Tom. Finally Tom pulled a very funny trick on Bill and said, "He who laughs last, laughs longest."* □ *Bill pulled another, even bigger trick on Tom and said, laughing, "He laughs best who laughs last."*

**hide one's head in the sand** See bury one's head in the sand.

**hide one's light under a bushel** to conceal one's good ideas or talents. (A biblical theme.) □ *Jane has some good ideas, but she doesn't speak very often. She hides her light under a bushel.* □ *Don't hide your light under a bushel. Share your gifts with other people.*

**high man on the totem pole** the person at the top of a hierarchy; the person in charge of an organization. (See also low man on the totem pole.) □ *I don't want to talk to a secretary. I demand to talk to the high man on the totem pole.* □ *Who's in charge around here? Who's high man on the totem pole?*

**hit a happy medium** See strike a happy medium.

**hit a snag** to run into a problem. □ *We've hit a snag with the building project.* □ *I stopped working on the roof when I hit a snag.*

**hit a sour note** See strike a sour note.

**hit bottom** to reach the lowest or worst point. □ *Our profits have hit bottom. This is our worst year ever.* □ *When my life hit bottom, I began to feel much better. I knew that if there was going to be any change, it would be for the better.*

**hitch a ride** See thumb a ride.

**hit (someone) like a ton of bricks** to surprise, startle, or shock someone. □ *Suddenly, the truth hit me like a ton of bricks.* □ *The sudden tax increase hit like a ton of bricks. Everyone became angry.*

**hit someone (right) between the eyes** to become completely apparent; to surprise or impress someone. (Also used literally.) □ *Suddenly, it hit me right between the eyes. John and Mary were in love.* □ *Then— as he was talking—the exact nature of the evil plan hit me between the eyes.*

**hit the bull's-eye** to achieve the goal perfectly. □ *Your idea really hit the bull's-eye. Thank you!* □ *Jill has a lot of insight. She knows how to hit the bull's-eye.*

**hit the nail (right) on the head** to do exactly the right thing; to do something in the most effective and efficient way. (A cliché.) □ *You've spotted the flaw, Sally. You hit the nail on the head.* □ *Bob doesn't say much, but every now and then he hits the nail right on the head.*

**hit the spot** to be exactly right; to be refreshing. □ *This cool drink really hits the spot.* □ *That was a delicious meal, dear. It hit the spot.*

**Hobson's choice** the choice between taking what is offered and getting nothing at all. (From the name of a stable owner in the seventeenth century who offered customers the hire of the horse nearest the door.) □ *We didn't really want that holiday cottage, but it was a case of Hobson's choice. We booked very late, and there was nothing else left.* □ *If you want a yellow car, it's Hobson's choice. The garage has only one.*

**hoist with one's own petard** harmed or disadvantaged by an action of one's own that was meant to harm someone else. (From a line in Shakespeare's *Hamlet*.) □ *She intended to murder her brother but was hoist with her own petard when she ate the poisoned food intended for him.* □ *The vandals were hoist with their own petard when they wanted to make an emergency call from the public telephone they had broken.*

**hold one's ground** See stand one's ground.

**hold one's head up** to have self-respect; to retain or display one's dignity. □ *I've nothing wrong. I can hold my head up in public.* Ⓣ *I'm so embarrassed and ashamed. I'll never be able to hold up my head again.*

**hold one's own** to do as well as anyone else. □ *I can hold my own in a footrace any day.* □ *She was unable to hold her own, and she had to quit.*

**hold one's peace** to remain silent. □ *Bill was unable to hold his peace any longer. "Don't do it!" he cried.* □ *Quiet, John. Hold your peace for a little while longer.*

**hold one's temper** See keep one's temper.

**hold one's tongue** to refrain from speaking; to refrain from saying something unpleasant. □ *I felt like scolding her, but I held my tongue.* □ *Hold your tongue, John. You can't talk to me that way.*

**Hold on to your hat!** See Hang on to your hat!

**hold out for something** to insist on getting something; to refuse to accept less than something. (Informal.) □ *The workers are holding out for a reasonable raise.* □ *The teachers are holding out for a reduction in class size.*

**hold out the olive branch** to offer to end a dispute and be friendly; to offer reconciliation. (The olive branch is a symbol of peace and reconciliation. A biblical reference.) □ *Jill was the first to hold out the* *olive branch after our argument.* □ *I always try to hold out the olive branch to someone I have hurt. Life is too short for a person to bear grudges for very long.*

**hold the fort** to take care of a place, such as a store or one's home. (From western movies.) □ *I'm going next door to visit Mrs. Jones. You stay here and hold the fort.* □ *You should open the store at eight o'clock and hold the fort until I get there at ten o'clock.*

**hold true** [for something] to be true; (for something) to remain true. □ *Does this rule hold true all the time?* □ *Yes, it holds true no matter what.*

**hold up one's end (of the bargain)** to do one's part as agreed; to attend to one's responsibilities as agreed. □ *Tom has to learn to cooperate. He must hold up his end of the bargain.* ⊤ *If you don't hold your end up, the whole project will fail.*

**hold water** to be able to be proved; to be correct or true. (Usually in the negative.) □ *Jack's story doesn't hold water. It sounds too unlikely.* □ *I don't think the police's theory will hold water. The suspect has an alibi.*

a **hole in one 1.** an instance of hitting a golf ball into a hole in only one try. (From the game of golf.) □ *John made a hole in one yesterday.* □ *I've never gotten a hole in one.* **2.** an instance of succeeding the first time. □ *It worked the first time I tried it—a hole in one.* □ *Bob got a hole in one on that sale. A lady walked in the door, and he sold her a car in five minutes.*

**holier-than-thou** excessively pious; acting as though one is more virtuous than other people. □ *Jack always adopts a holier-than-thou attitude toward other people, but people say he has been in prison.* □ *Jane used to be holier-than-thou, but she is marrying Tom, who is a crook.*

The **honeymoon is over.** a phrase said when the early, pleasant beginning of something has ended. (A cliché.) □ *Okay, the honeymoon is over. It's time to settle down and do some hard work.* □ *I knew the honeymoon was over when they started yelling at me to work faster.*

**honor someone's check** to accept someone's personal check. □ *The clerk at the store wouldn't honor my check. I had to pay cash.* □ *The bank didn't honor your check when I tried to deposit it. Please give me cash.*

**hope against all hope** to have hope even when the situation appears to be hopeless. □ *We hope against all hope that she'll see the right thing* *to do and do it.* □ *There is little point in hoping against all hope, except that it makes you feel better.*

**horn in (on someone)** to attempt to displace someone. □ *I'm going to ask Sally to the party. Don't you dare try to horn in on me!* □ *I wouldn't think of horning in.*

a **horse of a different color** See horse of another color.

a **horse of another color** AND a **horse of a different color** another matter altogether. □ *I was talking about the tree, not the bush. That's a horse of another color.* □ *Gambling is not the same as investing in the stock market. It's a horse of a different color.*

**horse sense** common sense; practical thinking. □ *Jack is no scholar, but he has a lot of horse sense.* □ *Horse sense tells me I should not be involved in that project.*

**hot on something** enthusiastic about something; very much interested in something; knowledgeable about something. (Informal.) □ *Jane is hot on animal rights.* □ *Jean is hot on modern ballet just now.*

**hot under the collar** very angry. (A cliché.) □ *The boss was really hot under the collar when you told him you lost the contract.* □ *I get hot under the collar every time I think about how unfair it is.*

**hue and cry** a loud public protest or opposition. □ *There was a hue and cry when the council wanted to build houses in the playing field.* □ *The decision to close the local school started a real hue and cry.*

**hunt high and low for someone or something** AND **search high and low for someone or something** to look carefully in every possible place for someone or something. □ *We looked high and low for the right teacher.* □ *The Smiths are searching high and low for the summer home of their dreams.*

**hush money** money paid as a bribe to persuade someone to remain silent and not reveal certain information. □ *Bob gave his younger sister hush money so that she wouldn't tell Jane that he had gone on a date with Sue.* □ *The crooks paid Fred hush money to keep their whereabouts secret.*

**If the shoe fits, wear it.** a proverb meaning that one should pay attention to something if it applies to oneself. □ *Some people here need to be quiet. If the shoe fits, wear it.* □ *This doesn't apply to everyone. If the shoe fits, wear it.*

**if worst comes to worst** in the worst possible situation; if things really get bad. (A cliché.) □ *If worst comes to worst, we'll hire someone to help you.* □ *If worst comes to worst, I'll have to borrow some money.*

**If you give one an inch, one will take a mile.** See Give one an inch, and one will take a mile.

**ill-gotten gains** money or other possessions acquired in a dishonest or illegal fashion. □ *Fred cheated at cards and is now living on his ill-gotten gains.* □ *Mary is enjoying her ill-gotten gains. She deceived an old lady into leaving her money in her will.*

**in a dead heat** finishing a race at exactly the same time; tied. (Here, *dead* means "exact" or "total.") □ *The two horses finished the race in a dead heat.* □ *They ended the contest in a dead heat.*

**in a flash** quickly; immediately. □ *I'll be there in a flash.* □ *It happened in a flash. Suddenly my wallet was gone.*

**in a huff** in an angry or offended manner. (*In* can be replaced with *into*. See the examples.) □ *He heard what we had to say, then left in a huff.* □ *She arrived in a huff and ordered us to bring her something to eat.* □ *She gets into a huff very easily.*

**in a mad rush** in a great hurry; in a busy rush. (*In* can be replaced with *into*. See the examples.) □ *I ran around all day today in a mad rush, looking for a present for Bill.* □ *Why are you always in a mad rush?* □ *I always get into a mad rush when I'm finishing a project.*

**in a pinch** if absolutely necessary; if there is no other alternative. □ *In a pinch, I could come tomorrow, but it's not really convenient.* □ *In a pinch, you could use margarine in this recipe, but butter is better.*

**in a (tight) spot** caught in a problem; in a difficult position. (*In* can be replaced with *into*. See the examples.) □ *Look, John, I'm in a tight spot. Can you lend me twenty dollars?* □ *I'm in a spot too. I need $300.* □ *I have never gotten into a tight spot.*

**in a vicious circle** in a situation in which the solution of one problem leads to a second problem, and the solution of the second problem brings back the first problem, etc. (*In* can be replaced with *into*. See the examples.) □ *Life is so strange. I seem to be in a vicious circle most of the time.* □ *I put lemon in my tea to make it sour, then sugar to make it sweet. I'm in a vicious circle.* □ *Don't let your life get into a vicious circle.*

**in a world of one's own** aloof; detached; self-centered. (*In* can be replaced with *into*. See the examples.) □ *John lives in a world of his own. He has very few friends.* □ *Mary walks around in a world of her own, but she's very intelligent.* □ *When she's thinking, she drifts into a world of her own.*

**in bad faith** without sincerity; with bad or dishonest intent; with duplicity. □ *It appears that you acted in bad faith and didn't live up to the terms of our agreement.* □ *If you do things in bad faith, you'll get a bad reputation.*

**in bad sorts** in a bad humor. □ *Bill is in bad sorts today. He's very grouchy.* □ *I try to be extra nice to people when I'm in bad sorts.*

**in bad taste** AND **in poor taste** rude; vulgar; obscene. □ *Mrs. Franklin felt that your joke was in bad taste.* □ *We found the play to be in poor taste, so we walked out in the middle of the second act.*

**in black and white** in writing or printing; made official by being written or printed. (Said of something, such as an agreement or a statement, that has been recorded in writing.) □ *I have it in black and white that I'm entitled to three weeks of vacation each year.* □ *It says right here in black and white that oak trees make acorns.* □ *Please put the agreement in black and white.*

**in broad daylight** publicly visible in the daytime. □ *The thief stole the car in broad daylight.* □ *There they were, selling drugs in broad daylight.*

**inch by inch** one inch at a time; little by little. □ *Traffic moved along inch by inch.* □ *Inch by inch, the snail moved across the stone.*

**in creation** See on earth.

**in deep water** in a dangerous or vulnerable situation; in a serious situation; in trouble. (As if one were swimming in, or fell into, water that is over one's head. *In* can be replaced with *into*. See the examples.) □ *John is having trouble with his taxes. He's in deep water.* □ *Bill is in deep water in algebra class. He's almost failing.* □ *He really got himself into deep water.*

**in fine feather** in good humor; in good health. (A cliché. *In* can be replaced with *into*. See the examples. Refers to a healthy and therefore beautiful bird.) □ *Hello, John. You appear to be in fine feather.* □ *Of course I'm in fine feather. I get lots of sleep.* □ *Good food and lots of sleep put me into fine feather.*

**in full swing** in progress; operating or running without restraint. (*In* can be replaced with *into*. See the examples.) □ *We can't leave now! The party is in full swing.* □ *Our program to help the starving people is in full swing. You should see results soon.* □ *Just wait until our project gets into full swing.*

**in good condition** See in good shape.

**in good shape** AND **in good condition** physically and functionally sound and sturdy. (Used for both people and things. *In* can be replaced with *into*. *Good* can be replaced with *better* or *the best*. See the examples.) □ *This car isn't in good shape.* □ *I'd like to have one that's in better condition.* □ *Mary is in good condition. She works hard to keep healthy.* □ *You have to make an effort to get into good shape.*

**in heat** in a period of sexual excitement; in estrus. (*Estrus* is the period of time in which female animals are most willing to breed. This expression is usually used for animals. It has been used for humans in a joking sense. *In* can be replaced with *into*. See the examples. See also in season.) □ *Our dog is in heat.* □ *She goes into heat every year at this time.* □ *When my dog is in heat, I have to keep her locked in the house.*

**in less than no time** very quickly. □ *I'll be there in less than no time.* □ *Don't worry. This won't take long. It'll be over with in less than no time.*

**in mint condition** in perfect condition. (Refers to the perfect state of a coin that has just been minted. See the examples.) □ *This is a fine* *car. It runs well and is in mint condition.* □ *We went through a house that was in mint condition, and we decided to buy it.*

**in name only** nominally; not actual, only by terminology. □ *The president is head of the country in name only. Congress makes the laws.* □ *Mr. Smith is the boss of the Smith Company in name only. Mrs. Smith handles all the business affairs.*

**in no mood to do something** not to feel like doing something; to wish not to do something. □ *I'm in no mood to cook dinner tonight.* □ *Mother is in no mood to put up with our arguing.*

**in nothing flat** in exactly no time at all. □ *Of course I can get there in a hurry. I'll be there in nothing flat.* □ *We covered the distance between New York and Philadelphia in nothing flat.*

**in one ear and out the other** [for something to be] ignored; [for something to be] unheard or unheeded. (A cliché. *In* can be replaced with *into*. See the examples.) □ *Everything I say to you goes into one ear and out the other!* □ *Bill just doesn't pay attention. Everything is in one ear and out the other.*

**in one fell swoop** See at one fell swoop.

**in one's birthday suit** naked; nude. (In the "clothes" in which one was born. *In* can be replaced with *into*. See the examples.) □ *I've heard that John sleeps in his birthday suit.* □ *We used to go down to the river and swim in our birthday suits.* □ *You have to get into your birthday suit to bathe.*

**in one's blood** See in the blood.

**in one's mind's eye** in one's mind. (Refers to visualizing something in one's mind.) □ *In my mind's eye, I can see trouble ahead.* □ *In her mind's eye, she could see a beautiful building beside the river. She decided to design such a building.*

**in one's or its prime** at one's or its peak or best time. □ *He rarely performs now, but in his prime, Bill was a wonderful singer.* □ *The program ended in its prime when we ran out of money.* □ *I could work long hours when I was in my prime.*

**in one's right mind** sane; rational and sensible. (Often in the negative.) □ *That was a stupid thing to do. You're not in your right mind.* □ *You can't be in your right mind! That sounds crazy!*

**in one's second childhood** being interested in things or people that normally interest children. □ *My father bought himself a toy train, and my mother said he was in his second childhood.* □ *Whenever I go to the river and throw stones, I feel as though I'm in my second childhood.*

**in one's spare time** in one's extra time; in the time not reserved for doing something else. □ *I write novels in my spare time.* □ *I'll try to paint the house in my spare time.*

**in over one's head** with more difficulties than one can manage. □ *Calculus is very hard for me. I'm in over my head.* □ *Ann is too busy. She's really in over her head.*

**in poor taste** See in bad taste.

**in print** [for a book] to be available for sale. (Compare with out of print.) □ *I think I can get that book for you. It's still in print.* □ *This is the only book in print on this subject.*

**in rags** in worn-out and torn clothing. □ *Oh, look at my clothing. I can't go to the party in rags!* □ *I think the new casual fashions make you look as if you're in rags.*

**in round figures** See in round numbers.

**in round numbers** AND **in round figures** as an estimated number; as a figure that has been rounded off to the closest whole number. (*In* can be replaced with *into*. See the examples.) □ *Please tell me in round numbers what it'll cost.* □ *I don't need the exact amount. Just give it to me in round figures.* □ *Bill put all the figures into round numbers to make the report easier to read.*

the **ins and outs of something** the details of something. (Informal.) □ *Jane knows about the plan generally, but not the ins and outs of it.* □ *I don't know the ins and outs of their quarrel.*

**in season 1.** currently available for selling. (Some foods and other things are available only at certain seasons. *In* can be replaced with *into*, especially when used with *come*. See the examples.) □ *Oysters are available in season.* □ *Strawberries aren't in season in January.* □ *When do strawberries come into season?* **2.** legally able to be caught or hunted. □ *Catfish are in season all year round.* □ *When are salmon in season?* **3.** [of a dog] in estrus. (See also in **heat.**) □ *My dog is in season every year at this time.* □ *When my dog is in season, I have to keep her locked in the house.*

**in seventh heaven** in a very happy state. (A cliché. This is the highest heaven, where God exists.) □ *Ann was really in seventh heaven when she got a car of her own.* □ *I'd be in seventh heaven if I had a million dollars.*

**in short order** very quickly. □ *I can straighten out this mess in short order.* □ *The people came in and cleaned the place up in short order.*

**in short supply** scarce. (*In* can be replaced with *into*. See the examples.) □ *Fresh vegetables are in short supply in the winter.* □ *Red cars are in short supply because everyone likes them and buys them.* □ *At this time of the year, fresh vegetables go into short supply.*

**in someone's (own) (best) interest(s)** to someone's own advantage; as a benefit to oneself. (Compare with in the interest(s) of something.) □ *It is not in your own interests to share your ideas with Jack. He will say that they are his.* □ *Jane thought it was in Bill's best interest to tell his mother about his illness.* □ *Most people do whatever is in their own best interests.*

**in stock** readily available, as with goods in a store. □ *I'm sorry, I don't have that in stock. I'll have to order it for you.* □ *We have all our Christmas merchandise in stock now.*

**in the air** everywhere; all about. (Also used literally.) □ *There is such a feeling of joy in the air.* □ *We felt a sense of tension in the air.*

**in the bargain** in addition to what was agreed on. (*In* can be replaced with *into*. See the examples.) □ *I bought a car, and they threw an air conditioner into the bargain.* □ *When I bought a house, I asked the seller to include the furniture in the bargain.*

**in the black** not in debt; in a financially profitable condition. (Refers to writing figures in black rather than in red, which would indicate a deficit. See also in the red. *In* can be replaced with *into*. See the examples.) □ *I wish my accounts were in the black.* □ *Sally moved the company into the black.*

**in the blood** AND **in one's blood** built into one's personality or character. □ *John's a great runner. It's in his blood.* □ *The whole family is very athletic. It's in the blood.*

**in the bullpen** [for a baseball pitcher to be] in a special place near a baseball field, warming up to pitch. (*In* can be replaced with *into*. See the examples.) □ *You can tell who is pitching next by seeing who is in* *the bullpen.* □ *Our best pitcher just went into the bullpen. He'll be pitching soon.*

**in the cards** in the future. □ *Well, what do you think is in the cards for tomorrow?* □ *I asked the boss if there was a raise in the cards for me.*

**in the doghouse** in trouble; in (someone's) disfavor. (As if a person would be sent outside for misbehavior, as one might send a dog from the comforts of the house to the discomforts of the yard. *In* can be replaced with *into*. See the examples.) □ *I'm really in the doghouse. I was late for an appointment.* □ *I hate being in the doghouse all the time. I don't know why I can't stay out of trouble.* □ *It's easy to get into the doghouse with her. She gets mad at the slightest thing.*

**in the doldrums** sluggish; inactive; in low spirits. (*In* can be replaced with *into*. See the examples.) □ *He's usually in the doldrums in the winter.* □ *I had some bad news yesterday, which put me into the doldrums.*

**in the flesh** bodily or physically present; in person. □ *I've heard that the queen is coming here in the flesh.* □ *Is she really here? In the flesh?* □ *I've wanted a computer for years, and now I've got one right here in the flesh.*

**in the gutter** [for a person to be] in a low state; depraved. (*In* can be replaced with *into*. See the examples.) □ *You had better straighten out your life, or you'll end up in the gutter.* □ *His bad habits put him into the gutter.*

**in the hole** in debt. (*In* can be replaced with *into*. See the examples.) □ *I'm $200 in the hole.* □ *Our finances go into the hole every month.*

**in the interest(s) of something** in order to advance or improve something. (Formal. Compare with in someone's (own) (best) interest(s).) □ *In the interest of health, people are asked not to smoke.* □ *The police imprisoned the suspects in the interests of public safety.*

**in the know** knowledgeable. (*In* can be replaced with *into*. See the examples.) □ *Let's ask Bob. He's in the know.* □ *I have no knowledge of how to work this machine. I think I can get into the know very quickly, though.*

**in the lap of luxury** in luxurious surroundings. (A cliché.) □ *John lives in the lap of luxury because his family is very wealthy.* □ *When I retire, I'd like to live in the lap of luxury.*

**in the limelight** AND **in the spotlight** at the center of attention. (The literal sense is also used. *Limelight* is an obsolete type of spotlight, and the word occurs only in this phrase. *In* can be replaced with *into*. See the examples.) □ *John will do almost anything to get himself into the limelight.* □ *I love being in the spotlight.* □ *All elected officials spend a lot of time in the limelight.*

**in the line of duty** as part of one's expected duties. □ *When soldiers fight people in a war, it's in the line of duty.* □ *In the line of duty, police officers often risk their lives in dangerous situations.*

**in the long run** over a long period of time; ultimately. (A cliché.) □ *We'd be better off in the long run buying one instead of renting one.* □ *In the long run, we'd be happier in the South.*

**in the money 1.** wealthy. □ *John is really in the money. He's worth millions.* □ *If I am ever in the money, I'll be generous.* **2.** in the winning position in a race or contest. (As if one had won the prize money.) □ *I knew when Jane raced around the final turn that she was in the money.* □ *The horses coming in first, second, and third are said to be in the money.*

**in the nick of time** just in time; at the last possible instant; just before it's too late. (A cliché.) □ *The doctor arrived in the nick of time. The patient's life was saved.* □ *I reached the airport in the nick of time.*

**in the pink (of condition)** in very good health; in very good condition, physically or emotionally. (*In* can be replaced with *into*. See the examples.) □ *The garden is lovely. All the flowers are in the pink of condition.* □ *Jane has to exercise hard to get into the pink of condition.* □ *I'd like to be in the pink, but I don't have the time.*

**in the prime of life** in the best and most productive period of one's life. (*In* can be replaced with *into*. See the examples.) □ *The good health of one's youth can carry over into the prime of life.* □ *He was struck down by a heart attack in the prime of life.*

**in the public eye** publicly; visible to all; conspicuous. (*In* can be replaced with *into*. See the examples.) □ *Elected officials find themselves constantly in the public eye.* □ *The mayor made it a practice to get into the public eye as much as possible.*

**in the red** in debt. (Refers to writing figures in red ink, rather than in black ink, when they show that one is in debt. See also **in the black**. *In* can be replaced with *into*. See the examples.) □ *My accounts are in* *the red at the end of every month.* □ *It's easy to get into the red if you don't pay close attention to the amount of money you spend.*

**in the right** on the moral or legal side of an issue; on the right side of an issue. □ *I felt I was in the right, but the judge ruled against me.* □ *It's hard to argue with Jane. She always believes that she's in the right.*

**in the same boat** in the same situation; having the same problem. (A cliché. *In* can be replaced with *into*. See the examples.) □ *TOM: I'm broke. Can you lend me twenty dollars? BILL: Sorry. I'm in the same boat.* □ *Jane and Mary are in the same boat. They both have been called for jury duty.*

**in the same breath** [stated or said] almost at the same time; as part of the same thought or conversation. □ *He told me I was lazy, but then in the same breath he said I was doing a good job.* □ *The teacher said that the students were working hard and, in the same breath, that they were not working hard enough.*

**in the spotlight** See in the limelight.

**in the twinkling of an eye** very quickly. (A biblical reference.) □ *In the twinkling of an eye, the deer had disappeared into the forest.* □ *I gave Bill ten dollars, and in the twinkling of an eye, he spent it.*

**in the wind** about to happen. (Also used literally.) □ *There are some major changes in the wind. Expect these changes to happen soon.* □ *There is something in the wind. We'll find out what it is soon.*

**in the world** See on earth.

**in the wrong** on the wrong or illegal side of an issue; guilty or in error. □ *I felt she was in the wrong, but the judge ruled in her favor.* □ *It's hard to argue with Jane. She always believes that everyone else is in the wrong.*

**in two shakes of a lamb's tail** in a very short time; very quickly. □ *Jane returned in two shakes of a lamb's tail.* □ *Fred was able to solve the problem in two shakes of a lamb's tail.*

**It never rains but it pours.** a proverb meaning that a lot of bad things tend to happen at the same time. □ *The car won't start, the stairs broke, and the dog died. It never rains but it pours.* □ *For years I was so healthy that I never even had a cold, but then I got pneumonia and was in the hospital for a week. It never rains but it pours.*

**jack-of-all-trades** someone who can do several different jobs instead of specializing in one. □ *John can do plumbing, carpentry, and roofing—a real jack-of-all-trades.* □ *Take your car to a trained mechanic, not a jack-of-all-trades.*

**job lot** a mixed collection of varying quality. (Informal.) □ *Mike found a valuable vase in that job lot he bought at the auction.* □ *There was nothing but junk in the job lot that I bought.*

**jockey for position** to try to push or work one's way into an advantageous position at the expense of others. □ *All the staff in that firm are jockeying for position. They all want the manager's job.* □ *It is unpleasant working for a firm where people are always jockeying for position.*

**Johnny-come-lately** someone who joins in (something) after it is under way. □ *Don't pay any attention to Sally. She's just a Johnny-come-lately and doesn't know what she's talking about.* □ *We've been here for thirty years. Why should some Johnny-come-lately tell us what to do?*

**Johnny-on-the-spot** someone who is in the right place at the right time. □ *Here I am, Johnny-on-the-spot. I told you I would be here at 12:20.* □ *Bill is late again. You can hardly call him Johnny-on-the-spot.*

**Join the club!** an expression indicating that the person spoken to is in the same, or a similar, unfortunate state as the speaker. (Informal.) □ *You've got nowhere to stay? Join the club! Neither have we.* □ *Did you lose your job, too? Join the club!*

**jumping-off point** a point or place from which to begin a venture. □ *The local library is a good jumping-off point for your research.* □ *The position in that firm would be a good jumping-off point for a job in advertising.*

**jump off the deep end** See *go off the deep end.*

**jump on the bandwagon** See *get on the bandwagon.*

**jump out of one's skin** to react strongly to a shock or surprise. (Usually with *nearly, almost,* etc.) □ *Oh! You really scared me. I nearly jumped out of my skin.* □ *Bill was so startled he almost jumped out of his skin.*

**jump the gun** to start before the starting signal. (Originally used in sports contests that are started by firing a gun.) □ *We all had to start the race again because Jane jumped the gun.* □ *When we took the test, Tom jumped the gun and started early.*

**jump the track 1.** [for something] to fall or jump off the rails or guides. (Usually said about a train.) □ *The train jumped the track, causing many injuries to the passengers.* □ *The engine jumped the track, but the other cars stayed on.* **2.** to change suddenly from one thing, thought, plan, or activity to another. □ *The entire project jumped the track, and we finally had to give up.* □ *John's mind jumped the track while he was in the play, and he forgot his lines.*

**just so 1.** in perfect order; neat and tidy. □ *Her hair is always just so.* □ *Their front garden is just so.* **2. Just so!** Precisely right!; Quite right! □ *BILL: The letter should arrive tomorrow. TOM: Just so!* □ *JANE: We must always try our best. MARTIN: Just so!*

**just what the doctor ordered** exactly what is required, especially for health or comfort. (A cliché.) □ *That meal was delicious, Bob. Just what the doctor ordered.* □ *BOB: Would you like something to drink? MARY: Yes, a cold glass of water would be just what the doctor ordered.*

**keep a civil tongue (in one's head)** to speak decently and politely. (Also with *have*.) □ *Please, John. Don't talk like that. Keep a civil tongue in your head.* □ *John seems unable to keep a civil tongue.* □ *He'd be welcome here if he had a civil tongue in his head.*

**keep an eye out (for someone or something)** to watch for the arrival or appearance of someone or something. (Also with *have*. The *an* can be replaced by *one's*.) □ *Please try to keep an eye out for the bus.* □ *Have your eye out for a raincoat on sale.* □ *Okay. I'll keep my eye out.*

**keep a stiff upper lip** to be cool and unmoved by unsettling events. (Also with *have*. See the note at keep a straight face.) □ *John always keeps a stiff upper lip.* □ *Now, Billy, don't cry. Keep a stiff upper lip.* □ *Bill can take it. He has a stiff upper lip.*

**keep a straight face** to make one's face stay free from laughter. (*Keep* can be replaced with *have*. *Keep* implies the exercise of effort, and *have* simply means to possess.) □ *It's hard to keep a straight face when someone tells a funny joke.* □ *I knew it was John who played the trick. He couldn't keep a straight face.* □ *John never has a straight face when he's telling a joke.*

**keep body and soul together** to feed, clothe, and house oneself. (A cliché.) □ *I hardly have enough money to keep body and soul together.* □ *How the old man was able to keep body and soul together is beyond me.*

**keep late hours** to stay up or stay out until very late; to work late. □ *I'm always tired because I keep late hours.* □ *If I didn't keep late hours, I wouldn't sleep so late in the morning.*

**keep on an even keel** to remain cool and calm. (Originally nautical.) □ *If Jane can keep on an even keel and not panic, she will be all right.* □ *Try to keep on an even keel and not get upset so easily.*

**keep one's ear to the ground** See have one's ear to the ground.

**keep one's eye on the ball 1.** to watch or follow the ball carefully, especially when one is playing a ball game; to follow the details of a ball game very carefully. □ *John, if you can't keep your eye on the ball, I'll have to take you out of the game.* □ *"Keep your eye on the ball," the coach roared at the players.* **2.** to remain alert to the events occurring around one. □ *If you want to get along in this office, you're going to have to keep your eye on the ball.* □ *Bill would do better in his classes if he would just keep his eye on the ball.*

**keep one's feet on the ground** See under get one's feet on the ground.

**keep one's head above water** See under get one's head above water.

**keep one's nose to the grindstone** See under put one's nose to the grindstone.

**keep one's temper** AND **hold one's temper** not to get angry; to hold back an expression of anger. □ *She should have learned to keep her temper when she was a child.* □ *Sally got thrown off the team because she couldn't hold her temper.*

**keep one's weather eye open** to watch for something (to happen); to be on the alert (for something); to be on guard. □ *Some trouble is brewing. Keep your weather eye open.* □ *Try to be more alert. Learn to keep your weather eye open.*

**keep one's word** to uphold one's promise. □ *I told her I'd be there to pick her up, and I intend to keep my word.* □ *Keeping one's word is necessary in the legal profession.*

**keep someone in stitches** to cause someone to laugh loud and hard, over and over. (Also with *have.* See the note at keep a straight face.) □ *The comedian kept us in stitches for nearly an hour.* □ *The teacher kept the class in stitches, but the students didn't learn anything.*

**keep someone on tenterhooks** to keep someone anxious or in suspense. (Also with *have.* See the note at keep a straight face.) □ *Please tell me now. Don't keep me on tenterhooks any longer!* □ *Now that we have her on tenterhooks, shall we let her worry, or shall we tell her?*

**keep someone or something hanging in midair** See under leave someone or something hanging in midair.

**keep someone or something in mind** AND **bear someone or something in mind** to remember and think about someone or something. □ *When you're driving a car, you must bear this in mind at all* times: *Keep your eyes on the road.* □ *As you leave home, keep your family in mind.*

**keep someone posted** to keep someone informed (of what is happening); to keep someone up to date. □ *If the price of corn goes up, I need to know. Please keep me posted.* □ *Keep her posted about the patient's status.*

**keep something on an even keel** to keep something in a steady and untroubled state. □ *The manager cannot keep the firm on an even keel any longer.* □ *When the workers are unhappy, it is difficult to keep the factory on an even keel.*

**keep something to oneself** to keep something a secret. (Notice the use of *but* in the examples. Compare with keep to oneself.) □ *I'm quitting my job, but please keep that to yourself.* □ *Keep it to yourself, but I'm quitting my job.* □ *John is always gossiping. He can't keep anything to himself.*

**keep something under one's hat** to keep something a secret; to keep something in one's mind (only). (If the secret stays under your hat, it stays in your mind. Note the use of *but* in the examples.) □ *Keep this under your hat, but I'm getting married.* □ *I'm moving away next month, but keep it under your hat.*

**keep something under wraps** to keep something concealed (until some future time). □ *We kept the plan under wraps until after the election.* □ *The automobile company kept the new model under wraps until most of the old models had been sold.*

**keep the home fires burning** to keep things going at one's home or other central location, maintaining the routine. (A cliché.) □ *My uncle kept the home fires burning when my sister and I went to school.* □ *The manager stays at the office and keeps the home fires burning while I'm out selling our products.*

**keep the wolf from the door** to maintain oneself at a minimal level; to keep from starving, freezing, etc. (A cliché.) □ *I don't make a lot of money, just enough to keep the wolf from the door.* □ *We have a small amount of money saved, hardly enough to keep the wolf from the door.*

**keep to oneself** to remain private; not to mix with other people very much. (Compare with keep something to oneself.) □ *We rarely see our neighbors. They mostly keep to themselves.* □ *Jean used to go out a lot, but she has kept to herself since her husband died.*

**keep up (with the Joneses)** to stay financially even with one's peers; to try hard to get the same amount of material goods that one's friends and neighbors have. (*Joneses* is the plural of *Jones*, a common American surname.) □ *Mr. and Mrs. Brown bought a new car simply to keep up with the Joneses.* □ *Keeping up with the Joneses can take all your money.*

**keep up (with the times)** to stay in fashion; to keep up with the news; to be contemporary or modern. □ *I try to keep up with the times. I want to know what's going on.* □ *I bought a whole new wardrobe because I want to keep up with the times.* □ *Sally learns all the new dances. She likes to keep up.*

**kick up a fuss** AND **kick up a row; kick up a storm** to become a nuisance; to misbehave and disturb (someone). (*Row* rhymes with *cow*. Note the variations in the examples.) □ *The customer kicked up such a fuss about the food that the manager came to apologize.* □ *I kicked up such a row that they threw me out.*

**kick up a row** See kick up a fuss.

**kick up a storm** See kick up a fuss.

**kick up one's heels** to celebrate; to act free or liberated. (As would a young colt.) □ *After the test was over, I just wanted to go out and kick up my heels.* □ *Some of the boys like to kick up their heels on the weekend.*

**kid stuff** a very easy task. (Informal.) □ *Climbing that hill is kid stuff.* □ *Driving an automatic car is kid stuff.*

**kill the fatted calf** to prepare an elaborate banquet (in someone's honor). (From the biblical story recounting the return of the prodigal son.) □ *When Bob got back from college, his parents killed the fatted calf and threw a great party.* □ *Sorry this meal isn't much, John. We didn't have time to kill the fatted calf.*

**kill the goose that laid the golden egg** to destroy the source of one's good fortune. (Based on an old fable.) □ *If you fire your best office worker, you'll be killing the goose that laid the golden egg.* □ *He sold his computer, which was like killing the goose that laid the golden egg.*

**kill time** to waste time. □ *Stop killing time. Get to work!* □ *We went over to the record shop just to kill time.*

**kill two birds with one stone** to solve two problems with one solution; to achieve two good results from one action. (A cliché.) □ *Bob needed to save money and also needed to get more exercise, so now he*

*jogs to work instead of taking the bus. He's killing two birds with one stone.*
□ *I have to cash a check and make a payment on my bank loan. I'll kill two birds with one stone by doing both in one trip to the bank.*

**kiss and make up** to forgive (someone) and be friends again. (Also used literally.) □ *They were very angry, but in the end they kissed and made up.* □ *I'm sorry. Let's kiss and make up.*

the **kiss of death** an act that puts an end to someone or something. □ *The mayor's veto was the kiss of death for the new law.* □ *Fainting on stage was the kiss of death for my acting career.*

**kiss something good-bye** to anticipate or experience the loss of something. □ *If you leave your camera on a park bench, you can kiss it good-bye.* □ *You kissed your wallet good-bye when you left it in the store.*

**knit one's brow** to wrinkle one's brow, especially by frowning. □ *The woman knit her brow and asked us what we wanted from her.* □ *While he read his book, John knit his brow occasionally. He must not have agreed with what he was reading.*

**knock on wood** a phrase said to cancel out imaginary bad luck. (Often said when one has just mentioned something good that one hopes will happen or will continue.) □ *My car has never given me any trouble— knock on wood.* □ *We plan to be in Florida by tomorrow evening—knock on wood.*

**knock someone cold 1.** to knock someone out. (Informal.) □ *The blow knocked the boxer cold.* □ *The attacker knocked the old man cold.* **2.** to stun someone; to shock someone. □ *The news of his death knocked me cold.* □ *Pat was knocked cold by the imprisonment of her son.*

**knock someone for a loop** See throw someone for a loop.

**know (all) the tricks of the trade** to possess the skills and knowledge necessary to do something. □ *Tom can repair car engines. He knows the tricks of the trade.* □ *If I knew all the tricks of the trade, I could be a better plumber.*

**know better** to be wise, experienced, or well taught. □ *Mary should have known better than to accept a lift from a stranger.* □ *Children should know better than to play in the road.*

**know-how** knowledge and skill. (Informal.) □ *Peter doesn't have the know-how to repair that car.* □ *Mary hasn't the know-how to work the computer.*

**know one's ABCs** to know the most basic things (like the alphabet) about something. □ *Bill can't do it. He doesn't even know his ABCs.* □ *You can't expect to write novels when you don't even know your ABCs.*

**know someone by sight** to know the name and recognize the face of someone. □ *I've never met the man, but I know him by sight.* □ *BOB: Have you ever met Mary? JANE: No, but I know her by sight.*

**know someone or something like a book** See know someone or something like the palm of one's hand.

**know someone or something like the back of one's hand** See know someone or something like the palm of one's hand.

**know someone or something like the palm of one's hand** AND **know someone or something like the back of one's hand; know someone or something like a book** to know someone or something very well. □ *Of course I know John. I know him like the back of my hand.* □ *We've spent so many hours together that I know him like a book.* □ *Bill knows this city like the palm of his hand.*

**know something from memory** to have memorized something so that one does not have to consult a written version; to know something well from seeing it very often. □ *Mary didn't need the script because she knew the play from memory.* □ *The conductor went through the entire concert without looking down at the music. He knew it from memory.*

**know something in one's bones** See feel something in one's bones.

**know something inside out** to know something thoroughly; to know about something thoroughly. □ *I know my geometry inside out.* □ *I studied and studied for my driver's test until I knew the rules inside out.*

**know the ropes** to know how to do something. □ *I can't do the job because I don't know the ropes.* □ *Ask Sally to do it. She knows the ropes.* ALSO: **show someone the ropes** to tell or show someone how something is to be done. □ *Since this was my first day on the job, the manager spent a lot of time showing me the ropes.*

**know the score** AND **know what's what** to know the facts; to know the facts about life and its difficulties. □ *Bob is so naive. He sure doesn't know the score.* □ *I know what you're trying to do. Oh, yes, I know what's what.*

**know what's what** See know the score.

**know which side one's bread is buttered on** to know what is most advantageous for oneself. (A cliché.) □ *He'll do it if his boss tells him to. He knows which side his bread is buttered on.* □ *Since John knows which side his bread is buttered on, he'll be there on time.*

**labor of love** a task that is either unpaid or poorly paid and that one does simply for one's own satisfaction or pleasure to please someone whom one likes or loves. □ *Jane made no money out of the biography she wrote. She was writing about the life of a friend, and the book was a labor of love.* □ *Mary hates knitting, but she made a sweater for her boyfriend. What a labor of love!*

**ladies' man** a man who likes the company of women and whose company is liked by women, the suggestion being that he likes to flirt with them. □ *John is a real ladies' man. He hates all-male parties.* □ *Bill is always flirting with the women at the club. He's a bit of a ladies' man.*

**lady-killer** a man who is very popular with women and who likes to flirt and make love with them; a man whom women cannot resist. □ *Fred used to be a real lady-killer, but now women laugh at him.* □ *Jack's wife doesn't know that he's a lady-killer and goes out with other women.*

the **land of Nod** sleep. (Humorous. From the fact that people sometimes nod when they are falling asleep. This is a pun, because the *land of Nod* is also the name of a place referred to in the Bible.) □ *The baby is in the land of Nod.* □ *Look at the clock! It's time we were all in the land of Nod.*

**landslide victory** a victory by a large margin; a very substantial victory, particularly in an election. □ *The mayor won a landslide victory in the election.* □ *The younger man won a landslide victory in the presidential election.*

**land someone with someone or something** to give or pass on someone or something unpleasant or unwanted to someone else. (Informal.) □ *John has landed me with his horrible little sister for the whole afternoon.* □ *No one wanted to judge the competition, so they landed Jean with the job.*

**land up somehow or somewhere** to finish somehow or somewhere; to come to be in a certain state or place at the end. (Usually in the wrong place or in a bad situation.) □ *We set out for Chicago but landed up in Detroit.* □ *He's so extravagant that he landed up in debt.*

**last but not least** last in sequence, but not last in importance. (An overused cliché. Often said in introductions.) □ *The speaker said, "And now, last but not least, I'd like to present Bill Smith, who will give us some final words."* □ *And last but not least, here is the loser of the race.*

**late in the day** far on in a project or activity; too late in a project or activity for action, decisions, etc., to be taken. (Also used literally.) □ *It was a bit late in the day for him to apologize.* □ *It's late in the day to change the plans.*

**laugh out of the other side of one's mouth** to change sharply from happiness to sadness. (A cliché.) □ *Now that you know the truth, you'll laugh out of the other side of your mouth.* □ *He was so proud that he won the election. He's laughing out of the other side of his mouth since they recounted the ballots and found out that he lost.*

**laugh something out of court** to dismiss something as ridiculous. □ *The committee laughed the suggestion out of court.* □ *Jack's request for a large salary increase was laughed out of court.*

**laugh up one's sleeve** to laugh secretly; to laugh quietly to oneself. □ *Jane looked very serious, but I knew she was laughing up her sleeve.* □ *I told Sally that her dress was darling, but I was laughing up my sleeve because her dress was too small.*

**a law unto oneself** one who makes one's own laws or rules; one who sets one's own standards of behavior. □ *You can't get Bill to follow the rules. He's a law unto himself.* □ *Jane is a law unto herself. She's totally unwilling to cooperate.*

**lay a finger on someone or something** to touch someone or something, even slightly, even with a finger. (Usually in the negative.) □ *Don't you dare lay a finger on my pencil. Go get your own!* □ *If you lay a finger on me, I'll scream.*

**lay an egg** to give a bad performance. □ *The cast of the play really laid an egg last night.* □ *I hope I don't lay an egg when it's my turn to sing.*

**lay down the law 1.** to state firmly what the rules are (for something). (A cliché.) □ *Before the meeting, the boss laid down the law. We all knew* *exactly what to do.* □ *The way she laid down the law means that I'll remember her rules.* **2.** to scold someone for misbehaving. □ *When the teacher caught us, he really laid down the law.* □ *Poor Bob. He really got it when his mother laid down the law.*

**lay it on thick** AND **pour it on thick; spread it on thick** to exaggerate praise, excuses, or blame. □ *Sally was laying it on thick when she said that Tom was the best singer she had ever heard.* □ *After Bob finished making his excuses, Sally said that he was pouring it on thick.* □ *Bob always spreads it on thick.*

**lay one's cards on the table** See put one's cards on the table.

**lay something on the line** See put something on the line.

**lay something to waste** See lay waste to something.

**lay waste to something** AND **lay something to waste** to destroy something (literally or figuratively). □ *The kids came in and laid waste to my clean house.* □ *The invaders laid the village to waste.*

**lead a dog's life** AND **live a dog's life** to lead a miserable life. □ *Poor Jane really leads a dog's life.* □ *I've been working so hard. I'm tired of living a dog's life.*

**lead someone down the garden path** to deceive someone. (A cliché.) □ *Now, be honest with me. Don't lead me down the garden path.* □ *That cheater really led her down the garden path.*

**lead someone on a merry chase** to lead someone in a purposeless pursuit. □ *What a waste of time. You really led me on a merry chase.* □ *Jane led Bill on a merry chase trying to find an antique lamp.*

**lead the life of Riley** AND **live the life of Riley** to live in luxury. (No one knows who Riley is.) □ *If I had a million dollars, I could lead the life of Riley.* □ *The treasurer took our money to Mexico, where he lived the life of Riley until the police caught him.*

**lead up to something** to prepare the way for something; to have something as a consequence. □ *His compliments were his way of leading up to asking for money.* □ *What were his actions leading up to?*

**learn something from the bottom up** to learn something thoroughly, from the very beginning; to learn all aspects of something, even the most lowly. □ *I learned my business from the bottom up.* □ *I started out sweeping the floors and learned everything from the bottom up.*

**leave a bad taste in someone's mouth** [for someone or something] to leave a bad feeling or memory with someone. □ *The whole business about the missing money left a bad taste in his mouth.* □ *It was a very nice party, but something about it left a bad taste in my mouth.* □ *I'm sorry that Bill was there. He always leaves a bad taste in my mouth.*

**leave a sinking ship** See desert a sinking ship.

**leave no stone unturned** to search in all possible places. (A cliché. As if one might find something under a rock.) □ *Don't worry. We'll find your stolen car. We'll leave no stone unturned.* □ *In searching for a nice place to live, we left no stone unturned.*

**leave one to one's fate** to abandon someone to whatever may happen—possibly death or some other unpleasant event. □ *We couldn't rescue the miners, and we were forced to leave them to their fate.* □ *Please don't try to help. Just go away and leave me to my fate.*

**leave someone for dead** to abandon someone as being dead. (The abandoned person may actually be alive.) □ *He looked so bad that they almost left him for dead.* □ *As the soldiers turned—leaving the enemy captain for dead—the captain fired at them.*

**leave someone high and dry 1.** to leave someone unsupported and unable to maneuver; to leave someone helpless. (Refers to a boat stranded on land or on a reef.) □ *All my workers quit and left me high and dry.* □ *All the children ran away and left Billy high and dry to take the blame for the broken window.* **2.** to leave someone without any money at all. □ *Mrs. Franklin took all the money out of the bank and left Mr. Franklin high and dry.* □ *Paying the bills always leaves me high and dry.*

**leave someone holding the baby** to leave someone with the responsibility for something, especially something difficult or unpleasant, often when it was originally someone else's responsibility. (Informal. Note the use of the passive in the first example.) □ *We all promised to look after the house when the owner was away, but I was left holding the baby on my own.* □ *It was her brother who promised to finish the work, and it was he who left her holding the baby.*

**leave someone holding the bag** to leave someone to take all the blame; to leave someone appearing guilty. □ *They all ran off and left me holding the bag. It wasn't even my fault.* □ *It was the mayor's fault, but he wasn't left holding the bag.*

**leave someone in peace** to stop bothering someone; to go away and let someone have peace. (Does not necessarily mean to go away from a person.) □ *Please go—leave me in peace.* □ *Can't you see that you're upsetting her? Leave her in peace.*

**leave someone in the lurch** to leave someone waiting for or anticipating one's actions. □ *Where were you, John? You really left me in the lurch.* □ *I didn't mean to leave you in the lurch. I thought we had canceled our meeting.*

**leave someone or something hanging in midair** to suspend dealing with someone or something; to leave someone waiting for an ending; to leave something waiting to be finished or continued. (Also used literally.) □ *She left her sentence hanging in midair.* □ *She left us hanging in midair when she paused.* □ *Tell me the rest of the story. Don't leave me hanging in midair.* □ *Don't leave the story hanging in midair.* ALSO: **keep someone or something hanging in midair** to maintain someone or something in a state of waiting to reach an ending or be completed. □ *Please don't keep us hanging in midair.*

**lend an ear (to someone)** to listen to someone. □ *Lend an ear to John. Hear what he has to say.* □ *I'd be delighted to lend an ear. I find great wisdom in everything John has to say.*

**lend oneself or itself to something** [for someone or something] to be adaptable to something; [for someone or something] to be useful for something. □ *This room doesn't lend itself to bright colors.* □ *John doesn't lend himself to casual conversation.*

**Let bygones be bygones.** a proverb meaning that one should forget the problems of the past. (Also a cliché.) □ *Okay, Sally, let bygones be bygones. Let's forgive and forget.* □ *Jane was unwilling to let bygones be bygones. She still won't speak to me.*

**let grass grow under one's feet** to do nothing; to stand still. (A cliché.) □ *Mary doesn't let the grass grow under her feet. She's always busy.* □ *Bob is too lazy. He's letting the grass grow under his feet.*

**let off steam** AND **blow off steam** to release excess energy or anger. □ *Whenever John gets a little angry, he blows off steam.* □ *Don't worry about John. He's just letting off steam.*

**let one's hair down** to become more intimate and begin to speak frankly. □ *Come on, Jane, let your hair down and tell me all about it.* T *I have a problem. Do you mind if I let down my hair?*

**Let sleeping dogs lie.** a proverb meaning that one should not search for trouble but should leave well enough alone—if something is not causing a problem, it is best just to leave it as it is. (Also a cliché.) □ *Don't mention that problem with Tom again. It's almost forgotten. Let sleeping dogs lie.* □ *You'll never be able to reform Bill. Leave him alone. Let sleeping dogs lie.*

**let someone off (the hook)** to release someone from a responsibility. □ *Please let me off the hook for Saturday. I have other plans.* □ *Okay, I'll let you off. You don't have to attend the meeting.*

**let something slide** to neglect something. □ *John let his lessons slide.* □ *Jane doesn't let her work slide.*

**let something slide by** See let something slip by.

**let something slip by** AND **let something slide by 1.** to forget or miss an important time or date. □ *I'm sorry I just let your birthday slip by.* □ *I let it slide by accidentally.* **2.** to waste a period of time. □ *You wasted the whole day by letting it slip by.* □ *We were having fun, and we let the time slide by.*

**let the cat out of the bag** AND **spill the beans** to reveal a secret or a surprise by accident. (Clichés.) □ *When Bill glanced at the door, he let the cat out of the bag. We knew then that he was expecting someone to arrive.* □ *We are planning a surprise party for Jane. Don't let the cat out of the bag.* □ *It's a secret. Try not to spill the beans.*

**let the chance slip by** to lose the opportunity (to do something). □ *When I was younger, I wanted to become a doctor, but I let the chance slip by.* □ *Don't let the chance slip by. Do it now!*

**lick one's lips** to show eagerness or pleasure about a future event. (Informal. From the habit of people licking their lips when they are about to enjoy eating something.) □ *The children licked their lips at the sight of the cake.* □ *The author's readers were licking their lips in anticipation of her new novel.* □ *The journalist was licking his lips when he went off to interview the disgraced politician.*

**lie through one's teeth** to lie boldly, obviously, and with no remorse. (A cliché.) □ *I knew she was lying through her teeth, but I didn't want to say so just then.* □ *I'm not lying through my teeth! I don't do that!*

the **life of the party** the type of person who is lively and helps make a party fun and exciting. □ *Bill is always the life of the party. Be sure to invite him.* □ *Bob isn't exactly the life of the party, but he's polite.*

**like a bat out of hell** with great speed and force. (A cliché. Use caution with the word *hell*.) □ *Did you see her leave? She left like a bat out of hell.* □ *The car sped down the street like a bat out of hell.*

**like a bolt out of the blue** suddenly and without warning. (A cliché. Refers to a bolt of lightning coming out of a clear blue sky.) □ *The news came to us like a bolt out of the blue.* □ *Like a bolt out of the blue, the boss came and fired us all.*

**like a bump on a log** unresponsive; immobile. (A cliché.) □ *I spoke to him, but he just sat there like a bump on a log.* □ *Don't stand there like a bump on a log. Give me a hand!*

**like a fish out of water** awkward; in a foreign or unaccustomed environment. (A cliché.) □ *At a formal dance, John is like a fish out of water.* □ *Mary was like a fish out of water at the bowling tournament.*

**like a lamb to the slaughter** AND **like lambs to the slaughter** [proceeding] quietly and without seeming to realize or complain about the likely difficulties or dangers of a situation. (Also without *like*, referring to one or those proceeding in this way. From the expression "lead someone like a lamb to the slaughter.") □ *Young men fighting in World War I were simply lambs to the slaughter.* □ *Our team's players went on the football field like lambs to the slaughter to meet the league leaders.* □ *When the boss called him into her office, Bill went like a lamb to the slaughter. He didn't know he was about to be fired.*

**like a sitting duck** AND **like sitting ducks** unguarded; unsuspecting and unaware. (Also without *like*. A cliché. The second phrase is the plural form. Refers to floating rather than flying ducks.) □ *He was waiting there like a sitting duck—a perfect target for a mugger.* □ *The soldiers were standing at the top of the hill like sitting ducks. It's a wonder they weren't all killed.* □ *We're sitting ducks out here in the open field. Let's hide under that tree.*

**like a three-ring circus** chaotic; exciting and busy. (A cliché.) □ *Our household is like a three-ring circus on Monday mornings.* □ *This meeting is like a three-ring circus. Quiet down and listen!*

**like lambs to the slaughter** See like a lamb to the slaughter.

**like looking for a needle in a haystack** [of a search] hopeless. (A cliché.) □ *Trying to find a white dog in the snow is like looking for a needle in a haystack.* □ *I tried to find my lost contact lens on the beach, but it was like looking for a needle in a haystack.*

**like nothing on earth** very untidy or very unattractive. (Informal.) □ *Joan arrived at the office looking like nothing on earth. She was all disheveled.* □ *In that electric yellow dress, Alice was like nothing on earth.*

**like sitting ducks** See like a sitting duck.

**like water off a duck's back** easily; without any apparent effect. (A cliché.) □ *Insults rolled off John like water off a duck's back.* □ *The bullets had no effect on the steel door. They fell away like water off a duck's back.*

**the line of least resistance** AND **the path of least resistance** the course of action that will cause the least trouble or effort. □ *Jane won't stand up for her rights. She always takes the line of least resistance.* □ *Joan never states her point of view. She takes the path of least resistance and agrees with everyone else.*

**the lion's share (of something)** the larger share of something. □ *The elder boy always takes the lion's share of the food.* □ *Jim was supposed to divide the cake into two equal pieces, but he took the lion's share.*

**a little bird told me** learned from a mysterious or secret source. (Often given as an evasive answer to someone who asks how you learned something. Rude in some circumstances.) □ *"All right," said Mary, "where did you get that information?" John replied, "A little bird told me."* □ *A little bird told me where I might find you.*

**little by little** slowly, a bit at a time. □ *Little by little, he began to understand what we were talking about.* □ *The snail crossed the stone little by little.*

A **little knowledge is a dangerous thing.** a proverb meaning that incomplete knowledge can embarrass or harm someone or something. □ *The doctor said, "Even though you've had a course in first aid, you shouldn't have treated your own illness. A little knowledge is a dangerous thing."* □ *John thought he knew how to take care of the garden, but he killed all the flowers. A little knowledge is a dangerous thing.*

**live a dog's life** See lead a dog's life.

**live and let live** to not interfere with other people's business or preferences. (A cliché.) □ *I don't care what they do! Live and let live, I always say.* □ *Your parents are strict. Mine just live and let live.*

**live beyond one's means** to spend more money than one can afford. □ *The Browns are deeply in debt because they are living beyond their means.* □ *I keep a budget so that I don't live beyond my means.*

**live by one's wits** to survive by being clever. □ *When you're in the kind of business I'm in, you have to live by your wits.* □ *John was orphaned at the age of ten and grew up living by his wits.*

**live from hand to mouth** to live in poor circumstances. □ *When both my parents were out of work, we lived from hand to mouth.* □ *We lived from hand to mouth during the war. Things were very difficult.*

**live in an ivory tower** to be aloof from the realities of living. (*Live* can be replaced by several expressions meaning to dwell or spend time, as in the examples. Also plural. Academics are often said to live in ivory towers.) □ *If you didn't spend so much time in your ivory tower, you'd know what people really think!* □ *Many professors are said to live in ivory towers. They don't know what the real world is like.*

**live off the fat of the land** to grow one's own food; to live on stored-up resources or abundant resources. (A cliché.) □ *If I had a million dollars, I'd invest it and live off the fat of the land.* □ *I'll be happy to retire soon and live off the fat of the land.* □ *Many farmers live off the fat of the land.*

**live out of a suitcase** to live briefly in a place, never unpacking one's luggage. □ *I hate living out of a suitcase. For my next vacation, I want to go to just one place and stay there the whole time.* □ *We were living out of suitcases in a motel while they repaired the damage the fire caused to our house.*

**live the life of Riley** See lead the life of Riley.

**live within one's means** to spend no more money than one has. □ *We have to struggle to live within our means, but we manage.* □ *John is unable to live within his means.*

**lock horns (with someone)** to get into an argument with someone. (Like bulls or stags fighting.) □ *Let's settle this peacefully. I don't want to lock horns with the boss.* □ *The boss doesn't want to lock horns either.*

**lock, stock, and barrel** absolutely every part or item. □ *We had to move everything out of the house—lock, stock, and barrel.* □ *We lost everything—lock, stock, and barrel—in the fire.*

**Long time no see.** a phrase indicating that one has not seen someone for a long time. □ *Hello, John. Long time no see.* □ *When John and Mary met on the street, they both said, "Long time no see."*

**look as if butter wouldn't melt in one's mouth** to appear to be cold and unfeeling (despite any information to the contrary). □ *Sally looks as if butter wouldn't melt in her mouth. She can be so cruel.* □ *What a sour face. He looks as if butter wouldn't melt in his mouth.*

**look daggers at someone** to give someone a dirty look. (As if one's line of vision were daggers aimed at someone.) □ *Tom must have been mad at Ann from the way he was looking daggers at her.* □ *Don't you dare look daggers at me. Don't even look cross-eyed at me!*

**look like a million dollars** to look very good. (A cliché.) □ *Oh, Sally, you look like a million dollars.* □ *Your new hairdo looks like a million dollars.*

**look like the cat that swallowed the canary** to appear as if one has just had a great success. (A cliché. Cats sometimes seem to appear pleased with themselves for things they have done.) □ *After the meeting, John looked like the cat that swallowed the canary. I knew he must have been a success.* □ *What happened? You look like the cat that swallowed the canary.*

**look the other way** to ignore (something) on purpose. (Also used literally.) □ *John could have prevented the problem, but he looked the other way.* □ *By looking the other way, he actually made the problem worse.*

**look to one's laurels** to take care not to lower or diminish one's reputation or position, especially in relation to that of someone who is potentially better. □ *With the arrival of the new member of the football team, James will have to look to his laurels to remain the highest scorer.* □ *The older members of the team will have to look to their laurels when young people join.*

**loom large** to be of great importance, especially when referring to a possible problem, danger, or threat. □ *The exams were looming large.* □ *Eviction was looming large when the students could not pay their rent.*

**lord it over someone** to dominate someone; to direct and control someone. □ *Mr. Smith seems to lord it over his wife.* □ *The boss lords it over everyone in the office.*

**lose face** to lose status; to become less respectable. □ *John is more afraid of losing face than losing money.* □ *Things will go better if you can explain to him where he was wrong without making him lose face.*

**lose heart** to lose one's courage or confidence. □ *Now, don't lose heart. Keep trying.* □ *What a disappointment! It's enough to make one lose heart.*

**lose oneself in something** to have all one's attention taken up by something. □ *I can lose myself in a book anytime.* □ *The children lose themselves in their favorite TV program on Saturdays.*

**lose one's grip** to lose control over something. □ *I can't seem to run things the way I used to. I'm losing my grip.* □ *They replaced the board of directors because it was losing its grip.*

**lose one's temper** to become angry. □ *Please don't lose your temper. It's not good for you.* □ *I'm sorry that I lost my temper.*

**lose one's train of thought** to forget what one was talking or thinking about. □ *Excuse me, I lost my train of thought. What was I saying?* □ *By asking a question, you made the speaker lose her train of thought.*

**lost in thought** busy thinking. □ *I'm sorry, I didn't hear what you said. I was lost in thought.* □ *Bill—lost in thought as always—went into the wrong room.*

**lost on someone** having no effect on someone; wasted on someone. (Informal.) □ *The joke was lost on Jean. She didn't understand it.* □ *The humor of the situation was lost on Mary. She was too upset to see it.*

**love at first sight** love established when two people first see one another. (A cliché.) □ *Bill was standing at the door when Ann opened it. It was love at first sight.* □ *It was love at first sight when they met, but it didn't last long.*

**lovely weather for ducks** rainy weather. (A cliché.) □ *BOB: Not very nice out today, is it? BILL: It's lovely weather for ducks.* □ *I don't like this rain, but it's lovely weather for ducks.*

**lower one's sights** to set one's goals lower. □ *Even though you get frustrated, don't lower your sights.* □ *I shouldn't lower my sights. If I work hard, I can do what I want.*

**lower one's voice** to speak more softly. □ *Please lower your voice, or you'll disturb the people who are working.* □ *He wouldn't lower his voice, so everyone heard what he said.*

**lower the boom on someone** to scold or punish someone severely; to crack down on someone and become very strict. (Originally nautical.) □ *If Bob won't behave better, I'll have to lower the boom on him.* □ *The teacher lowered the boom on the whole class for misbehaving.*

**low man on the totem pole** the least important person in a group; the person with the lowest status. (See also high man on the totem pole.) □ *I was the last to find out because I'm low man on the totem pole.* □ *I can't be of any help. I'm low man on the totem pole.*

**lull someone into a false sense of security** to lead someone into believing that all is well before attacking or doing something bad. □ *We lulled the enemy into a false sense of security by pretending to retreat. Then we launched an attack.* □ *The boss lulled us into a false sense of security by saying that our jobs were safe and then fired half the staff.*

**lunatic fringe** the more extreme members of a group. □ *Most of the members of that religious sect are quite reasonable, but she belongs to the lunatic fringe.* □ *Being diet-conscious is all very well, but there is a lunatic fringe that will hardly eat anything.*

**made to measure** [of clothing] made especially to fit the measurements of a particular person. □ *Jack has his suits made to measure because he's rather large.* □ *Having clothes made to measure is rather expensive.*

**maiden speech** a first public speech, especially a British Member of Parliament's first speech to the House of Commons. □ *The new mayor makes her maiden speech tonight.* □ *Our professor made her maiden speech to the conference yesterday.*

**maiden voyage** the first voyage of a ship or boat. □ *The liner sank on its maiden voyage.* □ *Jim is taking his yacht on its maiden voyage.*

**make a beeline for someone or something** to head straight toward someone or something. □ *Billy came into the kitchen and made a beeline for the cookies.* □ *After the game, we all made a beeline for John, who was serving cold drinks.*

**make a clean breast of something** to confess something. □ *You'll feel better if you make a clean breast of it. Now tell us what happened.* □ *I was forced to make a clean breast of the whole affair.*

**make a face** to twist one's face into a strange expression in order to show one's dislike, ridicule, etc., or in order to make someone laugh. □ *The comedian made faces in order to amuse the children.* □ *Jane made a face when she was asked to work late.*

**make a go of it** to make something work out all right. □ *It's a tough situation, but Ann is trying to make a go of it.* □ *We don't like living here, but we have to make a go of it.*

**make a great show of something** to make something obvious; to do something in a showy fashion. □ *Ann made a great show of wiping up the drink that John spilled.* □ *Jane displayed her irritation at our late arrival by making a great show of serving the cold dinner.*

**make a hit (with someone or something)** to please someone or something. □ *The singer made a hit with the audience.* □ *She was afraid she wouldn't make a hit.* □ *John made a hit with my parents last evening.*

**make a long story short** to bring a story to an end. (A cliché. A formula that introduces a summary of a story or a joke.) □ *And—to make a long story short—I never got back the money that I lent him.* □ *If I can make a long story short, let me say that everything worked out fine.*

**make a mountain out of a molehill** to make a major issue out of a minor one; to exaggerate the importance of something. (A cliché. Also plural. See the examples.) □ *Come on, don't make a mountain out of a molehill. It's not that important.* □ *Mary is always making mountains out of molehills.*

**make a nuisance of oneself** to be a constant bother. □ *I'm sorry to make a nuisance of myself, but I do need an answer to my question.* □ *Stop making a nuisance of yourself, and wait your turn.*

**make a run for it** to run fast to get away or get somewhere. □ *When the guard wasn't looking, the prisoner made a run for it.* □ *In the baseball game, the player on first base made a run for it, but he didn't make it to second base.*

**make a silk purse out of a sow's ear** to create something of value out of something of no value. (A cliché. Often in the negative.) □ *Don't bother trying to fix up this old bicycle. You can't make a silk purse out of a sow's ear.* □ *My mother made a lovely jacket out of an old coat. She succeeded in making a silk purse out of a sow's ear.*

**make cracks (about someone or something)** to ridicule or make jokes about someone or something. □ *Please stop making cracks about my haircut. It's the new style.* □ *Some people can't help making cracks. They are just rude.*

**make fast work of someone or something** See make short work of someone or something.

**make free with someone or something** See take liberties with someone or something.

**make good money** to earn a large amount of money. (Here, *good* means plentiful.) □ *Ann makes good money at her job.* □ *She must do something important, because she makes good money.*

**Make hay while the sun is shining.** a proverb meaning that one should make the most of good times and take advantage of opportunities while they are available. □ *There are lots of people here now. You should try to sell them soda pop. Make hay while the sun is shining.* □ *Go to school and get a good education while you're young. Make hay while the sun is shining.*

**make life miserable for someone** to make someone unhappy over a long period of time. □ *My shoes are tight, and they are making life miserable for me.* □ *Jane's boss is making life miserable for her.*

**make light of something** to treat something as if it were unimportant or humorous. □ *I wish you wouldn't make light of his problems. They're quite serious.* □ *I make light of my problems, and that helps me feel better.*

**make merry** to have fun; to have an enjoyable time. □ *The guests certainly made merry at the wedding.* □ *The children were making merry in the garden. They were dancing and playing.*

**make mincemeat of someone** (Informal.) **1.** to defeat someone completely. □ *Our football team made mincemeat of theirs.* □ *Bob made mincemeat of John in the tennis finals.* **2.** to scold or punish someone severely. □ *Jack's mother will make mincemeat of him when she sees the broken window.* □ *The teacher made mincemeat of Mike when he came to class without his homework.*

**make mischief** to cause trouble. □ *Bob loves to make mischief and get other people into trouble.* □ *Don't believe what Mary says. She's just trying to make mischief.*

**make oneself at home** to make oneself comfortable as if one were in one's own home. □ *Please come in and make yourself at home.* □ *I'm glad you're here. During your visit, just make yourself at home.*

**make short work of someone or something** AND **make fast work of someone or something** to finish with someone or something quickly. □ *I made short work of Tom so I could leave the office to play golf.* □ *Billy made fast work of his dinner so he could go out and play.*

**make someone or something tick** to cause someone or something to run or function. (Usually with *what*. Originally the kind of thing that would be said about a clock or a watch.) □ *I don't know what makes it tick.* □ *What makes John tick? I just don't understand him.* □ *I took apart the radio to find out what made it tick.*

**make someone's blood boil** to make someone very angry. □ *It just makes my blood boil to think of the amount of food that gets wasted around here.* □ *Whenever I think of that dishonest mess, it makes my blood boil.*

**make someone's blood run cold** to shock or horrify someone. □ *The terrible story in the newspaper made my blood run cold.* □ *I could tell you things about prisons that would make your blood run cold.*

**make someone's hair stand on end** to cause someone to be very frightened. □ *The horrible scream made my hair stand on end.* □ *The ghost story made our hair stand on end.*

**make someone's head spin** See make someone's head swim.

**make someone's head swim** AND **make someone's head spin 1.** to make someone dizzy or disoriented. □ *Riding in your car makes my head spin.* □ *Breathing the gas made my head swim.* **2.** to confuse or overwhelm someone. □ *All these numbers make my head swim.* □ *The physics lecture made my head spin.*

**make someone's mouth water** to make someone hungry (for something); to cause someone to salivate. □ *That beautiful salad makes my mouth water.* □ *Talking about food makes my mouth water.*

**make someone the scapegoat for something** to make someone take the blame for something. □ *They made Tom the scapegoat for the whole affair. It wasn't all his fault.* □ *Don't try to make me the scapegoat. I'll tell who really did it.*

**make something from scratch** to make something by starting with the basic ingredients. □ *We made the cake from scratch, using no prepared ingredients.* □ *I didn't have a ladder, so I made one from scratch.*

**make something up out of whole cloth** to create a story or a lie from no facts at all. (A cliché.) □ *I don't believe you. I think you made that up out of whole cloth.* T *Ann made up her explanation out of whole cloth. There was not a bit of truth in it.*

**make something worth someone's while** to make something profitable enough for someone to do. □ *If you deliver this parcel for me, I'll make it worth your while.* □ *The boss said he'd make it worth our while if we worked late.*

**make the feathers fly** See make the fur fly.

**make the fur fly** AND **make the feathers fly** to cause a fight or an argument. □ *When your mother gets home and sees what you've done, she'll really make the fur fly.* □ *When those two get together, they'll make the feathers fly. They hate each other.*

**make the grade** to be satisfactory; to be what is expected. □ *I'm sorry, but your work doesn't exactly make the grade.* □ *This meal doesn't just make the grade. It is excellent.*

**make up for lost time** to do much of something; to do something fast. □ *Because we took so long eating lunch, we have to drive faster to make up for lost time. Otherwise we'll be late.* □ *At the age of sixty, Bill learned to play golf. Now he plays every day. He's making up for lost time.*

a **man about town** a fashionable man who leads a sophisticated life. □ *He attends the opera and dines at the finest restaurants—quite a man about town.* □ *Jack's too much of a man about town to go to a football game.*

the **man in the street** the ordinary person. □ *Politicians rarely care what the man in the street thinks.* □ *The man in the street has little interest in literature.*

**manna from heaven** unexpected help or comfort; an unanticipated benefit or advantage. (Biblical.) □ *The arrival of the rescue team was like manna from heaven to the injured climber. He thought he would have been on the mountain all night.* □ *The offer of a new job just after she was fired from her old one was manna from heaven to Joan.*

**man-to-man** AND **woman-to-woman** speaking frankly and directly, one person to another. □ *Let's discuss this man-to-man so we know what each other thinks.* □ *The two mothers discussed their child-rearing problems woman-to-woman.*

**march to a different drummer** to believe in a different set of principles; to be unconventional in one's values. (A cliché.) □ *John marches to a different drummer. You can't assume he'll do what everyone else does.* □ *Grandpa says today's teenagers behave very badly, but perhaps they just march to a different drummer.*

a **matter of life and death** a matter of great urgency; an issue that will decide between living and dying. (Usually an exaggeration. Sometimes humorous.) □ *We must find a doctor. It's a matter of life and death.* □ *I must have some water. It's a matter of life and death.*

a **matter of opinion** the question of how good or bad someone or something is. □ *It's a matter of opinion how good the company is. John thinks it's great, and Fred thinks it's poor.* □ *Whether the committee is efficient is a matter of opinion.*

**mealy-mouthed** not frank or direct. (Informal.) □ *Jane's too mealy-mouthed to tell Frank she dislikes him. She just avoids him.* □ *Don't be so mealy-mouthed. It's better to speak plainly.*

**meet one's end** to die. □ *The dog met his end under the wheels of a car.* □ *I don't intend to meet my end until I'm 100 years old.*

**meet one's match** to encounter one's equal. □ *John played tennis with Bill yesterday, and it looks as if John has finally met his match.* □ *Listen to Jane and Mary argue. I always thought that Jane was loud, but she has finally met her match. Mary is just as loud!*

**meet someone halfway** to compromise with someone. □ *No, I won't give in, but I'll meet you halfway.* □ *They settled the argument by agreeing to meet each other halfway.*

**melt in one's mouth** to taste very good; [for food] to be very rich and satisfying. (A cliché.) □ *This cake is so good it'll melt in your mouth.* □ *John said that the food didn't exactly melt in his mouth.*

**mend (one's) fences** to restore good relations (with someone). (Also used literally.) □ *I think I had better get home and mend my fences. I had an argument with my daughter this morning.* □ *Sally called up her uncle to apologize and try to mend fences.*

**mend one's ways** to improve one's behavior. □ *John used to be very wild, but he's mended his ways.* □ *You'll have to mend your ways if you go out with Mary. She hates people to be late.*

**mention something in passing** to mention something casually; to mention something while talking about something else. □ *He just happened to mention in passing that the mayor had resigned.* □ *John mentioned in passing that he was nearly eighty years old.*

**middle-of-the-road** halfway between two extremes, especially political extremes. □ *Jane is very left-wing, but her husband is politically middle-of-the-road.* □ *I don't want to vote for either the left-wing or the right-wing candidate. I prefer someone with more middle-of-the-road views.*

**milestone in someone's life** a very important event or point in one's life. (From the stone at the side of a road showing the distance to or from a place.) □ *Joan's wedding was a milestone in her mother's life.* □ *The birth of a child is a milestone in every parent's life.*

**milk of human kindness** natural kindness and sympathy shown to others. (From Shakespeare's play *Macbeth*.) □ *Mary is completely hard and selfish—she has no milk of human kindness in her.* □ *Roger is too full of the milk of human kindness, and people take advantage of him.*

a **millstone about one's neck** a continual burden or handicap. □ *This huge and expensive house is a millstone about my neck.* □ *Bill's inability to read is a millstone about his neck.*

**mind one's own business** to attend only to the things that concern one. □ *Leave me alone, Bill. Mind your own business.* □ *I'd be fine if John would mind his own business.*

**mind one's p's and q's** to mind one's manners; to pay attention to small details of behavior. (From an old caution to children learning the alphabet or to typesetters to watch carefully for the difference between p and q.) □ *When we go to the mayor's reception, please mind your p's and q's.* □ *I always mind my p's and q's when I eat at a restaurant with white tablecloths.*

**mind you** a phrase indicating that something should be taken into consideration. □ *He's very well dressed, but mind you he's got plenty of money to buy clothes.* □ *Jean is unfriendly to me, but mind you she's never very nice to anyone.*

a **mine of information** someone or something that is full of information. □ *Grandfather is a mine of information about World War I.* □ *The new encyclopedia is a positive mine of useful information.*

**miscarriage of justice** a wrong or mistaken decision, especially one made in court of law. □ *Sentencing the old man on a charge of murder proved to be a miscarriage of justice.* □ *Punishing the pupil for cheating was a miscarriage of justice. He was innocent.*

**miss (something) by a mile** to fail to hit something by a great distance. (A cliché.) □ *Ann shot the arrow and missed the target by a mile.* □ *"Good grief, you missed by a mile," shouted Sally.*

**miss the point** to fail to understand the point, purpose, or intent. □ *I'm afraid you missed the point. Let me explain it again.* □ *You keep explaining, and I keep missing the point.*

a **mixed bag** a varied collection of people or things. (Refers to a bag of game brought home after a day's hunting.) □ *The new pupils are a mixed bag—some bright, some positively stupid.* □ *The furniture I bought is a mixed bag. Some of it is valuable, and the rest is worthless.*

**moment of truth** the point at which someone has to face the reality of a situation. □ *The moment of truth is here. Turn over your exam papers and begin.* □ *Now for the moment of truth, when we find out whether we have the building permit or not.*

**Money burns a hole in someone's pocket.** a phrase meaning that someone spends as much money as possible, and that having money makes a person want to spend it. (As if the money were trying as hard as possible to get out of the pocket.) □ *Sally can't seem to save anything. Money burns a hole in her pocket.* □ *If money burns a hole in your pocket, you'll never have any for emergencies.*

**Money is no object.** It does not matter how much something costs. □ *Please show me your finest automobile. Money is no object.* □ *I want the best earrings you have. Don't worry about how much they cost, because money is no object.*

**Money is the root of all evil.** a proverb meaning that money is the basic cause of all wrongdoing. (In the Bible, this appears as "the love of money is the root of all evil.") □ *Why do you work so hard to make money? It will just cause you trouble. Money is the root of all evil.* □ *Any thief in prison can tell you that money is the root of all evil.*

**Money talks.** Money gives one power and influence to help get things done or to get one's own way. □ *Don't worry. I know how to get things done. Money talks.* □ *I can't compete against rich old Mrs. Jones. She'll get her way because money talks.*

**monkey business** peculiar or out-of-the-ordinary activities, especially mischievous or illegal ones. □ *There's been some monkey business in connection with the firm's accounts.* □ *Bob left the firm quite suddenly. I think there was some monkey business between him and the boss's wife.*

the **morning after (the night before)** the morning after a night spent drinking, when one has a hangover. □ *Oh, I've got a headache. Talk* *about the morning after the night before!* □ *It looked like a case of the morning after the night before, and Frank asked for some aspirin.*

**move heaven and earth to do something** to make a major effort to do something. (A cliché.) □ *"I'll move heaven and earth to be with you, Mary," said Bill.* □ *I had to move heaven and earth to get there on time.*

**move up (in the world)** to advance (oneself) and become success-ful. □ *The harder I work, the more I move up in the world.* □ *Keep your eye on John. He's really moving up.*

**much ado about nothing** a lot of excitement about nothing. (A cliché. This is the title of a play by Shakespeare. Do not confuse *ado* with *adieu.*) □ *All the commotion about the new tax law turned out to be much ado about nothing.* □ *Your promises always turn out to be much ado about nothing.*

**nail in someone's or something's coffin** something that will harm or destroy someone or something. □ *Every word of criticism that Bob said about the firm was a nail in his coffin.* □ *I knew the boss would fire him. Losing the export order was the final nail in the company's coffin.*

**name-dropping** See under drop someone's name.

**neck and neck** exactly even, especially in a race or a contest. □ *John and Tom finished the race neck and neck.* □ *Mary and Ann were neck and neck in the spelling contest. Their scores were tied.*

**neither fish nor fowl** not any recognizable thing. (A cliché.) □ *The car that they drove up in was neither fish nor fowl. It must have been made out of spare parts.* □ *This proposal is neither fish nor fowl. I can't tell what you're proposing.*

**neither hide nor hair** no sign or indication (of someone or something). (A cliché.) □ *We could find neither hide nor hair of him. I don't know where he is.* □ *There has been no one here—neither hide nor hair—for the last three days.*

**new blood** See fresh blood.

**a new lease on life** a renewed and revitalized outlook on life; a new start in living. (A cliché.) □ *Getting the job offer was a new lease on life.* □ *When I got out of the hospital, I felt as if I had a new lease on life.*

**a new one on someone** something one has not heard before and that one is not ready to believe. (Informal. The *someone* is often *me*.) □ *Jack's poverty is a new one on me. He always seems to have plenty of money.* □ *The firm's difficulties are a new one on me. I thought that they were doing very well.*

**next to nothing** hardly anything; almost nothing. □ *This car's worth next to nothing. It's full of rust.* □ *I bought this antique chair for next to nothing.*

**night owl** someone who usually stays up very late. □ *Ann's a real night owl. She never goes to bed before 2 A.M. and sleeps until noon.* □ *Jack's a night owl and is at his best after midnight.*

**nine days' wonder** something that is of interest to people only for a short time. □ *Don't worry about the story about you in the newspaper. It'll be a nine days' wonder, and then people will forget.* □ *The elopement of Jack and Ann was a nine days' wonder. Now people never mention it.*

**nip and tuck** almost even; almost tied. □ *The horses ran nip and tuck for the first half of the race. Then my horse pulled ahead.* □ *In the football game last Saturday, both teams were nip and tuck throughout the game.*

**nip something in the bud** to put an end to something at an early stage. (A cliché. As if one were pinching the flowering bud from an annoying plant.) □ *John is getting into bad habits, and it's best to nip them in the bud.* □ *There was trouble in the classroom, but the teacher nipped it in the bud.*

**nobody's fool** a sensible and wise person who is not easily deceived. □ *Mary is nobody's fool. She knows Jack would try to cheat her.* □ *Ann looks as though she's not very bright, but she's nobody's fool.*

**nod off** to fall asleep. (Informal.) □ *Jack nodded off during the minister's sermon.* □ *Father always nods off after Sunday lunch.*

**no (ifs, ands, or) buts about it** absolutely no discussion, dissension, or doubt about something. (A cliché.) □ *I want you there exactly at eight, no ifs, ands, or buts about it.* □ *This is the best television set available for the money, no buts about it.*

**no joke** a serious matter. (Informal.) □ *It's no joke when you miss the last train.* □ *It's certainly no joke when you have to walk home.*

**no laughing matter** a serious matter. (A cliché.) □ *Be serious. This is no laughing matter.* □ *This disease is no laughing matter. It's quite deadly.*

**none other than** the very person. □ *The new building was opened by none other than the president.* □ *Jack's wife turned out to be none other than my cousin.*

**none the wiser** not knowing any more. □ *I was none the wiser about the project after the lecture. It was a complete waste of time.* □ *Ann tried to explain the situation tactfully to Jack, but in the end, he was none the wiser.*

**none the worse for wear** no worse because of use or effort. □ *I lent my car to John. When I got it back, it was none the worse for wear.* □ *I had a hard day today, but I'm none the worse for wear.*

**none too** not very; not at all. □ *The towels in the bathroom were none too clean.* □ *It was none too warm in their house.*

**no skin off someone's nose** See no skin off someone's teeth.

**no skin off someone's teeth** AND **no skin off someone's nose** no difficulty for someone; no concern of someone. (A cliché.) □ *It's no skin off my nose if she wants to act that way.* □ *She said it was no skin off her teeth if we wanted to sell the house.*

**no spring chicken** no longer young. □ *I don't get around very well anymore. I'm no spring chicken, you know.* □ *Even though John is no spring chicken, he still plays tennis twice a week.*

**not able to see the forest for the trees** allowing many details of a problem to obscure the problem as a whole. (A cliché. *Not able to* is often expressed as *can't*.) □ *The solution is obvious. You missed it because you can't see the forest for the trees.* □ *She suddenly realized that she hadn't been able to see the forest for the trees.*

**not born yesterday** experienced; knowledgeable in the ways of the world. □ *I know what's going on. I wasn't born yesterday.* □ *Sally knows the score. She wasn't born yesterday.*

**not have a leg to stand on** [for a person's argument or a case] to have no support. □ *You may think you're in the right, but you don't have a leg to stand on.* □ *My lawyer said I didn't have a leg to stand on, so I shouldn't sue the company.*

**nothing but** only; just. □ *Joan drinks nothing but milk.* □ *Fred buys nothing but expensive clothes.*

**nothing but skin and bones** AND **all skin and bones** very thin or emaciated. □ *Bill has lost so much weight. He's nothing but skin and bones.* □ *That old horse is all skin and bones. I won't ride it.*

**nothing short of something** more or less the same as something bad; as bad as something. □ *His behavior was nothing short of criminal.* □ *Climbing those mountains alone is nothing short of suicide.*

**Nothing ventured, nothing gained.** a proverb meaning that one cannot achieve anything if one does not try. □ *Come on, John. Give it a* *try. Nothing ventured, nothing gained.* □ *I felt as if I had to take the chance. Nothing ventured, nothing gained.*

**not hold water** to make no sense; to be illogical. (Said of ideas, arguments, etc., not people. Like a vessel or container that leaks, the idea has flaws or "holes" in it.) □ *Your argument doesn't hold water.* □ *This scheme won't work because it won't hold water.*

**not know enough to come in out of the rain** to be very stupid. (A cliché.) □ *Bob's so stupid. He doesn't know enough to come in out of the rain.* □ *You can't expect very much from somebody who doesn't know enough to come in out of the rain.*

**not know someone from Adam** not to know someone at all. (A cliché.) □ *I wouldn't recognize John if I saw him. I don't know him from Adam.* □ *What does she look like? I don't know her from Adam.*

**not long for this world** to be about to die. (A cliché.) □ *Our dog is nearly twelve years old and not long for this world.* □ *I'm so tired. I think I'm not long for this world.*

**not open one's mouth** AND **not utter a word** to say nothing at all; not to say anything; not to tell something (to anyone). □ *Don't worry, I'll keep your secret. I won't even open my mouth.* □ *Have no fear. I won't utter a word.* □ *I don't know how they found out. I didn't even open my mouth.*

**not see further than the end of one's nose** to care only about what is actually present or obvious; not to care about the future or about what is happening elsewhere or to other people. □ *Mary can't see further than the end of her nose. She doesn't care about what will happen to the environment in the future as long as she's comfortable now.* □ *Jack's been accused of not seeing further than the end of his nose. He refuses to expand the firm and look for new markets.*

**not set foot somewhere** to stay out of or away from somewhere; not to go somewhere. □ *I wouldn't set foot in John's room. I'm very angry with him.* □ *He never set foot here.*

**not sleep a wink** not to sleep at all; to be sleepless; not to close one's eyes in sleep even as long as it takes to blink. □ *I couldn't sleep a wink last night.* □ *Ann hasn't been able to sleep a wink for a week.*

**not someone's cup of tea** not something one prefers. (A cliché.) □ *Playing cards isn't her cup of tea.* □ *Sorry, that's not my cup of tea.*

**not up to scratch** AND **not up to snuff** not adequate. □ *Sorry, your paper isn't up to scratch. Please do it over again.* □ *The performance was not up to snuff.*

**not up to snuff** See not up to scratch.

**not utter a word** See not open one's mouth.

**nowhere near** not nearly. □ *We have nowhere near enough coal for the winter.* □ *They're nowhere near ready for the game.*

**nuts and bolts (of something)** the basic facts about something; the practical details of something. □ *Tom knows all about the nuts and bolts of the chemical process.* □ *Ann is familiar with the nuts and bolts of public relations.*

**odd man out** an unusual or atypical person or thing. □ *I'm odd man out because I'm not wearing a tie.* □ *Unless you want to be odd man out, you had better learn to work a computer.*

the **odds are against one** one's chances are slim; there is little chance of one succeeding; the situation is not favorable for one. (Also with other forms of the verb *be*. See the examples.) □ *You can give it a try, but the odds are against you.* □ *I knew the odds were against me, but I ran in the race anyway—and I won!*

**odor of sanctity** an atmosphere of excessive holiness or piety. (Derogatory.) □ *I'm uncomfortable in their house. There's such an odor of sanctity, with Bibles and holy pictures everywhere.* □ *People are nervous of Jane's odor of sanctity. She's always praying for people or doing good works and never has any fun.*

**of all the nerve** how shocking; how dare (someone). (The speaker is exclaiming that someone is being very insolent or rude.) □ *How can you talk to me that way! Of all the nerve!* □ *Imagine anyone coming to a formal dance in jeans. Of all the nerve!*

**off base** unrealistic; inexact; wrong. □ *I'm afraid you're off base when you state that this problem will take care of itself.* □ *You're way off base! Let me show you the facts.*

**off-color 1.** not the exact color (that one wants). □ *The book cover used to be red, but now it's a little off-color.* □ *The wall was painted off-color. I think it was meant to be orange.* **2.** rude, vulgar, or impolite. □ *That joke you told was off-color and embarrassed me.* □ *The nightclub act was a bit off-color.*

**off duty** not working at one's job. □ *I'm sorry, I can't talk to you until I'm off duty.* □ *The police officer couldn't help me because he was off duty.*

**off the air** [relating to radio or television stations and programs] not broadcasting or being broadcast. (Compare with *on the air*.) □ *The radio* audience won't hear what you say when you're off the air. □ When the performers were off the air, the director told them how well they had done.

**off the record** unofficial; informal. □ *This is off the record, but I disagree with the mayor on this matter.* □ *Although her comments were off the record, the newspaper published them anyway.*

**off the top of one's head** [to state something] rapidly and without having to think or remember. □ *I can't think of the answer off the top of my head.* □ *Jane can tell you the correct amount off the top of her head.*

**off to a running start** with a good, fast beginning, possibly a head start. □ *I got off to a running start in math this year.* □ *The horses got off to a running start.*

**of the first water** of the finest quality. (Originally a measurement of the quality of a pearl.) □ *This is a very fine pearl—a pearl of the first water.* □ *Tom is of the first water—a true gentleman.*

**on active duty** in battle or ready to go into battle. (Military.) □ *The soldier was on active duty for ten months.* □ *That was a long time to be on active duty.*

**on a fool's errand** involved in a useless journey or task. □ *Bill went for an interview, but he was on a fool's errand. The job had already been filled.* □ *I was sent on a fool's errand to buy some flowers. I knew the shop would be shut by then.*

**on all fours** on one's hands and knees. □ *I dropped a contact lens and spent an hour on all fours looking for it.* □ *The baby is on all fours most of the time.*

**on a waiting list** [for someone's name to be] on a list of people waiting for an opportunity to do something. (*A* can be replaced with *the.*) □ *I couldn't get a seat on the plane, but I got on a waiting list.* □ *There is no room for you, but we can put your name on the waiting list.*

**once in a blue moon** very rarely. (A cliché.) □ *I seldom go to a movie—maybe once in a blue moon.* □ *I don't go into the city except once in a blue moon.*

**on cloud nine** very happy. □ *When I got my promotion, I was on cloud nine.* □ *When the check came, I was on cloud nine for days.*

**on duty** at work; currently doing one's work. □ *I can't help you now, but I'll be on duty in about an hour.* □ *Who is on duty here? I need some help.*

**on earth** AND **in creation; in the world** of all things, places, or people; out of all the possibilities; given all options. (Used as an intensifier after *who, what, when, where,* or *how* to express surprise or amazement.) □ *What on earth do you mean?* □ *How in creation do you expect me to do that?* □ *Who in the world do you think you are?* □ *When on earth do you expect me to do this?*

**One good turn deserves another.** a proverb meaning that a good deed should be repaid with another good deed. □ *If he does you a favor, you should do him a favor. One good turn deserves another.* □ *Glad to help you out. One good turn deserves another.*

**one in a hundred** See one in a thousand.

**one in a million** See one in a thousand.

**one in a thousand** AND **one in a hundred; one in a million** unique; one of a very few. □ *He's a great guy. He's one in million.* □ *Mary's one in a hundred—such a hard worker.*

**One man's meat is another man's poison.** a proverb meaning that one person's preference may be disliked by another person. □ *John just loves his new fur hat, but I think it is horrible. Oh, well, one man's meat is another man's poison.* □ *The neighbors are very fond of their dog even though it's ugly, loud, and smelly. I guess one man's meat is another man's poison.*

**one's back is to the wall** See under have one's back to the wall.

**One's bark is worse than one's bite.** Although one appears threatening, one will not actually do much damage. □ *Don't worry about Bob. He won't hurt you. His bark is worse than his bite.* □ *She may scream and yell, but have no fear. Her bark is worse than her bite.*

**one's better half** one's spouse. (Usually refers to a wife.) □ *I think we'd like to come for dinner, but I'll have to ask my better half.* □ *I have to go home now to my better half. We are going out tonight.*

**one's days are numbered** one faces death or dismissal. (A cliché.) □ *If I don't get this contract, my days are numbered at this company.* □ *Uncle Tom has a terminal disease. His days are numbered.*

**one's eyes are bigger than one's stomach** one has taken or asked for more food than one can eat. □ *I can't eat all this. I'm afraid that my eyes were bigger than my stomach.* □ *Take one piece of cake instead of two. I think your eyes are bigger than your stomach.* ALSO: **have eyes bigger than one's stomach** to have a desire for more food than one could possibly eat. □ *I know I have eyes bigger than my stomach, so I won't take a lot of food.*

**one's hands are tied** See under have one's hands tied.

**one's heart is in one's mouth** See under have one's heart in one's mouth.

**one's heart is set on something** See under have one's heart set on something.

**one's number is up** one's time to die—or to suffer some other unpleasantness—has come. □ *John is worried. He thinks his number is up.* □ *When my number is up, I hope it all goes fast.*

**one's tail is between one's legs** See under have one's tail between one's legs.

**one's words stick in one's throat** See under have one's words stick in one's throat.

**on one's feet 1.** standing up; standing on one's feet. □ *Get on your feet. They are playing the national anthem.* □ *I've been on my feet all day, and they hurt.* **2.** well and healthy, especially after an illness. □ *I hope to be back on my feet next week.* □ *Mary is glad to be on her feet again after being sick for three weeks.*

**on one's honor** on one's solemn oath; [promised] sincerely, speaking as an honorable person. □ *On my honor, I'll be there on time.* □ *He promised on his honor that he'd pay me back next week.*

**on one's mind** occupying one's thoughts; currently being thought about. □ *You've been on my mind all day.* □ *Do you have something on your mind? You look so serious.*

**on one's or its last legs** almost completely worn out, exhausted, or broken down; close to dying or ending. □ *This building is on its last legs. It should be torn down.* □ *I feel as if I'm on my last legs. I'm really tired.*

**on one's toes** alert. □ *You have to be on your toes if you want to be in this business.* □ *My boss keeps me on my toes.*

**on pins and needles** anxious; in suspense. (A cliché. Compare with pins and needles.) □ *I've been on pins and needles all day, waiting for you to call with the news.* □ *We were on pins and needles until we heard that your plane landed safely.*

**on second thought** having given something more thought; having reconsidered something. □ *On second thought, maybe you should sell your house and move into an apartment.* □ *On second thought, let's not go to a movie.*

**on someone's doorstep** See at someone's doorstep.

**on someone's head** on someone's own self. (Usually with *blame*. *On* can be replaced with *upon*.) □ *All the blame fell on their heads.* □ *I don't think that all the criticism should be on my head.*

**on someone's say-so** on someone's authority; with someone's permission. □ *I can't do it on your say-so. I'll have to get a written request.* □ *BILL: I canceled the contract with the Jones Company. BOB: On whose say-so?*

**on someone's shoulders** on someone's own self. (Usually with *responsibility*. *On* can be replaced with *upon*.) □ *Why should all the assignments fall on my shoulders?* □ *She carries a tremendous amount of responsibility on her shoulders.*

**on target** on schedule; exactly as predicted. □ *Your estimate of the cost was right on target.* □ *My prediction was not on target.*

**on the air** [relating to a radio or television station or program] broadcasting or being broadcast. (Compare with **off the air**.) □ *The radio station came back on the air shortly after the storm.* □ *We were on the air for two hours.*

**on the average** generally; usually; in general. □ *On the average, you can expect about a 10 percent failure.* □ *This report looks okay, on the average.*

**on the bench 1.** directing a session of court. (Said of a judge.) □ *I have to go to court tomorrow. Who's on the bench?* □ *It doesn't matter who's on the bench. You'll get a fair hearing.* **2.** sitting, waiting for a chance to play in a game. (In team sports such as basketball, football, and soccer.) □ *Bill is on the bench now. I hope he gets to play.* □ *John played during the first quarter, but now he's on the bench.*

**on the block 1.** on a city block. □ *John is the biggest kid on the block.* □ *We had a party on the block last weekend.* **2.** on sale at auction; on the auction block. □ *We couldn't afford to keep up the house, so it was put on the block to pay the taxes.* □ *That's the finest painting I've ever seen on the block.*

**on the button** exactly right; in exactly the right place; at exactly the right time. □ *That's it! You're right on the button.* □ *He got here at one o'clock on the button.*

**on the contrary** in opposition to what has just been said. □ *I'm not ill. On the contrary, I'm very healthy.* □ *She's not in a bad mood. On the contrary, she's as happy as a lark.*

**on the dot** at exactly the right time. □ *I'll be there at noon on the dot.* □ *I expect to see you here at eight o'clock on the dot.*

**on the go** busy; moving about busily. □ *I'm usually on the go all day long.* □ *I hate being on the go all the time.*

**on the heels of something** soon after something. □ *There was a rainstorm on the heels of the windstorm.* □ *The team held a victory celebration on the heels of their winning season.*

**on the horizon** soon to happen. □ *Do you know what's on the horizon?* □ *Who can tell what's on the horizon?*

**on the horns of a dilemma** having to decide between two things, people, etc.; balanced between one choice and another. □ *Mary found herself on the horns of a dilemma. She didn't know which to choose.* □ *I make up my mind easily. I'm not on the horns of a dilemma very often.*

**on the hour** at the beginning of the hour or of each hour; precisely when the numbered hour begins—for example, at 3:00, not at 3:08 or 3:30. □ *I have to take this medicine every hour on the hour.* □ *I expect to see you there on the hour, not one minute before and not one minute after.*

**on the house** [something that is] given away free by a merchant. □ *"Here," said the waiter, "have a cup of coffee on the house."* □ *I went to a restaurant last night. I was the ten thousandth customer, so my dinner was on the house.*

**on the level** See (strictly) on the level.

**on the market** available for sale; offered for sale. □ *I had to put my car on the market.* □ *This is the finest home computer on the market.*

**on the mend** getting well; healing. □ *My cold was terrible, but I'm on the mend now.* □ *What you need is some hot chicken soup. Then you'll really be on the mend.*

**on the move** moving; happening busily. □ *What a busy day. Things are really on the move at the store.* □ *When all the buffalo were on the move across the plains, it must have been very exciting.*

**on the off chance** because of a slight possibility [that something may happen or might be the case]; just in case. □ *I went to the theater on the off chance that there would still be tickets available for tonight's show.* □ *We didn't think we would get into the football stadium, but we went on the off chance.*

**on the QT** quietly; secretly. □ *The company president was making payments to his wife on the QT.* □ *The mayor accepted a bribe on the QT.*

**on the spot 1.** at exactly the right place; in the place where one is needed. □ *Fortunately, a lifeguard was on the spot when little Billy fell into the swimming pool.* □ *I expect you to be on the spot when and where trouble arises.* **2.** in trouble; in a difficult situation. □ *There is a problem in the department I manage, and I'm really on the spot.* □ *I hate to be on the spot when it's not my fault.*

**on the spur of the moment** suddenly; spontaneously. □ *We decided to go on the spur of the moment.* □ *I had to leave town on the spur of the moment.*

**on the tip of one's tongue** about to be said; almost remembered. (As if a word were about to leap from one's tongue and be spoken.) □ *I have his name right on the tip of my tongue. I'll think of it in a second.* □ *John had the answer on the tip of his tongue, but Ann said it first.*

**on the wagon** not drinking alcohol; no longer drinking alcohol. (Refers to a "water wagon.") □ *None for me, thanks. I'm on the wagon.* □ *Look at John. I don't think he's on the wagon anymore.*

**on the wrong track** going the wrong way; following the wrong set of assumptions. □ *You'll never get the right answer. You're on the wrong track.* □ *They won't get it figured out because they are on the wrong track.*

**on thin ice** in a risky situation. □ *If you try that, you'll really be on thin ice. That's too risky.* □ *If you don't want to find yourself on thin ice,* *you must be sure of your facts.* ALSO: **skate on thin ice** to be in a risky situation. (Also used literally.) □ *I try to stay well informed so I don't end up skating on thin ice when the teacher asks me a question.*

**on tiptoe** standing or walking on the front part of the feet (the balls of the feet) with no weight put on the heels. (This is done to gain height or to walk quietly.) □ *I had to stand on tiptoe in order to see over the fence.* □ *I came in late and walked on tiptoe so I wouldn't wake anybody.*

**on top** victorious over something; famous or notorious for something. □ *I have to study day and night to keep on top.* □ *Bill is on top in his field.*

**on top of the world** feeling wonderful; glorious; ecstatic. (A cliché.) □ *Wow, I feel on top of the world.* □ *Since he got a new job, he's on top of the world.*

**on trial** being tried in court. □ *My sister is on trial today, so I have to go to court.* □ *They placed the suspected thief on trial.*

**on vacation** taking a trip; taking time off from work. □ *Where are you going on vacation this year?* □ *I'll be away on vacation for three weeks.*

**open a can of worms** to uncover a set of problems; to create unnecessary complications. (*Can of worms* means "mess." Also with *open up* and with various modifiers such as *new, whole, another*, as in the examples.) □ *Now you are opening a whole new can of worms.* □ *How about cleaning up this mess before you open up another can of worms?*

an **open-and-shut case** something, usually a legal case or a problem, that is simple and straightforward without complications. □ *The murder trial was an open-and-shut case. The defendant was caught with the murder weapon.* □ *Jack's death was an open-and-shut case of suicide. He left a suicide note.*

an **open book** someone or something that is easy to interpret and understand. □ *Jane's an open book. I always know what she is going to do next.* □ *The council's intentions are an open book. It's trying to save money.* □ *My life is an open book. I have no secrets.*

**open one's heart (to someone)** to reveal one's inmost thoughts to someone. □ *I always open my heart to my spouse when I have a problem.* □ *It's a good idea to open your heart every now and then.*

**open Pandora's box** to uncover a lot of unsuspected problems. (A cliché. From Greek mythology.) □ *When I asked Jane about her problems,*

*I didn't know I had opened Pandora's box.* □ *You should be cautious with people who are upset. You don't want to open Pandora's box.*

**open secret** something that is supposed to be secret but is known to a great many people. □ *Their engagement is an open secret. Only their friends are supposed to know, but in fact, the whole town knows.* □ *It's an open secret that Fred's looking for a new job.*

the **order of the day** something necessary or usual at a certain time. □ *Warm clothes are the order of the day when camping in the winter.* □ *Going to bed early was the order of the day when we were young.*

the **other side of the tracks** the poorer part of a town, often near the railroad tracks. (Especially with *from the* or *live on the.*) □ *Who cares if she's from the other side of the tracks?* □ *I came from a poor family—we lived on the other side of the tracks.*

An **ounce of prevention is worth a pound of cure.** a proverb meaning that it is easier and better to prevent something bad than to deal with the results. □ *When you ride in a car, buckle your seat belt. An ounce of prevention is worth a pound of cure.* □ *Every child should be vaccinated against polio. An ounce of prevention is worth a pound of cure.*

**out and about** able to go out and travel around; well enough to go out. □ *Beth has been ill, but now she's out and about.* □ *As soon as I feel better, I'll be able to get out and about.*

**out cold** AND **out like a light** unconscious; deeply asleep. □ *I fell and hit my head. I was out cold for about a minute.* □ *Tom fainted! He's out like a light!*

**out in left field** offbeat; unusual and eccentric. □ *Sally is a lot of fun, but she's sort of out in left field.* □ *What a strange idea. It's really out in left field.*

**out like a light** See out cold.

**out of a clear blue sky** AND **out of the blue** suddenly; without warning. (A cliché.) □ *Then, out of a clear blue sky, he told me he was leaving.* □ *Mary appeared on my doorstep out of the blue.*

**out of (all) proportion** of an exaggerated proportion; of an unrealistic proportion compared with something else. (Often said about something that is given more attention or importance than it deserves.) □ *This problem has grown out of all proportion.* □ *Yes, this thing is way out of proportion.* ALSO: **blow something out of (all) proportion** to cause something to be unrealistically proportioned relative to something else, especially to cause something to be given more than the appropriate amount of attention or importance. □ *The press has blown this issue out of all proportion.* □ *Let's be reasonable. Don't blow this thing out of proportion.*

**out of circulation** [of someone] not interacting socially with other people. □ *I don't know what's happening, because I've been out of circulation for a while.* □ *My cold has kept me out of circulation for a few weeks.*

**out of commission** broken, unserviceable, or inoperable. □ *My watch is out of commission and is running slowly.* □ *I can't run in the marathon because my knees are out of commission.*

**out of gas** tired; exhausted; worn out. (Also used literally for cars and other machines powered by gasoline.) □ *What a day! I've been working since morning, and I'm really out of gas.* □ *This electric clock is out of gas. I'll have to get a new one.* ALSO: **run out of gas** to become worn out; to become exhausted. (Also used literally of cars, etc., using up all the gasoline available.) □ *If I don't get enough sleep at night, I run out of gas in the middle of the afternoon.*

**out of hand** immediately and without consulting anyone; without delay. □ *I can't answer that out of hand. I'll check with the manager and call you back.* □ *The offer was so good that I accepted it out of hand.*

**out of luck** without good luck; having bad fortune. □ *If you wanted some ice cream, you're out of luck.* □ *I was out of luck. I got there too late to get a seat.*

**out of one's element** not in a natural or comfortable situation. □ *When it comes to computers, I'm out of my element.* □ *Sally's out of her element in math.*

**out of one's head** See out of one's mind.

**out of one's mind** AND **out of one's head; out of one's senses** silly and senseless; crazy; irrational. □ *Why did you do that? You must be out of your mind!* □ *Good grief, Tom! You have to be out of your head!* □ *She's acting as if she were out of her senses.*

**out of one's senses** See out of one's mind.

**out of order 1.** not following correct parliamentary procedure. □ *I was declared out of order by the president.* □ *Ann inquired, "Isn't a motion to table the question out of order at this time?"* **2.** See out of service.

**out of practice** performing poorly due to a lack of practice. □ *I used to be able to play the piano extremely well, but now I'm out of practice.* □ *The baseball players lost the game because they were out of practice.*

**out of print** [for a book] to be no longer available for sale. (Compare with in print.) □ *The book you want is out of print, but perhaps I can find a used copy for you.* □ *It was published nearly ten years ago, so it's probably out of print.*

**out of season 1.** not now available for sale. □ *Sorry, oysters are out of season. We don't have any.* □ *Watermelon is out of season in the winter.* **2.** not now legally able to be hunted or caught. □ *Are salmon out of season?* □ *I caught a trout out of season and had to pay a fine.*

**out of service** AND **out of order** inoperable; not currently operating. □ *Both elevators are out of order, so I had to use the stairs.* □ *The washroom is temporarily out of service.*

**Out of sight, out of mind.** a proverb meaning that if one does not see something, one will not think about it. □ *When I go home, I put my schoolbooks away so I won't worry about doing my homework. After all, out of sight, out of mind.* □ *Jane dented the fender on her car. It's on the right side, so she doesn't have to look at it. As they say, out of sight, out of mind.*

**out of sorts** not feeling well; grumpy and irritable. □ *I've been out of sorts for a day or two. I think I might be getting the flu.* □ *The baby is out of sorts. Maybe she's getting a tooth.*

**out of the blue** See out of a clear blue sky.

**out of the corner of one's eye** [seeing something] at a glance; glimpsing (something). □ *Out of the corner of my eye, I saw someone do it. It might have been Jane.* □ *I only saw the accident out of the corner of my eye. I don't know who is at fault.*

**out of the frying pan into the fire** from a bad situation to a worse situation. (A cliché. If it was hot in the pan, it is hotter in the fire.) □ *When I tried to argue about my fine for a traffic violation, the judge charged me with contempt of court. I really went out of the frying pan into the fire.* □ *I got deeply in debt. Then I really got out of the frying pan into the fire when I lost my job.*

**out of the hole** out of debt. □ *I get paid next week, and then I can get out of the hole.* □ *I can't seem to get out of the hole. I keep spending more money than I earn.*

**out of the question** not possible; not permitted. □ *I'm sorry, but it's out of the question.* □ *You can't go to Florida this spring. We can't afford it. It's out of the question.*

**out of the red** out of debt. (Compare with in the red.) □ *This year our firm is likely to get out of the red before fall.* □ *If we can cut down on expenses, we can get out of the red fairly soon.*

**out of the running** no longer being considered; eliminated from a contest. □ *After the first part of the diving meet, three members of our team were out of the running.* □ *After the scandal was made public, I was out of the running. I withdrew from the election.*

**out of the woods** past a critical phase; out of the unknown. □ *When the patient got out of the woods, everyone relaxed.* □ *I can give you a better prediction for your future health when you are out of the woods.*

**out of thin air** apparently out of nowhere; as if from nothing. □ *Suddenly—out of thin air—the messenger appeared.* □ *You just made that up out of thin air.*

**out of this world** wonderful; extraordinary. (A cliché.) □ *This pie is just out of this world.* □ *How lovely you look—simply out of this world!*

**out of tune (with someone or something) 1.** not in musical harmony with someone or something. □ *The oboe is out of tune with the flute.* □ *The chorus was out of tune with the soloist.* □ *They are all out of tune.* **2.** not in (figurative) harmony or agreement. □ *Your proposal is out of tune with my ideas of what we should be doing.* □ *Bill's ideas were out of tune with the company's objectives.*

**out of turn** not at the proper time; not in the proper order. □ *We were permitted to be served out of turn, because we had to leave early.* □ *Bill tried to register out of turn and was sent to the back of the line.*

**out on a limb** in or into a dangerous position; taking a chance, especially by doing something differently from the way others do it. (Often with go.) □ *I don't want to go out on a limb, but I think I'd agree to your request.* □ *She really went out on a limb when she gave him permission to leave early.* □ *As the only one who supports the plan, Bill is really out on a limb.*

**out on the town** celebrating at one or more places in a town. □ *I'm really tired. I was out on the town until dawn.* □ *We went out on the town to celebrate our wedding anniversary.*

**out to lunch 1.** eating lunch outside the office. □ *I'm sorry, but Sally Jones is out to lunch. May I take a message?* □ *She's been out to lunch for nearly two hours. When will she be back?* **2.** unalert; uninformed; spacey. □ *Ann is really out to lunch these days.* □ *Bill didn't get much sleep last night, and he's out to lunch today.*

**over someone's head** too difficult or clever for someone to understand. (Treated grammatically as a distance above one's head or understanding.) □ *The children have no idea what the new teacher is talking about. Her ideas are way over their heads.* □ *She started a physics course, but it turned out to be miles over her head.*

**over the hill** old; too old to do something. □ *Now that Mary's forty, she thinks she's over the hill.* □ *Most teenagers think that their parents are over the hill, no matter what their ages are.*

**over the hump** past the difficult part. □ *This is a difficult project, but we're over the hump now.* □ *I'm halfway through—over the hump—and it looks as if I may get finished after all.*

**over the long haul** for a relatively long period of time. □ *Over the long haul, it might be better to invest in stocks.* □ *Over the long haul, everything will turn out all right.*

**over the short haul** for the immediate future. □ *Over the short haul, you'd be better off to put your money in the bank.* □ *Over the short haul, you may wish you had done something different. But things will work out all right.*

**over the top** to or at a point where one has achieved more than one's goal. □ *Our fund-raising campaign went over the top by $3,000.* □ *We didn't go over the top. We didn't even get half of what we planned to collect.*

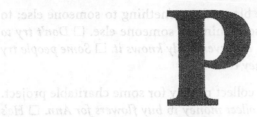

**packed (in) like sardines** packed very tightly. (A cliché.) □ *It was terribly crowded there. We were packed in like sardines.* □ *The bus was full. The passengers were packed like sardines.* □ *They packed us in like sardines.*

**paddle one's own canoe** to do something by oneself; to be alone. (A cliché.) □ *I've been left to paddle my own canoe too many times.* □ *Sally isn't with us. She's off paddling her own canoe.*

**pad the bill** to put unnecessary items on a bill to make the total cost higher. □ *The plumber had padded the bill with things we didn't need.* □ *I was falsely accused of padding the bill.*

**paint the town red** to have a wild celebration during a night on the town. □ *Let's all go out and paint the town red!* □ *Oh, do I feel awful. I was out all last night, painting the town red.*

**part and parcel of something** an essential part of something; something that is unavoidably included as part of something else. □ *Fear of crime is part and parcel of life in the city.* □ *Bill refused to accept pain and illness as part and parcel of growing older.*

**part someone's hair** to come very close to someone. □ *That plane flew so low that it nearly parted my hair.* □ *He punched at me and missed. He only parted my hair.*

the **party line** the official ideas and attitudes that are adopted by the leaders of a particular group and that the other members are expected to accept. □ *Tom has left the club. He refused to follow the party line.* □ *Many politicians accept the party line without thinking.*

The **party's over.** a phrase said when a happy or fortunate time has come to an end. (Informal.) □ *We go back to school tomorrow. The party's over.* □ *The staff did hardly any work under the old management, but they'll find the party's over now.*

**pass the buck** to pass the blame for something to someone else; to give the responsibility for something to someone else. □ *Don't try to pass the buck! It's your fault, and everybody knows it.* □ *Some people try to pass the buck whenever they can.*

**pass the hat** to attempt to collect money for some charitable project. □ *Bob is passing the hat to collect money to buy flowers for Ann.* □ *He's always passing the hat for something.*

the **path of least resistance** See line of least resistance.

**pay an arm and a leg (for something)** AND **pay through the nose (for something)** to pay too much money for something. □ *I hate to have to pay an arm and a leg for a tank of gas.* □ *If you shop around, you won't have to pay an arm and a leg.* □ *Why should you pay through the nose?* ALSO: **cost an arm and a leg** to cost too much. □ *It cost an arm and a leg, so I didn't buy it.*

**pay one's debt (to society)** to serve a sentence for a crime, usually in prison. □ *The judge said that Mr. Simpson had to pay his debt to society.* □ *Mr. Brown paid his debt in state prison.*

**pay one's dues** to have earned one's right to something through hard work or suffering. □ *He worked hard to get to where he is today. He paid his dues and did what he was told.* □ *I have every right to be here. I paid my dues!*

**pay the piper** to face the results of one's actions; to receive punishment for something. (A cliché.) □ *You can put off paying your debts only so long. Eventually you'll have to pay the piper.* □ *You can't get away with that forever. You'll have to pay the piper someday.*

**pay through the nose (for something)** See pay an arm and a leg (for something).

A **penny for your thoughts.** a proverb indicating that one would be happy to know what someone else is thinking about. (As if to say, "I will give you a penny for your thoughts.") □ *You look sad. A penny for your thoughts.* □ *Bill stood quietly, looking at the ocean. "A penny for your thoughts," Sue said.*

A **penny saved is a penny earned.** a proverb meaning that money saved through thrift is just as valuable as money earned through employment—both increase one's wealth equally. (Sometimes used to explain stinginess.) □ *"I don't want to pay that much for the book," said*

Mary. "After all, a penny saved is a penny earned." □ John buys only the cheapest foods so he can put more money in the bank. "A penny saved is a penny earned," he says.

**penny-wise and pound-foolish** a proverb meaning that it is foolish to lose a lot of money to save a little money. (A cliché.) □ *Sally shops very carefully to save a few cents on food, then charges the food to a credit card that costs a lot in annual interest. That's being penny-wise and pound-foolish.* □ *John drives thirty miles to buy gas for three cents a gallon less than it costs here. He's really penny-wise and pound-foolish.*

**Perish the thought.** Do not even consider thinking of something. (Literary.) □ *If you should become ill—perish the thought—I'd take care of you.* □ *I'm afraid that we need a new car. Perish the thought.*

**pick and choose** to choose very carefully from a number of possibilities; to be selective. □ *You must take what you are given. You cannot pick and choose.* □ *Jane is so beautiful. She can pick and choose from a whole range of suitors.*

**pick up the tab** to pay the bill. □ *Whenever we go out, my father picks up the tab.* □ *Order whatever you want. The company is picking up the tab.*

**piece of the pie** AND **slice of the cake** a share of something. □ *There's so much work to do that everyone must get a slice of the cake.* □ *The firm makes huge profits, and the workers want a piece of the pie.*

**pie in the sky** a future reward, especially after death. (A cliché. Also part of a longer phrase, "You'll get pie in the sky when you die," which is a line from a song by U.S. radical labor organizer Joe Hill.) □ *Are you nice to people just because of pie in the sky, or do you really like them?* □ *Don't hold out for a big reward—you know, pie in the sky.*

**pins and needles** a tingling feeling in some part of one's body. (Compare with on pins and needles.) □ *I've got pins and needles in my legs.* □ *Mary gets pins and needles if she crosses her arms for long.*

**pipe dream** a wish or an idea that is impossible to achieve or carry out. (From the dreams or visions induced by the smoking of an opium pipe.) □ *Going to the West Indies is a pipe dream. We'll never have enough money.* □ *Your hopes of winning a lot of money are just a silly pipe dream.*

**pitch in (and help)** to get busy and help with something. □ *Pick up a paintbrush and pitch in and help.* □ *Why don't some of you pitch in? We need all the help we can get.*

**pitch someone a curve** See throw someone a curve.

**play along with someone or something** to agree to cooperate or conspire with someone or someone's plan; to pretend to agree to cooperate or conspire with someone or someone's plan. (See also the following entry.) □ *I refused to play along with the treasurer when he outlined his plan.* □ *It might be wise to play along with the kidnappers, at least for a little while.* □ *I'll play along with your scheme until the others get here, but I don't like it.*

**play ball (with someone)** to cooperate with someone. (See the previous entry.) □ *Look, friend, if you play ball with me, everything will work out all right.* □ *Things would go better for you if you'd learn to play ball.*

**play both ends (against the middle)** to scheme in a way that pits two sides against each other for one's own gain. □ *I told my brother that Mary doesn't like him. Then I told Mary that my brother doesn't like her. They broke up, so now I can have the car this weekend. I succeeded in playing both ends against the middle.* □ *If you try to play both ends, you're likely to get in trouble with both sides.*

**play by ear** See play something by ear.

**play cat and mouse (with someone)** to capture and release someone over and over. (A cliché.) □ *The police played cat and mouse with the suspect until they had sufficient evidence to make an arrest.* □ *Tom had been playing cat and mouse with Ann. Finally she got tired of it and broke up with him.*

**played out** (Informal.) **1.** exhausted. □ *I'm played out after looking after the baby.* □ *Bob's always played out after he's been gardening.* **2.** no longer of interest or influence. □ *Jane's political ideas are all played out.* □ *That particular religious sect is played out now.*

**play fast and loose (with someone or something)** to act carelessly, thoughtlessly, and irresponsibly. □ *I'm tired of your playing fast and loose with me. Leave me alone.* □ *Bob got fired for playing fast and loose with the company's money.* □ *If you play fast and loose like that, you can get into a lot of trouble.*

**play it safe** to be or act safe; to do something safely. □ *You should play it safe and take your umbrella.* □ *If you have a cold or the flu, play it safe and go to bed.*

**play one's cards close to one's vest** See play one's cards close to the vest.

**play one's cards close to the vest** AND **play one's cards close to one's vest** [for someone] to work or negotiate in a careful and private manner. (Refers to holding one's playing cards close so that no one can possibly see what one is holding.) □ *It's hard to figure out what John is up to because he plays his cards close to the vest.* □ *Don't let them know what you're planning. Play your cards close to your vest.*

**play second fiddle (to someone)** to be in a subordinate position to someone. □ *I'm tired of playing second fiddle to John.* □ *I'm better trained than he, and I have more experience. I shouldn't play second fiddle.*

**play something by ear 1.** to be able to play a piece of music after just listening to it a few times, without looking at the notes. □ *I can play "Stardust" by ear.* □ *Some people can play Chopin's music by ear.* **2.** AND **play by ear** to play a musical instrument well, without formal training. □ *John can play the piano by ear.* □ *If I could play by ear, I wouldn't have to take lessons—or practice!*

**play (the) devil's advocate** to put forward arguments against or objections to a proposition, which one may actually agree with, purely to test the validity of the proposition. (The devil's advocate was given the role of opposing the canonization of a saint in the medieval Church in order to prove that the grounds for canonization were sound.) □ *I agree with your plan. I'm just playing the devil's advocate so you'll know what the opposition will say.* □ *Mary offered to play devil's advocate and argue against our case so that we would find out any flaws in it.*

**play the field** to date many different people rather than dating one person. □ *When Tom told Ann good-bye, he said he wanted to play the field.* □ *He said he wanted to play the field while he was still young.*

**play the fool** to act in a silly manner in order to amuse other people. □ *The teacher told Tom to stop playing the fool and sit down.* □ *Fred likes playing the fool, but we didn't find him funny last night.*

**play to the gallery** to perform in a manner that will get the strong approval of the audience; to perform in a manner that will get the approval of the lower elements in the audience. □ *John is a competent* actor, but he has a tendency to play to the gallery. □ When he made the rude remark, he was just playing to the gallery.

**play with fire** to take a big risk. □ *If you accuse her of stealing, you'll be playing with fire.* □ *I wouldn't try that if I were you—unless you like playing with fire.*

**please oneself** AND **suit oneself** to do what one wishes. (Informal.) □ *We don't mind whether you stay or not. Suit yourself!* □ *The boss preferred me to work late, but he told me to please myself.*

The **plot thickens.** a phrase said when things are becoming more complicated or interesting. □ *The police assumed that the woman was murdered by her ex-husband, but he has an alibi. The plot thickens.* □ *John is supposed to be going out with Mary, but I saw him last night with Sally. The plot thickens.*

**poetic justice** the appropriate but chance receiving of rewards or punishments by those deserving them. □ *It was poetic justice that Jane won the race after Mary tried to get her banned.* □ *The car thieves tried to steal a car with no gas. That's poetic justice.*

**point the finger at someone** to blame someone; to identify someone as the guilty person. □ *Don't point the finger at me! I didn't take the money.* □ *The manager refused to point the finger at anyone in particular and said the whole staff were sometimes guilty of being late.*

**poke fun (at someone)** to make fun of someone; to ridicule someone. □ *Stop poking fun at me! It's not nice.* □ *Bob is always poking fun.*

**poke one's nose in(to something)** AND **stick one's nose in(to something)** to interfere with something; to be nosy about something. □ *I wish you'd stop poking your nose into my business.* □ *She was too upset for me to stick my nose in and ask what was wrong.*

**pop the question** to ask someone to marry one. □ *I was surprised when he popped the question.* □ *I've been waiting for years for someone to pop the question.*

the **pot calling the kettle black** [an instance of] someone with a fault accusing someone else of having the same fault. (A cliché.) □ *Ann is always late, but she was rude enough to tell everyone when I was late. Now, that's the pot calling the kettle black!* □ *You're calling me thoughtless? That's really a case of the pot calling the kettle black.*

**pound a beat** to walk a route. (Usually said of a police patrol officer.) □ *The patrolman pounded the same beat for years and years.* □ *Pounding a beat will wreck your feet.*

**pound the pavement** to walk through the streets, looking for a job. □ *I spent two months pounding the pavement after the factory I worked for closed.* □ *Hey, Bob. You'd better get busy pounding those nails unless you want to be out pounding the pavement.*

**pour cold water on something** AND **dash cold water on something; throw cold water on something** to discourage doing something; to reduce enthusiasm for something. □ *When my father said I couldn't have the car, he poured cold water on my plans.* □ *John threw cold water on the whole project by refusing to participate.*

**pour it on thick** See lay it on thick.

**pour money down the drain** to waste money. □ *What a waste! You're just pouring money down the drain.* □ *Don't buy any more of that low-quality merchandise. That's just pouring money down the drain.*

**pour oil on troubled water** to calm things down. (A cliché. If oil is poured onto rough seas during a storm, the water will become more calm.) □ *That was a good thing to say to John. It helped pour oil on troubled water. Now he looks happy.* □ *Bob is the kind of person who pours oil on troubled water.*

the **powers that be** the people who are in authority. □ *The powers that be have decided to send back the immigrants.* □ *I have applied for a license, and the powers that be are considering my application.*

**practice what you preach** to do what you advise other people to do. (A cliché.) □ *If you'd practice what you preach, you'd be better off.* □ *You give good advice. Why not practice what you preach?*

**precious few** AND **precious little** very few; very little. (Informal.) □ *We get precious few tourists here in the winter.* □ *There's precious little food in the house, and we have no money.*

**precious little** See precious few.

**press one's luck** See push one's luck.

**press someone to the wall** See push someone to the wall.

**Pretty is as pretty does.** a proverb meaning that one should do pleasant things if one wishes to be considered pleasant. (A cliché.) □ *Now,*

*Sally. Let's be nice. Pretty is as pretty does.* □ *My great-aunt always used to say to my sister, "Pretty is as pretty does."*

**prick up one's ears** to listen more closely. □ *At the sound of my voice, my dog pricked up her ears.* □ *I pricked up my ears when I heard my name mentioned.*

**prime mover** the force that sets something going; someone or something that starts something off. □ *The assistant manager was the prime mover in getting the manager fired.* □ *Discontent with his job was the prime mover in John's deciding to emigrate.*

**promise someone the moon** See promise the moon (to someone).

**promise the moon (to someone)** AND **promise someone the moon** to make extravagant promises to someone. □ *Bill will promise you the moon, but he won't live up to his promises.* □ *My boss promised the moon but only paid the minimum wage.*

**pull oneself up (by one's own bootstraps)** to achieve (something) through one's own efforts. (A cliché.) □ *They simply don't have the resources to pull themselves up by their own bootstraps.* □ *If I could have pulled myself up, I'd have done it by now.*

**pull out all the stops** to use all one's energy and effort in order to achieve something. (From the stops of a pipe organ. The more that are pulled out, the louder it gets.) □ *You'll have to pull out all the stops if you're going to pass the exam.* □ *The doctors will pull out all the stops to save the child's life.*

**pull out (of something)** to leave or abandon a place or situation. (Informal.) □ *The soldiers pulled out of their dangerous position and marched on.* □ *Our team pulled out of the competition.*

**pull someone's leg** to kid, fool, or trick someone. □ *You don't mean that. You're just pulling my leg.* □ *Don't believe him. He's just pulling your leg.*

**pull someone's or something's teeth** to reduce the power of someone or something. □ *The mayor tried to pull the teeth of the new law.* □ *The city council pulled the teeth of the new mayor.*

**pull something out of a hat** AND **pull something out of thin air** to produce something as if by magic. □ *This is a serious problem, and we just can't pull a solution out of a hat.* □ *I'm sorry, but I don't have a pen. What do you want me to do, pull one out of thin air?*

**pull something out of thin air** See pull something out of a hat.

**pull the rug out (from under someone)** to make someone ineffective. □ *The treasurer pulled the rug out from under the mayor.* □ *Things were going along fine until the treasurer pulled the rug out.*

**pull the wool over someone's eyes** to deceive someone. (A cliché.) □ *You can't pull the wool over my eyes. I know what's going on.* □ *Don't try to pull the wool over her eyes. She's too smart.*

**pull up stakes** to move to another place. (As if one were pulling up tent stakes.) □ *I've been here long enough. It's time to pull up stakes.* □ *I hate the thought of having to pull up stakes.*

**push off** to go away. (Informal.) □ *We told the children to push off.* □ *Push off! We don't want you here.*

**push one's luck** AND **press one's luck** to expect continued good fortune; to expect to continue to escape bad luck. □ *You're okay so far, but don't push your luck.* □ *Bob pressed his luck too much and got into a lot of trouble.*

**push someone to the wall** AND **press someone to the wall** to force someone into a position where there is only one choice to make; to put someone in a defensive position. □ *There was little else I could do. They pushed me to the wall.* □ *When we pressed him to the wall, he told us where the cookies were hidden.*

**put a bee in someone's bonnet** See under have a bee in one's bonnet.

**put all one's eggs in one basket** to risk everything at once. (If the basket is dropped, all the eggs are lost. A cliché. Often in the negative.) □ *Don't put all your eggs in one basket. Then everything won't be lost if there is a catastrophe.* □ *John only applied to the one college he wanted to go to. He put all his eggs in one basket.*

**put in a good word (for someone)** to say something (to someone) in support of someone else. □ *I hope you get the job. I'll put in a good word for you.* □ *Yes, I want the job. If you see the boss, please put in a good word.*

**put in one's oar** to give help; to interfere by giving advice; to add one's assistance to the general effort. □ *I'm sorry. I shouldn't have put in my oar.* T *You don't need to put your oar in. I don't need your advice.*

**put in one's two cents(' worth)** to add one's comments (to something). (Implies that one's comments may not be of great value but need to be stated anyway.) □ *Can I put in my two cents' worth?* ⊤ *Sure, go ahead—put your two cents in.*

**put on a brave face** to try to appear happy or satisfied when faced with misfortune or danger. ⊤ *We've lost all our money, but we must put a brave face on for the sake of the children.* □ *Jim's lost his job and is worried, but he's putting on a brave face.*

**put on airs** to act superior. □ *Stop putting on airs. You're just human like the rest of us.* □ *Ann is always putting on airs. You'd think she was a queen.*

**put one's best foot forward** to act or appear at one's best; to try to make a good impression. (A cliché.) □ *When you apply for a job, you should always put your best foot forward.* □ *I try to put my best foot forward whenever I meet someone for the first time.*

**put one's cards on the table** AND **lay one's cards on the table** to reveal everything; to be open and honest with someone. (As one might do at certain points in a number of different card games to make an accounting of the cards one has been holding.) □ *Come on, John, lay your cards on the table. Tell me what you really think.* □ *Why don't we both put our cards on the table?*

**put one's dibs on something** See have dibs on something.

**put one's foot in it** See put one's foot in one's mouth.

**put one's foot in one's mouth** AND **put one's foot in it; stick one's foot in one's mouth** to say something that one regrets; unintentionally to say something stupid, insulting, or hurtful. □ *When I told Ann that her hair was more beautiful than I had ever seen it, I really put my foot in my mouth. It was a wig.* □ *I put my foot in it by telling John's secret.*

**put one's hand to the plow** to begin to do a big and important task; to undertake a major effort. (A cliché. Rarely literal.) □ *If John would only put his hand to the plow, he could do an excellent job.* □ *You'll never accomplish anything if you don't put your hand to the plow.*

**put one's nose to the grindstone** to keep busy doing one's work. (Also with *have* and *get*, as in the examples.) □ *The boss told me to put my nose to the grindstone.* □ *I've had my nose to the grindstone ever since I started working here.* □ *If the other people in this office would get their* *noses to the grindstone, more work would get done.* ALSO: **keep one's nose to the grindstone** to keep busy continuously over a period of time. □ *The manager told me to keep my nose to the grindstone or be fired.*

**put one's shoulder to the wheel** to get busy. □ *You won't accomplish anything unless you put your shoulder to the wheel.* □ *I put my shoulder to the wheel and finished the job quickly.*

**put one through one's paces** to make one demonstrate what one can do; to make one do one's job thoroughly. □ *The boss really put me through my paces today. I'm tired.* □ *I tried out for a part in the play, and the director really put me through my paces.*

**put on one's thinking cap** to start thinking in a serious manner. (A cliché. Usually used with children.) □ *All right now, let's put on our thinking caps and do some arithmetic.* □ *It's time to put on our thinking caps, children.*

**put someone or something out to pasture** to retire someone or something. (Originally said of a horse that was too old to work.) □ *Please don't put me out to pasture. I have lots of good years left.* □ *This car is very old and keeps breaking down. It's time to put it out to pasture.*

**put someone or something to bed 1.** [with *someone*] to help someone—usually a child—get into a bed. □ *Come on, Billy, it's time for me to put you to bed.* □ *I want Grandpa to put me to bed.* **2.** [with *something*] to complete work on something and send it on to the next step in production, especially in publishing. □ *This edition is finished. Let's put it to bed.* □ *Finish editing this book and put it to bed.*

**put someone or something to sleep 1.** to kill someone or something. (Euphemistic.) □ *We had to put our dog to sleep.* □ *The robber said he'd put us to sleep forever if we didn't cooperate.* **2.** to cause someone or something to sleep, perhaps through drugs or anesthesia. □ *The doctor put the patient to sleep before the operation.* □ *I put the cat to sleep by stroking its tummy.* **3.** [with *someone*] to bore someone. □ *That dull lecture put me to sleep.* □ *Her long story really put me to sleep.*

**put someone's nose out of joint** to offend someone; to cause someone to feel slighted or insulted. □ *I'm afraid I put his nose out of joint by not inviting him to the picnic.* □ *There is no reason to put your nose out of joint. I meant no harm.*

**put someone through the wringer** to give someone a difficult time. (As one squeezes water from clothing in an old-fashioned wringer washing machine.) □ *They are really putting me through the wringer at school.* □ *The boss put Bob through the wringer over this contract.*

**put someone to shame** to make someone ashamed; to embarrass someone, especially by doing or achieving more than that person; to show someone up. □ *Your excellent efforts put us all to shame.* □ *I put him to shame by telling everyone about his bad behavior.*

**put someone to the test** to test someone; to see what someone can achieve. □ *I think I can jump that far, but no one has ever put me to the test.* □ *I'm going to put you to the test right now!*

**put something on ice** AND **put something on the back burner** to delay or postpone something; to put something on hold. □ *I'm afraid that we'll have to put your project on ice for a while.* □ *Just put your idea on the back burner and keep it there till we get some money.*

**put something on paper** to write something down; to write or type an agreement on paper. □ *You have a great idea for a novel. Now put it on paper.* □ *I'm sorry, I can't discuss your offer until I see something in writing. Put it on paper, and then we'll talk.*

**put something on the back burner** See put something on ice.

**put something on the cuff** to buy something on credit; to add to one's credit balance. (As if one were making a note of the purchase on one's shirt cuff.) □ *I'll take two of those, and please put them on the cuff.* □ *I'm sorry, Tom. We can't put anything more on the cuff.*

**put something on the line** AND **lay something on the line** to speak very firmly and directly about something. (Perhaps this refers to a battle line.) □ *She was very mad. She put it on the line, and we have no doubt about what she meant.* □ *All right, you kids! I'm going to lay it on the line. Don't ever do that again if you know what's good for you.*

**put something through its paces** to demonstrate how well something operates; to demonstrate all the things something can do. □ *I was down by the barn, watching Sally put her horse through its paces.* □ *This is an excellent can opener. Watch me put it through its paces.*

**put the cart before the horse** to have or do things in the wrong order; to have things confused and mixed up. (Refers to an imaginary hitching up of a horse cart in such a way that the cart would move in front of the horse rather than being pulled behind it. A cliché. Also with *have*.) □ *You're eating your dessert before the rest of the meal! That's* *putting the cart before the horse.* □ *Slow down and do your work step by step. Don't put the cart before the horse!* □ *John has the cart before the horse in most of his projects.*

**put two and two together** to figure something out from the information available. (A cliché.) □ *Well, I put two and two together and came up with an idea of who did it.* □ *Don't worry. John won't figure it out. He can't put two and two together.*

**put up a (brave) front** to appear to be brave (even if one is not). □ *Mary is frightened, but she's putting up a brave front.* □ *If she weren't putting up a front, I'd be more frightened than I am.*

**put upon someone** to make use of someone to an unreasonable degree; to take advantage of someone for one's own benefit. (Typically passive.) □ *My mother was always put upon by her neighbors. She was too nice to refuse their requests for help.* □ *Jane feels put upon by her husband's parents. They're always coming to stay with her.*

**put words into someone's mouth** to speak for another person without permission. □ *Stop putting words into my mouth. I can speak for myself.* □ *The lawyer was scolded for putting words into the witness's mouth.*

**Put your money where your mouth is!** a command to stop talking or boasting and make a bet; a command to take action to support what one says. (A cliché.) □ *I'm tired of your bragging about your skill at betting. Put your money where your mouth is!* □ *You talk about contributing to charity, but you don't do it. Put your money where your mouth is!*

**quake in one's boots** See shake in one's boots.

**quick on the draw** See quick on the trigger.

**quick on the trigger** AND **quick on the draw 1.** quick to draw a gun and shoot. □ *Some of the old cowboys were known to be quick on the trigger.* □ *Wyatt Earp was particularly quick on the draw.* **2.** quick to respond to anything. □ *John gets the right answer before anyone else. He's really quick on the trigger.* □ *Sally will probably win the quiz game. She's really quick on the draw.*

**quick on the uptake** quick to understand (something). (Compare with slow on the uptake.) □ *Just because I'm not quick on the uptake, it doesn't mean I'm stupid.* □ *Mary understands jokes before anyone else because she's so quick on the uptake.*

**quite something** something very good or remarkable. (Informal. The word *something* is always used in this expression.) □ *You should see their new house. It's quite something.* □ *Mary's mother has bought a new hat for the wedding, and it's quite something.*

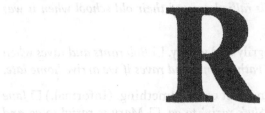

**rack one's brain(s)** to try very hard to think of something. ☐ *I racked my brains all afternoon but couldn't remember where I had put the book.* ☐ *Don't waste any more time racking your brain. Go borrow the book from the library.*

**rain cats and dogs** to rain very hard. (A cliché.) ☐ *It's raining cats and dogs. Look at it pour!* ☐ *I'm not going out in that storm. It's raining cats and dogs.*

**rain or shine** whether it rains or the sun shines; no matter what. (A cliché.) ☐ *Don't worry. I'll be there rain or shine.* ☐ *We'll hold the picnic—rain or shine.*

**raise one's sights** to set higher goals for oneself. ☐ *A year ago, Bill didn't think he would finish high school. Now he has raised his sights and is planning to go to college.* ☐ *Instead of collecting $1,000 for charity, let's raise our sights and try to collect $2,000.*

**raise some eyebrows** to shock or surprise people mildly (by doing or saying something). (*Some* can be replaced with *a few, someone's, a lot of*, etc.) ☐ *What you just said may raise some eyebrows, but it shouldn't make anyone really angry.* ☐ *John's sudden marriage to Ann raised a few eyebrows.*

**rake someone over the coals** AND **haul someone over the coals** to give someone a severe scolding. ☐ *My mother hauled me over the coals for coming in late last night.* ☐ *The manager raked me over the coals for being late again.*

**rake something up** to uncover something unpleasant and remind people about it. ☐ *The young journalist raked up the old scandal about the president.* ☐ *The politician's opponents are trying to rake up some unpleasant details about his past.*

**rally (a)round someone or something** to come together to support someone or something. ☐ *The family rallied around Jack when he lost* his job. □ *The former pupils rallied around their old school when it was in danger of being closed.*

**rant and rave** to shout angrily and wildly. □ *Bob rants and raves when anything displeases him.* □ *Father rants and raves if we arrive home late.*

**rarin' to go** extremely keen to act or do something. (Informal.) □ *Jane can't wait to start her job. She's rarin' to go.* □ *Mary is rarin' to go and can't wait for her university term to start.*

**rat race** a fierce struggle for success, especially in one's career or business. □ *Bob is tired of the rat race. He's retired and lives in the country.* □ *The money market is a rat race, and many people who work in it die of the stress.*

**reach first base (with someone or something)** See get to first base (with someone or something).

**read between the lines** to infer something (from something else); to try to understand what is meant by something that is not written clearly or openly. (Does not necessarily refer to written or printed information.) □ *After listening to what she said, if you read between the lines, you can begin to see what she really means.* □ *Don't believe everything you hear. Learn to read between the lines.*

**read someone like a book** to understand someone very well. □ *I've got John figured out. I can read him like a book.* □ *Of course I understand you. I read you like a book.*

**read someone the riot act** to give someone a severe scolding. □ *The manager read me the riot act for coming in late.* □ *The teacher read the students the riot act for their failure to do their assignments.*

**rear its ugly head** [for something unpleasant] to appear or become obvious after lying hidden. □ *Jealousy reared its ugly head and destroyed their marriage.* □ *The question of money always rears its ugly head in matters of business.*

**recite something chapter and verse** to give detailed information; to quote something in great detail, especially some source of authority. (A reference to the method of referring to biblical text.) □ *Just tell us not to smoke here. You don't have to recite the company's rules chapter and verse!* □ *The suspect recited his associates' activities chapter and verse.*

**red tape** excessively complex rules, regulations, and formal procedures, especially in government and public departments. (From the color of the tape used by government departments to tie up bundles of documents.) □ *Because of red tape, it took Frank weeks to get a visa.* □ *Red tape prevented Jack's wife from joining him abroad.*

**ride roughshod over someone or something** to treat someone or something with disdain or scorn. □ *Tom seems to ride roughshod over his friends.* □ *You shouldn't have come into our town to ride roughshod over our laws and our traditions.*

**ride the gravy train** to live in luxury. □ *If I had a million dollars, I sure could ride the gravy train.* □ *I wouldn't like loafing. I don't want to ride the gravy train.*

**riding for a fall** risking failure or an accident, usually due to overconfidence. □ *Tom drives too fast, and he seems too sure of himself. He's riding for a fall.* □ *Bill needs to eat better and get more sleep. He's riding for a fall.*

**right off the bat** immediately; first thing. (Seems to refer to a ball leaving the baseball bat, but probably referred to a cricket bat originally.) □ *When he was learning to ride a bicycle, he fell on his head right off the bat.* □ *The new manager demanded new office furniture right off the bat.*

**right under someone's nose** See under someone's (very) nose.

**ring down the curtain (on something)** AND **bring down the curtain (on something)** to bring something to an end; to declare something to be at an end. □ *It's time to ring down the curtain on our relationship. We have nothing in common anymore.* □ *We've tried our best to make this company a success, but it's time to bring down the curtain.* □ *After many years the old man brought down the curtain and closed the restaurant.*

**ring in the new year** to celebrate the beginning of the new year at midnight on December 31. (As if ringing church bells to celebrate the new year.) □ *We are planning a big party to ring in the new year.* □ *How did you ring in the new year?*

**ring true** to sound or seem true or likely. (From testing the quality of metal or glass by striking it and listening to the noise made.) □ *The pupil's excuse for being late doesn't ring true.* □ *Do you think that Mary's explanation for her absence rang true?*

**ripe old age** a very old age. □ *Mr. Smith died last night, but he was a ripe old age—ninety-nine.* □ *All the Smiths seem to live to a ripe old age.*

**rise and shine** to get out of bed and be lively and energetic. (Informal. Often a command.) □ *Come on children! Rise and shine! We're going to the seaside.* □ *Father always calls out "Rise and shine!" in the morning when we want to go on sleeping.*

**risk one's neck (to do something)** to risk physical harm in order to accomplish something. □ *Look at that traffic! I refuse to risk my neck just to cross the street to buy a paper.* □ *I refuse to risk my neck at all.*

**road hog** someone who drives carelessly and selfishly. (Informal.) □ *Look at that road hog driving in the middle of the road and stopping other drivers from passing him.* □ *That road hog nearly knocked the children over. He was driving too fast.*

**rob Peter to pay Paul** to take from one person or source just to give to another, so one still has not gained anything oneself. (A cliché. Usually concerns debts.) □ *Why borrow money to pay your bills? That's just robbing Peter to pay Paul.* □ *There's no point in robbing Peter to pay Paul. You still will be in debt.*

**rob the cradle** to marry or date someone who is much younger than oneself. (As if one were consorting with an infant.) □ *I hear that Bill is dating Ann. Isn't that sort of robbing the cradle? She's much younger than he is.* □ *Uncle Bill—who is nearly eighty—married a thirty-year-old woman. That is really robbing the cradle.*

**rock the boat** to cause trouble where none is welcome; to disturb a situation that is otherwise stable and satisfactory. (Often in the negative.) □ *Look, Tom, everything is going fine here. Don't rock the boat!* □ *You can depend on Tom to mess things up by rocking the boat.*

**roll in** to come in large numbers or amounts. (Informal.) □ *We didn't expect many people at the party, but they just kept rolling in.* □ *Money is simply rolling in for our fund-raiser.*

**rolling in something** having large amounts of something, usually money. (Informal.) □ *That family is rolling in money.* □ *Jack doesn't need to earn money. He's rolling in it.*

A **rolling stone gathers no moss.** a proverb meaning that a person who keeps changing jobs or residences accumulates no possessions or responsibilities. (This may be intended as a criticism or as a positive comment, depending on whether one views the accumulation as being good or bad.) □ *"John just can't seem to stay in one place. He should settle down," said Sally. "You know, a rolling stone gathers no moss."* □ *Bill has no furniture to bother with because he keeps on the move. He says that a rolling stone gathers no moss.*

**roll out the red carpet for someone** See under get the red-carpet treatment.

**Rome wasn't built in a day.** a proverb meaning that important or complex things don't happen overnight. (A cliché.) □ *Don't expect a lot to happen right away. Rome wasn't built in a day, you know.* □ *Don't be anxious about how fast you are learning. Rome wasn't built in a day.*

**rooted to the spot** unable to move because of fear or surprise. □ *Joan stood rooted to the spot when she saw the ghostly figure.* □ *Mary was rooted to the spot when the thief snatched her bag.*

**root something out** to get rid of something completely; to destroy something. ⊤ *No government will ever root out crime completely.* □ *The headmaster wants to root troublemakers out of the school.*

**rough it** to live in simple or uncomfortable conditions without the usual amenities. (Informal.) □ *The students are roughing it in a shack with no running water.* □ *Bob and Jack had nowhere to live, so they had to rough it in a tent until they found an apartment.*

**rub elbows with someone** AND **rub shoulders with someone** to associate with someone; to work closely with someone. □ *I don't care to rub elbows with someone who acts like that!* □ *I rub shoulders with John at work. We are good friends.*

**rub salt in a wound** to deliberately make someone's unhappiness, shame, or misfortune worse. □ *Don't rub salt in the wound by telling me how enjoyable the party was.* □ *Jim is feeling miserable about losing his job, and Fred is rubbing salt in the wound by saying how good his replacement is.*

**rub shoulders with someone** See rub elbows with someone.

**rub someone's fur the wrong way** AND **rub someone the wrong way** to irritate someone. (As if one were stroking an animal's fur, such as that of a pet cat, in the wrong direction, thus irritating the animal. The second entry form is derived from the first.) □ *I'm sorry I rubbed* *your fur the wrong way. I didn't mean to upset you.* □ *Don't rub her the wrong way!*

**rub someone's nose in something** to remind someone of something one has done wrong; to remind someone of something bad or unfortunate that has happened. (From a method of house-training animals.) □ *When Bob failed his exam, his brother rubbed his nose in it.* □ *Mary knows she shouldn't have broken her engagement. Don't rub her nose in it.*

**rub someone the wrong way** See rub someone's fur the wrong way.

**ruffle someone's feathers** to upset or annoy someone. (A bird's feathers become ruffled if it is angry or afraid.) □ *You certainly ruffled Mrs. Smith's feathers by criticizing her garden.* □ *Try to be tactful and not ruffle people's feathers.*

**rule of thumb** a general principle developed through experiential rather than scientific means. (From the use of one's thumb to make quick and rough measurements.) □ *As a rule of thumb, you can expect a new battery to last about a year.* □ *A good rule of thumb is to assume that each person will eat five shrimp. If you are cooking for four people, you will need twenty shrimp.*

**rule the roost** to be the boss or manager, especially at home. □ *Who rules the roost at your house?* □ *Our new office manager really rules the roost.*

**run a fever** AND **run a temperature** to have a body temperature higher than normal; to have a fever. □ *I ran a fever when I had the flu.* □ *The baby is running a temperature and is grouchy.*

**run (around) in circles** See run around like a chicken with its head cut off.

**run around like a chicken with its head cut off** AND **run (around) in circles** to run around frantically and aimlessly; to be in a state of chaos. (A cliché.) □ *I spent all afternoon running around like a chicken with its head cut off.* □ *If you run around in circles, you'll never get anything done.* □ *Get organized and stop running in circles.*

**run a taut ship** See run a tight ship.

**run a temperature** See run a fever.

**run a tight ship** AND **run a taut ship** to run a ship or an organization in an orderly and disciplined manner. (*Taut* and *tight* mean the same thing. *Taut* is correct nautical use.) □ *The new office manager really runs a tight ship.* □ *Captain Jones is known for running a taut ship.*

**run for it** to try to escape by running. (Informal.) □ *The guard's not looking. Let's run for it!* □ *The convict tried to run for it, but the guard caught him.*

**run for one's life** to run away to save one's life. □ *The dam has burst! Run for your life!* □ *The zookeeper told us all to run for our lives.*

**run high** [for feelings] to be in a state of excitement or anger. □ *Feelings were running high as the general election approached.* □ *The mood of the crowd ran high when they saw the man beat the child.*

**run in the family** [for a characteristic] to appear in all (or most) members of a family. □ *My grandparents lived well into their nineties, and it runs in the family. Most of my relatives have lived to be quite old.* □ *My brothers and I have red hair. It runs in the family.*

**run into a stone wall** to come to a barrier against further progress. (Also used literally.) □ *We've run into a stone wall in our investigation.* □ *Algebra was hard for Tom, but he really ran into a stone wall with geometry.*

**run out of gas** See under out of gas.

**run someone or something to earth** to find something after a search. (From chasing a fox into its hole during a hunt.) □ *Jean finally ran her long-lost cousin to earth in Paris.* □ *After months of searching, I ran a copy of Jim's book to earth.*

**run someone ragged** to force someone to work hard and fast; to keep someone or something busy to the point of exhaustion. □ *This busy season is running us all ragged at the store.* □ *What a busy day. I ran myself ragged.*

**run something up** to cause something to rise sharply in amount. ⊤ *Joan has run up a huge account in her parents' name.* □ *Fred has run a large bill up at the local garage and cannot pay it.*

**run to seed** AND **go to seed** to become worn out and uncared for. (Said especially of a lawn that needs care.) □ *Look at that lawn. The whole thing has run to seed.* □ *Pick things up around here. This place is going to seed. What a mess!*

**run to something 1.** to be sufficient for something; to have enough money for something. □ *Our budget doesn't run to vacations abroad.* □ *We just can't run to a new car.* **2.** to add up to a certain amount of money. □ *In the end, the bill ran to thousands of dollars.* □ *His account ran to more than I expected.*

**sacred cow** something that is regarded by some people with such respect and veneration that they don't like it being criticized by anyone in any way. (From the fact that the cow is regarded as sacred in Hinduism.) □ *University education is a sacred cow in the Smith family. Fred is regarded as a failure because he left school at sixteen.* □ *Don't talk about eating meat to Pam. Vegetarianism is one of her sacred cows.*

**saddle someone with something** to give someone something undesirable, annoying, or difficult to deal with. (Informal.) □ *Mary says she doesn't want to be saddled with a baby, but her husband would love one.* □ *Jim saddled Eddie with the most boring job so that he would leave.*

**safe and sound** safe and whole or healthy. (A cliché.) □ *It was a rough trip, but we got there safe and sound.* □ *I'm glad to see you here safe and sound.*

the **salt of the earth** the most worthy of people; a very good or worthy person. (Biblical.) □ *Mrs. Jones is the salt of the earth. She is the first to help anyone in trouble.* □ *Frank's mother is the salt of the earth. She has five children of her own and yet fosters three others.*

**saved by the bell** rescued from a difficult or dangerous situation just in time by something that brings the situation to a sudden end. (From the sounding of a bell marking the end of a round in a boxing match.) □ *James didn't know the answer to the question, but he was saved by the bell when the teacher was called away from the room.* □ *I couldn't think of anything to say to the woman at the bus stop, but I was saved by the bell when the bus arrived.*

**save something for a rainy day** to reserve something—usually money—for some future need. (A cliché. *Save something* can be replaced with *put something aside, hold something back, keep something,* etc.) □ *I've saved a little money for a rainy day.* □ *Keep some extra candy for a rainy day.*

**save the day** to produce a good result when a bad result was expected. □ *The team was expected to lose, but Sally made many points and saved the day.* □ *Your excellent speech saved the day.*

**scarcer than hens' teeth** See (as) scarce as hens' teeth.

**scrape the bottom of the barrel** to select from among the worst; to choose from what is left over. (As if one were down to the very last and worst choices.) □ *You've bought a bad-looking car. You really scraped the bottom of the barrel to get that one.* □ *The worker you sent over was the worst I've ever seen. Send me another—and don't scrape the bottom of the barrel.*

**scratch the surface** to just begin to find out about something; to examine only the superficial aspects of something. □ *The investigation of the governor's staff revealed some suspicious dealing. It is thought that the investigators have just scratched the surface.* □ *We don't know how bad the problem is. We've only scratched the surface.*

**scream bloody murder** See cry bloody murder.

**screw up one's courage** to build up one's courage. □ *I guess I have to screw up my courage and go to the dentist.* □ *I spent all morning screwing up my courage to take my driver's test.*

**scrimp and save** to be very thrifty; to live on very little money, often in order to save up for something. □ *We had to scrimp and save in order to send the children to college.* □ *The Smiths scrimp and save all year in order to go on a vacation.*

the **seamy side of life** the most unpleasant or roughest aspect of life. (Informal. A reference to the inside of a garment, where the seams show.) □ *Doctors in that neighborhood really see the seamy side of life.* □ *Mary saw the seamy side of life when she worked at a homeless shelter.*

**search high and low for someone or something** See hunt high and low for someone or something.

**search something with a fine-tooth comb** See go over something with a fine-tooth comb.

**second nature to someone** easy and natural for someone. □ *Swimming is second nature to Jane.* □ *Driving is no problem for Bob. It's second nature to him.*

**second-rate** not of the best quality; inferior. □ *Fred's a second-rate tennis player compared with Jim.* □ *The government is building second-rate housing.*

**see double** to see two of everything instead of one. □ *When I was driving, I saw two people on the road instead of one. I'm seeing double. There's something wrong with my eyes.* □ *Mike thought he was seeing double when he saw Mary with her twin sister. He didn't know she had a twin.*

**see eye to eye (about something)** AND **see eye to eye on something** to view something in the same way (as someone else). □ *John and Ann see eye to eye about the new law. Neither of them likes it.* □ *That's interesting, because they rarely see eye to eye.*

**see eye to eye on something** See eye to eye (about something).

**seeing that** considering; since. □ *Seeing that she has no money, Sally won't be going shopping.* □ *Seeing that it's raining, we won't go to the beach.*

**see stars** to see flashing lights after receiving a blow to the head. □ *I saw stars when I bumped my head on the attic ceiling.* □ *The little boy saw stars when he fell headfirst onto the concrete.*

**see the (hand)writing on the wall** to know that something is certain to happen. (A cliché. Biblical. Often refers to something bad.) □ *If you don't improve your performance, they'll fire you. Can't you see the writing on the wall?* □ *I know I'll fail the course. I can see the handwriting on the wall.*

**see the light (at the end of the tunnel)** to foresee an end to one's problems after a long period of time. □ *I had been horribly ill for two months before I began to see the light at the end of the tunnel.* □ *I began to see the light one day in early spring. At that moment, I knew I'd get well.*

**see the light (of day)** to come to the end of a very busy time. □ *Finally, when the holiday season was over, we could see the light of day. We had been so busy!* □ *When business lets up for a while, we'll be able to see the light.*

**see things** to imagine one sees someone or something that is not there. □ *Jean says that she saw a ghost, but she was just seeing things.* □ *I thought I was seeing things when Bill walked into the room. Someone had told me he was in Europe.*

**sell like hotcakes** [for something] to be sold very fast. □ *The delicious candy sold like hotcakes.* □ *The fancy new cars were selling like hotcakes.*

**sell someone a bill of goods** to get someone to believe something that isn't true; to deceive someone. □ *Don't pay any attention to what John says. He's just trying to sell you a bill of goods.* □ *I'm not selling you a bill of goods. What I say is true.*

**sell someone or something short** to underestimate someone or something; to fail to see the good qualities of someone or something. □ *This is a very good restaurant. Don't sell it short.* □ *When you say that John isn't interested in music, you're selling him short. Did you know he plays the violin quite well?*

**send one about one's business** to send someone away, usually in an unfriendly way. □ *Is that annoying man on the telephone again? Please send him about his business.* □ *Ann, I can't clean up the house with you running around. I'm going to have to send you about your business.*

**send someone packing** to send someone away; to dismiss someone, possibly rudely. □ *I couldn't stand him anymore, so I sent him packing.* □ *The maid proved to be so incompetent that I had to send her packing.*

**send someone to the showers** to send a player out of the game and off the field, court, etc. (From sports.) □ *John played so badly that the coach sent him to the showers after the third quarter.* □ *After the fistfight, the coaches sent both players to the showers.*

**separate the men from the boys** to separate the competent from those who are less competent. □ *This is the kind of task that separates the men from the boys.* □ *This project is very difficult. It'll separate the men from the boys.*

**separate the sheep from the goats** to divide people into two groups according to whether they meet a certain standard. (Biblical.) □ *Working in a place like this really separates the sheep from the goats.* □ *We can't go on with the game until we separate the sheep from the goats. Let's see who can jump the farthest.*

**serve as a guinea pig** [for someone] to be experimented on; to allow some sort of test to be performed on one. (A cliché.) □ *Practice on someone else! I don't want to serve as a guinea pig!* □ *Jane agreed to serve as a guinea pig and try out the new flavor of ice cream.*

**serve someone right** [for an act or event] to punish someone fairly (for doing something). □ *John copied off my test paper. It would serve him right if he fails the test.* □ *It'd serve John right if he got arrested.*

**set foot somewhere** to go or enter somewhere. (Often in the negative.) □ *If I were you, I wouldn't set foot in that town.* □ *I wouldn't set foot in her house! Not after the way she spoke to me.*

**set great store by someone or something** to have positive expectations for someone or something; to have high hopes for someone or something. □ *I set great store by my computer and its ability to help me in my work.* □ *We set great store by John because of his quick mind.*

**set one back on one's heels** to surprise, shock, or overwhelm someone. □ *Her sudden announcement set us all back on our heels.* □ *The manager scolded me, and that really set me back on my heels.*

**set one's heart on something** See under have one's heart set on something.

**set one's sights on something** to select something as one's goal. □ *I set my sights on a master's degree from the state university.* □ *Don't set your sights on something you cannot possibly do.*

**set someone's teeth on edge 1.** [for a sour or bitter taste] to irritate one's mouth and make it feel funny. □ *Have you ever eaten a lemon? It'll set your teeth on edge.* □ *I can't stand food that sets my teeth on edge.* **2.** [for a person or a noise] to be irritating or get on one's nerves. □ *Please don't scrape your fingernails on the blackboard! It sets my teeth on edge!* □ *Here comes Bob. He's so annoying. He really sets my teeth on edge.*

**set the world on fire** to do exciting things that bring fame and glory. (Frequently in the negative.) □ *I'm not very ambitious. I don't want to set the world on fire.* □ *You don't have to set the world on fire. Just do a good job.*

**settle up with someone** to pay someone what one owes; to pay one one's share of something. □ *I must settle up with Jim for the bike I bought from him.* □ *Fred paid the whole restaurant bill, and we all settled up with him later.*

**shades of someone or something** reminders of someone or something; things reminiscent of someone or something. □ *When I met Jim's mother, I thought, "shades of Aunt Mary."* □ *"Shades of high school," said Jack as the university lecturer rebuked him for being late.*

**shaggy-dog story** a kind of funny story that relies on its length and its sudden ridiculous ending for its humor. □ *Don't let John tell a shaggy-dog story. It'll go on for hours.* □ *Mary didn't get the point of Fred's shaggy-dog story.*

**shake in one's boots** AND **quake in one's boots** to be afraid; to shake from fear. □ *I was shaking in my boots because I had to go see the manager.* □ *Stop quaking in your boots, Bob. I'm not going to fire you.*

**shape up or ship out** to either improve one's performance or one's behavior or quit and leave. (A cliché.) □ *Okay, Tom. That's the end. Shape up or ship out!* □ *John was late again, so I told him to shape up or ship out.*

**shed crocodile tears** to shed false tears; to pretend that one is weeping. □ *The child wasn't hurt, but she shed crocodile tears anyway.* □ *He thought he could get his way if he shed crocodile tears.*

**ships that pass in the night** people who meet each other briefly by chance and are unlikely to meet again. □ *Mary would have liked to see Jim again, but to him they were ships that passed in the night.* □ *When you travel a lot on business, your encounters are just so many ships that pass in the night.*

The **shoe is on the other foot.** a proverb meaning that one is experiencing the same things that one caused another person to experience. (Note the variations in the examples.) □ *The teacher is taking a course in summer school and is finding out what it's like when the shoe is on the other foot.* □ *When the policeman was arrested, he learned what it was like to have the shoe on the other foot.*

**shoot from the hip** to speak directly and frankly. □ *John tends to shoot from the hip, but he speaks the truth.* □ *Don't pay any attention to John. He means no harm. It's just his nature to shoot from the hip.*

**shotgun wedding** a forced wedding. (Informal. From the bride's father having threatened the bridegroom with a shotgun to force him to marry.) □ *Mary was six months pregnant when she married Bill. It was a real shotgun wedding.* □ *Bob would never have married Jane if she hadn't been pregnant, but because she was, Jane's father saw to it that there was a shotgun wedding.*

a **shot in the arm** a boost; something that gives someone energy. □ *Thank you for cheering me up. It was a real shot in the arm.* □ *Your friendly greeting card was just what I needed—a shot in the arm.*

**shoulder to shoulder** side by side; with a shared purpose. □ *The two armies fought shoulder to shoulder against the joint enemy.* □ *The strikers said they would stand shoulder to shoulder against the management.*

**should have stood in bed** should have stayed in bed. (Has nothing to do with standing up.) □ *What a horrible day! I should have stood in bed.* □ *The minute I got up and heard the news this morning, I knew I should have stood in bed.*

**show one's face** to appear (somewhere). (Usually in the negative.) □ *After what she said, she had better not show her face around here again.* □ *If I don't say I'm sorry, I'll never be able to show my face again.*

**show one's hand** to reveal one's intentions to someone. (From card games.) □ *I don't know whether Jim's intending to marry Jane or not. He's not one to show his hand.* □ *If you want to get a raise, don't show the boss your hand too soon.*

**show one's (true) colors** to show what one is really like or what one is really thinking. □ *Whose side are you on, John? Come on. Show your colors.* □ *It's hard to tell what Mary is thinking. She never shows her true colors.*

**show someone the ropes** See under know the ropes.

**signed, sealed, and delivered** formally and officially signed; [for a formal document to be] executed. (A cliché.) □ *Here is the deed to the property—signed, sealed, and delivered.* □ *I can't begin work on this project until I have the contract signed, sealed, and delivered.*

**sign one's own death warrant** to do something that ensures the failure of one's endeavors. (A cliché.) □ *I wouldn't ever gamble a large sum of money. That would be signing my own death warrant.* □ *The killer signed his own death warrant when he walked into the police station and gave himself up.*

**sign on the dotted line** to place one's signature on a contract or other important paper. (A cliché.) □ *This agreement isn't properly concluded until we both sign on the dotted line.* □ *Here are the papers for the purchase of your car. As soon as you sign on the dotted line, that beautiful, shiny automobile will be all yours!*

**silly season** the time of year, usually in the summer, when there is a lack of important news and newspapers contain articles about unimportant or trivial things instead. □ *It must be the silly season. There's a* *story here about peculiarly shaped potatoes.* □ *There's a piece on the front page about people with big feet. Talk about the silly season.*

**sing someone's praises** to praise someone highly and enthusiastically. □ *The boss is singing the praises of his new secretary.* □ *The theater critics are singing the praises of the young actor.*

**sink one's teeth into something** (A cliché.) **1.** to take a bite of some kind of food, usually a special kind of food. □ *I can't wait to sink my teeth into a nice juicy steak.* □ *Look at that chocolate cake! Don't you want to sink your teeth into that?* **2.** to get a chance to do, learn, or control something. □ *That appears to be a very challenging assignment. I can't wait to sink my teeth into it.* □ *Being the manager of this department is a big task. I'm very eager to sink my teeth into it.*

**sink or swim** to either fail or succeed. (A cliché.) □ *After I've studied and learned all I can, I have to take the test and sink or swim.* □ *It's too late to help John now. It's sink or swim for him.*

**sit at someone's feet** to admire someone greatly; to be influenced by someone's teaching; to be taught by someone. □ *Jack sat at the feet of Picasso when he was studying in Europe.* □ *Tom would love to sit at the feet of the musician Yehudi Menuhin.*

**sit on its hands** See under sit on one's hands.

**sit on one's hands** to do nothing; to fail to help. (Not literal.) □ *When we needed help from Mary, she just sat on her hands.* □ *We need the cooperation of everyone. You can't sit on your hands!* ALSO: **sit on its hands** [for an audience] to refuse to applaud. (Not literal.) □ *We saw a very poor performance of the play. The audience sat on its hands the entire time.*

**sit on the fence** not to take sides in a dispute; not to make a clear choice between two possibilities. □ *When Jane and Tom argue, it is best to sit on the fence, because then you won't offend either of them.* □ *No one knows which of the candidates Joan will vote for. She's sitting on the fence.*

**sit tight** to wait; to wait patiently. (Does not necessarily refer to sitting.) □ *Just relax and sit tight. I'll be right with you.* □ *We were waiting in line for the gates to open, when someone came out and told us to sit tight because it wouldn't be much longer before we could go in.*

**sitting on a powder keg** in a risky or explosive situation; in a situation where something serious or dangerous may happen at any time.

(Not literal. A powder keg is a keg of gunpowder.) □ *Things are very tense at work. The whole office is sitting on a powder keg.* □ *The fire at the oil field seems to be under control for now, but all the workers there are sitting on a powder keg.*

**sitting target** someone or something in a position that is easily attacked. □ *The old man was a sitting target for the burglars. He lived alone and did not have a telephone.* □ *People recently hired will be sitting targets if the firm needs to reduce staff.*

**sit up and take notice** to become alert and pay attention. □ *A loud noise from the front of the room caused everyone to sit up and take notice.* □ *The company wouldn't pay any attention to my complaints. When I had my lawyer write them a letter, they sat up and took notice.*

**six of one and half a dozen of the other** about the same one way or another. (A cliché.) □ *It doesn't matter to me which way you do it. It's six of one and half a dozen of the other.* □ *What difference does it make? They're both the same—six of one and half a dozen of the other.*

**sixth sense** a supposed power to know or feel things that are not perceptible by the five senses of sight, hearing, smell, taste, and touch. □ *My sixth sense told me to avoid going home by my usual route. Later, I discovered there had been a fatal accident there.* □ *Jane's sixth sense demanded that she not trust Tom, even though he seemed honest enough.*

**skate on thin ice** See under on thin ice.

**skeleton in the closet** a hidden and shocking secret; a secret fact about oneself. (Often in the plural. As if one had hidden the grisly remains of a murder in the closet.) □ *You can ask anyone about how reliable I am. I don't mind. I don't have any skeletons in the closet.* □ *My uncle was in jail for a day once. That's our family's skeleton in the closet.*

The **sky's the limit.** There is no limit to the success that can be achieved or the money that can be gained or spent. □ *If you take a job with us, you'll find the promotion prospects very good. The sky's the limit, in fact.* □ *The new salespeople were told that the sky was the limit when it came to potential earnings.*

**slap in the face** an insult; an act that causes disappointment or discouragement. □ *Losing the election was a slap in the face for the club president.* □ *Failing to get into a good college was a slap in the face to Tom after his years of study.*

**sleep in** to oversleep; to sleep late in the morning. □ *If you sleep in again, you'll lose your job.* □ *Get an alarm clock to stop you from sleeping in.*

**sleep like a log** to sleep very soundly. (A cliché.) □ *Nothing can wake me up. I usually sleep like a log.* □ *Everyone in our family sleeps like a log, so no one heard the fire engines in the middle of the night.*

**sleep on something** to think about something overnight; to weigh a decision overnight. □ *I don't know whether I should agree to do it. Let me sleep on it.* □ *I slept on it, and I've decided to accept your offer.*

**slice of the cake** See piece of the pie.

**slip of the tongue** an error in speaking in which a word is pronounced incorrectly, or in which the speaker says something unintentionally. (As if one's tongue had made a misstep.) □ *I didn't mean to tell her that. It was a slip of the tongue.* □ *I failed to understand the instructions because the speaker made a slip of the tongue at an important point.*

**slip one's mind** [for something that was to be remembered] to be forgotten. (As if a thought had slipped out of one's brain.) □ *I meant to go to the grocery store on the way home, but it slipped my mind.* □ *My birthday slipped my mind. I guess I wanted to forget it.*

**slip through someone's fingers** to get away from someone; for someone to lose track (of something or someone). □ *I had a copy of the book you want, but somehow it slipped through my fingers.* □ *There was a detective following me, but I managed to slip through his fingers.*

**Slow and steady wins the race.** a proverb meaning that deliberateness and determination will lead to a person to success. □ *I worked my way through college in six years. Now I know what they mean when they say, "Slow and steady wins the race."* □ *Don't give up just because you can't produce results as quickly as the others. Remember, slow and steady wins the race.*

**slow on the uptake** slow to understand something. (Compare with quick on the uptake.) □ *I'm a little slow on the uptake today. I didn't get much sleep last night.* □ *Bill is really slow on the uptake. You'll have to explain it twice.*

**smack-dab in the middle** right in the middle. □ *I want a big helping of mashed potatoes with a glob of butter smack-dab in the middle.* □ *Tom* and Sally were having a terrible argument, and I was trapped—smack-dab in the middle.

**small fry 1.** children. □ *Peter's taking all the small fry to the zoo.* □ *Time for bed, small fry.* **2.** unimportant people or things. □ *The police have only caught the small fry. The leader of the gang is still free.* □ *The small fry are helping each other compete against the larger businesses.*

**small print** the part of a document that is not easily noticed, often because of the smallness of the print, and that often contains important information. □ *You should have read the small print before signing the contract.* □ *You should always read the small print of an insurance policy.*

**small-time** small; on a small scale. □ *Our business is just small-time now, but it's growing.* □ *He's a small-time crook.*

**smear campaign (against someone)** a campaign aimed at damaging someone's reputation by making accusations and spreading rumors. □ *The politician's opponents are engaging in a smear campaign against him.* □ *Jack started a smear campaign against Tom so that Tom wouldn't get the manager's job.*

**smile on someone or something** to be favorable to someone or something. □ *Fate smiled on me, and I got the job.* □ *Lady Luck smiled on our venture, and we made a profit.*

**smooth sailing** progress made without any difficulty; an easy situation. □ *Once you've passed that exam, it will be all smooth sailing.* □ *Working there was not all smooth sailing. The boss had a very hot temper.*

**soil one's hands** See get one's hands dirty.

**so quiet you could hear a pin drop** See so still you could hear a pin drop.

**so still you could hear a pin drop** AND **so quiet you could hear a pin drop** very quiet. (A cliché. Also with *can*.) □ *When I came into the room, it was so still you could hear a pin drop. Then everyone shouted, "Happy birthday!"* □ *Please be quiet. Be so quiet you can hear a pin drop.*

**sound off** to speak loudly and freely about something, especially when complaining. (Informal.) □ *The people at the bus stop were sounding off about the poor transportation services.* □ *Bob was sounding off about the government's economic policies.*

**sow one's wild oats** to do wild and foolish things in one's youth. (Often assumed to have some sort of sexual meaning, with wild oats referring to a young man's semen.) □ *Bill was out sowing his wild oats last night, and he's in jail this morning.* □ *Mrs. Smith told Mr. Smith that he was too old to be sowing his wild oats.*

**speak for themselves** See speaks for itself.

**speak of the devil** a phrase said when someone whose name has just been mentioned appears or is heard from. (A cliché.) □ *Well, speak of the devil! Hello, Tom. We were just talking about you.* □ *I had just mentioned Sally when—speak of the devil—she walked in the door.*

**speaks for itself** AND **speak for themselves** to have an obvious meaning; not to need explaining; to need no explanation. □ *The facts speak for themselves. Tom's guilty.* □ *The result of the test speaks for itself. You need to work harder.*

**speak the same language** [for people] to have similar ideas, tastes, etc. □ *Jane and Jack get along very well. They really speak the same language about almost everything.* □ *Bob and his father didn't speak the same language when it came to politics.*

**speak with a forked tongue** to tell lies; to try to deceive someone. □ *Jean's mother sounds very charming, but she speaks with a forked tongue.* □ *People tend to believe Fred because he seems plausible, but we know he speaks with a forked tongue.*

**spill the beans** See let the cat out of the bag.

**split the difference** to divide the difference between two amounts (with someone else). □ *You want to sell for $120, and I want to buy for $100. Let's split the difference and close the deal at $110.* □ *I don't want to split the difference. I want $120.*

**spoon-feed someone** to treat someone with too much care or help; to teach someone with methods that are too easy and do not stimulate the learner to independent thinking. □ *The teacher spoon-feeds the pupils by dictating notes on the novel instead of getting the children to read the books themselves.* □ *You mustn't spoon-feed the new recruits by telling them what to do all the time. They must use their initiative.*

a **sporting chance** a reasonably good chance. □ *If you hurry, you have a sporting chance of catching the bus.* □ *The firm has only a sporting chance of getting the export order.*

**spread it on thick** See lay it on thick.

**spread like wildfire** to spread rapidly and without control. (A cliché.) □ *The epidemic is spreading like wildfire. Everyone is getting sick.* □ *John told a joke that was so funny it spread like wildfire.*

**spread oneself too thin** to do so many things that one can do none of them well; to spread one's efforts or attention too widely. □ *It's a good idea to get involved in a lot of activities, but don't spread yourself too thin.* □ *I'm too busy these days. I'm afraid I've spread myself too thin.*

**square deal** a fair and honest transaction; fair treatment. (Informal.) □ *All the workers want is a square deal, but their boss underpays them.* □ *You always get a square deal with that travel agent.*

**square meal** a nourishing, filling meal. (Informal.) □ *All you've eaten today is junk food. You should sit down to a square meal.* □ *The tramp hadn't had a square meal in weeks.*

**a square peg in a round hole** a misfit. (A cliché.) □ *John can't seem to get along with the people he works with. He's just a square peg in a round hole.* □ *I'm not a square peg in a round hole. It's just that no one understands me.*

**square up to someone or something** to face someone or something bravely; to tackle someone or something. □ *You'll have to square up to the bully, or he'll make your life miserable.* □ *It's time to square up to your financial problems. You can't just ignore them.*

**square up with someone** to pay someone what one owes; to pay one's share of something to someone. (Informal.) □ *I'll square up with you later if you pay the whole bill now.* □ *Bob said he would square up with Tom for his share of the gas.*

**squeak by 1.** to barely manage. □ *We don't really have enough supplies, but I think we can squeak by if necessary.* □ *Mary just squeaked by on her budget this month.* **2.** See the following entry.

**squeak by (someone or something)** to just get past or beyond someone or something. □ *The guard was almost asleep, so I squeaked by him.* □ *The large table almost blocked the hall, but I could just squeak by.*

**stab someone in the back** to betray someone. □ *I thought we were friends! Why did you stab me in the back?* □ *You don't expect a person whom you trust to stab you in the back.*

**stand corrected** to admit that one has been wrong. □ *I realize that I accused him wrongly. I stand corrected.* □ *We appreciate now that our conclusions were wrong. We stand corrected.*

**standing joke** a subject that regularly and over a period of time causes amusement whenever it is mentioned. □ *Uncle Jim's driving was a standing joke. He used to drive incredibly slowly.* □ *Their mother's inability to make a decision was a standing joke among the brothers all their lives.*

**stand one's ground** AND **hold one's ground** to stand up for one's rights; to resist an attack. □ *The lawyer tried to confuse me when I was giving testimony, but I managed to stand my ground.* □ *Some people were trying to crowd us off the beach, but we held our ground.*

**stand on one's own two feet** to be independent and self-sufficient, rather than being supported by someone else. □ *I'll be glad when I have a good job and can stand on my own two feet.* □ *When Jane gets out of debt, she'll be able to stand on her own two feet again.*

**stand out a mile** See stick out a mile.

**stand up and be counted** to state one's support (for someone or something); to come out for someone or something. □ *If you believe in more government help for farmers, write your representative—stand up and be counted.* □ *I'm generally in favor of what you propose, but not enough to stand up and be counted.*

**stare someone in the face** [for something] to be very obvious to someone; [for something] to be very easy for someone to see or understand. (Informal.) □ *Her child's need for special teachers must have been staring Sally in the face, but she ignored it.* □ *It's staring Dick in the face that the boss is displeased with him.*

**start from scratch** to start from the beginning; to start from nothing. □ *Whenever I bake a cake, I start from scratch. I never use a cake mix.* □ *I built every bit of my own house. I started from scratch and did everything with my own hands.* □ *We lost everything in the flood and had to start again from scratch.*

**start (off) with a clean slate** to start out again afresh; to ignore the past and start over again. □ *I plowed under all last year's flowers so I could start with a clean slate next spring.* □ *If I start off with a clean slate, then I'll know exactly what each plant is.*

**stay put** not to move; to stay where one is. (Informal.) □ *We've decided to stay put and not to buy a new house.* □ *If the children just stay put, their parents will collect them soon.*

**steal a base** to sneak from one base to another in baseball. □ *The runner stole second base, but he nearly got put out on the way.* □ *Tom runs so slowly that he never tries to steal a base.*

**steal a march (on someone)** to get some sort of an advantage over someone without being noticed. □ *I got the contract because I was able to steal a march on my competitor.* □ *You have to be clever and fast—not dishonest—to steal a march.*

**steal someone's thunder** to lessen someone's force or authority. (Not literal.) □ *What do you mean by coming in here and stealing my thunder? I'm in charge here!* □ *Someone stole my thunder by leaking my announcement to the press.*

**steal the show** See steal the spotlight.

**steal the spotlight** AND **steal the show** to give the best performance in a show, play, or some other event; to get attention for oneself. □ *The lead in the play was very good, but the butler stole the show.* □ *Ann always tries to steal the spotlight when she and I make a presentation.*

**step on it** See step on the gas.

**step on someone's toes** AND **tread on someone's toes** to interfere with or offend someone. (Note examples with *anyone*.) □ *When you're in public office, you have to avoid stepping on anyone's toes.* □ *Ann trod on someone's toes during the last campaign and lost the election.*

**step on the gas** AND **step on it** to hurry up. □ *I'm in a hurry, driver. Step on it!* □ *I can't step on the gas, mister. There's too much traffic.*

**step out of line** to misbehave; to do something offensive. □ *I'm terribly sorry. I hope I didn't step out of line.* □ *John is a lot of fun to go out with, but he has a tendency to step out of line.*

**stew in one's own juice** to be left alone to suffer one's anger or disappointment. □ *John has such a terrible temper. When he got mad at us, we just let him go away and stew in his own juice.* □ *After John stewed in his own juice for a while, he decided to come back and apologize to us.*

**stick one's foot in one's mouth** See put one's foot in one's mouth.

**stick one's neck out** to take a risk. □ *Why should I stick my neck out to do something for her? What's she ever done for me?* □ *He made a risky investment. He stuck his neck out because he thought he could make some money.*

**stick one's nose in(to something)** See poke one's nose in(to something).

**stick out a mile** AND **stand out a mile** to be very obvious. (Informal.) □ *It stands out a mile that Tom and Jane have quarreled.* □ *The firm's lack of good management sticks out a mile.*

**stick to one's guns** to remain firm in one's convictions; to stand up for one's rights. □ *I'll stick to my guns on this matter. I'm sure I'm right.* □ *Bob can be persuaded to do it our way. He probably won't stick to his guns on this point.*

**Still waters run deep.** a proverb meaning that a quiet person is probably thinking deep or important thoughts. □ *Jane is so quiet. She's probably thinking. Still waters run deep, you know.* □ *It's true that still waters run deep, but I think that Jane is really half asleep.*

**stir up a hornet's nest** to create trouble or difficulties. □ *What a mess you have made of things. You've really stirred up a hornet's nest.* □ *Bill stirred up a hornet's nest when he discovered the theft.*

a **stone's throw (away)** a short distance (away); a relatively short distance (away). (May refer to distances in feet or miles.) □ *John saw Mary across the street, just a stone's throw away.* □ *Philadelphia is just a stone's throw from New York City.*

**stop (just) short (of something)** not to go as far as something; to stop before something. (The *something* is often an action, as in the examples.) □ *Fortunately Bob stopped short of hitting Tom.* □ *He was about to hit him, but he stopped short at the last moment.* □ *The boss criticized Jane's work, but he stopped just short of firing her.* □ *Jack drove the car to the end of the driveway and stopped just short of the garage door.* □ *I read almost the whole book but stopped short of the last chapter.*

**straight from the horse's mouth** from an authoritative or dependable source. (A cliché.) □ *I know it's true! I heard it straight from the horse's mouth!* □ *This comes straight from the horse's mouth, so it has to be believed.*

**straight from the shoulder** sincerely; frankly; holding nothing back. (A cliché.) □ *Sally always speaks straight from the shoulder. You never have to guess what she really means.* □ *Bill gave a good presentation—straight from the shoulder and brief.*

**straight out** frankly; directly. (Informal.) □ *Bob told Pam straight out that he didn't want to marry her.* □ *Jim was told straight out to start working harder.*

**stretch one's legs** to walk around after sitting down or lying down for a time. □ *We wanted to stretch our legs during intermission.* □ *After sitting in the car all day, the travelers decided to stretch their legs.*

**(strictly) on the level** honest; dependably open and fair. □ *How can I be sure you're on the level?* □ *You can trust Sally. She's strictly on the level.*

**strike a balance (between two things)** to find a satisfactory compromise between two extremes. □ *The political party must strike a balance between the right wing and the left wing.* □ *Jane is overdressed for the party, and Sally is underdressed. What a pity they didn't strike a balance.*

**strike a chord (with someone)** to cause someone to remember something; to remind someone or something; to be familiar. □ *The woman in the portrait struck a chord with me, and I realized that it was my grandmother.* □ *His name strikes a chord, but I don't know why.*

**strike a happy medium** AND **hit a happy medium** to find a compromise position; to arrive at a position halfway between two unacceptable extremes. □ *Ann likes very spicy food, but Bob doesn't care for spicy food at all. We are trying to find a restaurant that strikes a happy medium.* □ *Tom is either very happy or very sad. He can't seem to hit a happy medium.*

**strike a match** to light a match. □ *Mary struck a match and lit a candle.* □ *When Sally struck a match to light a cigarette, Jane said quickly, "No smoking, please."*

**strike a sour note** AND **hit a sour note** to signify something unpleasant. □ *Jane's sad announcement struck a sour note at the annual banquet.* □ *News of the crime hit a sour note in our holiday celebration.*

**strike it rich** to acquire wealth suddenly. □ *If I could strike it rich, I wouldn't have to work anymore.* □ *Sally ordered a dozen oysters and found a huge pearl in one of them. She struck it rich!*

**strike someone funny** to seem funny to someone. □ *Sally has a great sense of humor. Everything she says strikes me funny.* □ *Why are you laughing? Did something I said strike you funny?*

**strike someone's fancy** to appeal to someone. □ *I'll have some ice cream, please. Chocolate strikes my fancy right now.* □ *Why don't you go to the store and buy a hat that strikes your fancy?*

**strike up a friendship** to become friends (with someone). □ *I struck up a friendship with John while we were on a business trip together.* □ *If you're lonely, you should go out and try to strike up a friendship with someone you like.*

**strike while the iron is hot** to do something at the best possible time, while there is an appropriate opportunity. (A cliché.) □ *He was in a good mood, so I asked for a loan of $200. I thought I'd better strike while the iron was hot.* □ *Please go to the bank and settle this matter now! They are willing to be reasonable. You've got to strike while the iron is hot.*

**stuff and nonsense** nonsense. □ *Come on! Don't give me all that stuff and nonsense!* □ *I don't understand this book. It's all stuff and nonsense as far as I am concerned.*

**stuff the ballot box** to put fraudulent ballots into a ballot box; to cheat in counting the votes in an election. □ *The election judge was caught stuffing the ballot box in the election yesterday.* □ *Election officials are supposed to guard against stuffing the ballot box.*

**stumbling block** something that prevents or obstructs progress. □ *We'd like to buy that house, but the high price is the stumbling block.* □ *Jim's lack of experience is a stumbling block to getting a job.*

**suit oneself** See *please oneself.*

**suit someone to a T** AND **fit someone to a T** to be very appropriate for someone. □ *This kind of job suits me to a T.* □ *This is Sally's kind of house. It fits her to a T.*

**swan song** the last work or performance of a playwright, musician, actor, etc., before death or retirement. □ *His portrayal of Lear was the actor's swan song.* □ *We didn't know that the singer's performance last night was her swan song.*

**sweep something under the carpet** AND **brush something under the carpet** to try to hide something unpleasant, shameful, etc., from the attention of others. □ *The boss said he couldn't sweep the theft under the carpet, that he'd have to call in the police.* □ *The headmaster tried to brush the children's truancy under the carpet, but the inspector wanted to investigate it.*

**sweet nothings** affectionate but unimportant or meaningless words spoken to a loved one. □ *Jack was whispering sweet nothings in Joan's ear when they were dancing.* □ *The two lovers sat in the cinema exchanging sweet nothings.*

**swim against the current** See swim against the tide.

**swim against the tide** AND **swim against the current** to do the opposite of what everyone else does; to go against the trend. □ *Bob tends to do what everybody else does. He isn't likely to swim against the tide.* □ *Mary always swims against the current. She's a very contrary person.*

**tag along** to go along with or follow someone, often when uninvited or unwanted. (Informal.) □ *Jean always tags along when Tim and Sally go out on a date.* □ *I took my children to the zoo, and the neighbor's children tagged along.*

the **tail wagging the dog** [a situation in which] a small part [is] controlling the whole thing. (Also with *be*, as in the examples.) □ *John was just hired yesterday, and today he's bossing everyone around. It's a case of the tail wagging the dog.* □ *Why is this small matter so important? Now the tail is wagging the dog!*

**take a back seat (to someone)** to defer to someone; to give control to someone. □ *I decided to take a back seat to Mary and let her manage the project.* □ *I had done the best I could, but it was time to take a back seat and let someone else run things.*

**take a leaf out of someone's book** to behave or to do something in the way that someone else would. (A *leaf* is a page.) □ *When you act like that, you're taking a leaf out of your sister's book, and I don't like it!* □ *You had better do it your way. Don't take a leaf out of my book. I don't do it well.*

**take a load off one's feet** See get a load off one's feet.

**take a nosedive** See go into a nosedive.

**take cold** See catch cold.

**take forty winks** to take a nap; to go to sleep. □ *I think I'll go to bed and take forty winks. See you in the morning.* □ *Why don't you go take forty winks and call me in about an hour?*

**take it or leave it** to accept something the way it is or not have it at all. □ *This is my last offer. Take it or leave it.* □ *It's not much, but it's the only food we have. You can take it or leave it.*

**take liberties with someone or something** AND **make free with someone or something** to use or abuse someone or something. □ *You are overly familiar with me, Mr. Jones. One might think you were taking liberties with me.* □ *I don't like it when you make free with my lawn mower. You should at least ask when you want to borrow it.*

**take one's cue from someone** to use someone else's behavior or reactions as a guide to one's own. (From the theatrical cue as a signal to speak, etc.) □ *If you don't know which cutlery to use at the dinner, just take your cue from John.* □ *The other children took their cue from Tommy and ignored the new boy.*

**take one's death (of cold)** See catch one's death (of cold).

**take one's medicine** to accept the punishment or the bad fortune that one deserves. (Also used literally.) □ *I know I did wrong, and I know I have to take my medicine.* □ *Billy knew he was going to get spanked, and he didn't want to take his medicine.*

**take someone or something at face value** to accept someone or something as actually being the way someone or something appears. (From the value printed on the "face" of a coin or currency.) □ *Don't just take her offer at face value. Think of the implications.* □ *Joan tends to take people at face value, so she is always getting hurt when they behave unexpectedly.*

**take someone or something by storm** to overwhelm someone or something; to attract a great deal of attention from someone or something. (A cliché.) □ *Jane is madly in love with Tom. He took her by storm at the office party, and they've been together ever since.* □ *The singer took the world of opera by storm with her performance in* Carmen.

**take someone or something for granted** to accept someone or something—without gratitude—as a matter of course. □ *We tend to take a lot of things for granted.* □ *Mrs. Franklin complained that Mr. Franklin takes her for granted.*

**take someone's breath away** to overwhelm someone with beauty or grandeur. □ *The magnificent painting took my breath away.* □ *Ann looked so beautiful that she took my breath away.*

**take someone under one's wing** to take over and care for a person. □ *John wasn't doing well in geometry until the teacher took him under her wing.* □ *I took the new workers under my wing, and they learned the job quickly.*

**take something in stride** to accept something as natural or expected. □ *The argument surprised him, but he took it in stride.* □ *It was a very rude remark, but Mary took it in stride.*

**take something lying down** to endure something unpleasant without fighting back. □ *He insulted me publicly. You don't expect me to take that lying down, do you?* □ *I'm not the kind of person who'll take something like that lying down.*

**take something on faith** to accept or believe something on the basis of little or no evidence. □ *Please try to believe what I'm telling you. Just take it on faith.* □ *Surely you can't expect me to take a story like that on faith.*

**take something on the chin** to experience and endure a direct blow or assault. □ *The bad news was a real shock, and John took it on the chin.* □ *The worst luck comes my way, and I always end up taking it on the chin.*

**take something with a grain of salt** See take something with a pinch of salt.

**take something with a pinch of salt** AND **take something with a grain of salt** to listen to a story or an explanation with considerable doubt. □ *You must take anything she says with a grain of salt. She doesn't always tell the truth.* □ *They took my explanation with a pinch of salt. I was sure they didn't believe me.*

**take the bitter with the sweet** to accept the bad things along with the good things. (A cliché.) □ *We all have disappointments. You have to learn to take the bitter with the sweet.* □ *There are good days and bad days, but every day you take the bitter with the sweet. That's life.*

**take the bull by the horns** to meet a challenge directly. (A cliché.) □ *If we are going to solve this problem, someone is going to have to take the bull by the horns.* □ *This threat isn't going to go away by itself. We are going to take the bull by the horns and settle this matter once and for all.*

**take the law into one's own hands** to attempt to administer the law; to act as a judge and jury for someone who has done something wrong. □ *Citizens don't have the right to take the law into their own hands.* □ *The shopkeeper took the law into his own hands when he tried to arrest the thief.*

**take the stand** to go to and sit in the witness chair on the witness stand in a courtroom. □ *I was in court all day, waiting to take the stand.* □ *The lawyer asked the witness to take the stand.*

**take the words (right) out of one's mouth** [for someone else] to say what one was about to say oneself. □ *John said exactly what I was going to say. He took the words out of my mouth.* □ *I agree with you, and I wanted to say the same thing. You took the words right out of my mouth.*

**take to one's heels** to run away. □ *The little boy said hello and then took to his heels.* □ *The robber took to his heels when he saw the police coming.*

**take up one's abode somewhere** to settle down and live somewhere. (Literary.) □ *I took up my abode downtown near my office.* □ *We decided to take up our abode in a warmer climate.*

**talk a blue streak** to say a lot and talk very rapidly. □ *Billy didn't talk until he was six, and then he started talking a blue streak.* □ *I can't understand anything Bob says. He talks a blue streak, and I can't follow his thinking.*

**talk in circles** to talk in a confusing or roundabout manner. □ *I couldn't understand a thing he said. All he did was talk in circles.* □ *We argued for a long time and finally decided that we were talking in circles.*

the **talk of the town** the subject of gossip; someone or something that everyone is talking about. □ *Joan's argument with the city council is the talk of the town.* □ *Fred's father is the talk of the town since the police arrested him.*

**talk shop** to talk about business matters at a social event (where business talk is out of place). □ *All right, everyone, we're not here to talk shop. Let's have a good time.* □ *Mary and Jane stood by the punch bowl, talking shop.*

**talk through one's hat** to talk nonsense; to brag and boast. □ *John isn't really as good as he says. He's just talking through his hat.* □ *Stop talking through your hat, and start being sincere!*

**talk until one is blue in the face** to talk until one is exhausted. □ *I talked until I was blue in the face, but I couldn't change her mind.* □ *She had to talk until she was blue in the face in order to convince him.*

**tall story** AND **tall tale** a story that is difficult or impossible to believe; a lie. □ *Jim's alibi sounds like a tall tale to me.* □ *To get a day off work,*

*Jack told a tall story about his grandmother dying. Both of his grandmothers are already dead.*

**tall tale** See tall story.

**tarred with the same brush** having the same faults or bad points as someone else. □ *Jack and his brother are tarred with the same brush. They're both crooks.* □ *The Smith children are tarred with the same brush. They're all lazy.*

**teach one's grandmother to suck eggs** to try to tell or show someone more knowledgeable or experienced than oneself how to do something. □ *Don't suggest showing Mary how to knit. It will be teaching your grandmother to suck eggs. She's an expert.* □ *Don't teach your grandmother to suck eggs. Jack has been playing tennis for years.*

**tear one's hair (out)** to be anxious, frustrated, or angry. □ *I was so nervous, I was about to tear my hair.* □ *I had better get home. My parents will be tearing their hair out.*

**teething troubles** difficulties and problems experienced in the early stages of a project, activity, etc. □ *There have been a lot of teething troubles with the new computer system.* □ *We have got over the teething troubles connected with the new building complex.*

**tell its own story** AND **tell its own tale** [for the state of something] to indicate clearly what has happened. □ *The upturned boat told its own tale. The oarsman had drowned.* □ *The girl's tear-stained face told its own story.*

**tell its own tale** See tell its own story.

**tell one to one's face** to tell (something) to someone directly. □ *I'm sorry that Sally feels that way about me. I wish she had told me to my face.* □ *I won't tell Tom that you're mad at him. You should tell him to his face.*

**tell tales out of school** to tell secrets or spread rumors. □ *I wish that John would keep quiet. He's telling tales out of school again.* □ *If you tell tales out of school a lot, people won't ever trust you.*

**a tempest in a teapot** an uproar about practically nothing. (A cliché.) □ *This isn't a serious problem—just a tempest in a teapot.* □ *Even a tempest in a teapot can take a lot of time to get settled.*

**thankful for small blessings** grateful for any benefits or advantages one has, especially in a generally difficult situation. □ *We have very little money, but we must be grateful for small blessings. At least we have enough food.* □ *Bob was badly injured in the accident, but at least he's still alive. Let's be thankful for small blessings.*

**thank one's lucky stars** to be thankful for one's luck. (A cliché.) □ *You can thank your lucky stars that I was there to help you.* □ *I thank my lucky stars that I studied the right things for the test.*

**That's the last straw.** AND **That's the straw that broke the camel's back.** That is the final difficulty or problem that makes the burden too great or that makes the task too difficult, because many problems or difficulties have already preceded it. (A cliché. As if one were loading a camel's back with straw, and one final straw makes the weight too heavy.) □ *Now it's raining! That's the last straw. The picnic is canceled!* □ *When Sally became sick, that was the straw that broke the camel's back.*

**That's the straw that broke the camel's back.** See That's the last straw.

**That's the ticket.** That is exactly what is needed. (A cliché.) □ *That's the ticket, John. You're doing it just the way it should be done.* □ *That's the ticket! I knew you could do it.*

**That takes care of that.** That is settled. (A cliché.) □ *That takes care of that, and I'm glad it's over.* □ *I spent all morning dealing with this matter, and that takes care of that.*

**There are plenty of other fish in the sea.** There are many other choices. (A cliché. Used to refer to persons.) □ *When John broke up with Ann, I told her not to worry. There are plenty of other fish in the sea.* □ *It's too bad that your secretary quit, but there are plenty of other fish in the sea.*

**There's more than one way to skin a cat.** a proverb meaning that there is more than one way to do something. □ *If that approach won't work, try another. There's more than one way to skin a cat.* □ *Don't worry, I'll figure out a way to get it done. There's more than one way to skin a cat.*

**There's no accounting for taste.** a proverb meaning that there is no explanation for people's preferences. (Usually said about something that one personally dislikes or believes to reflect bad taste.) □ *Look at that purple and orange car! There's no accounting for taste.* □ *Some people* seemed to like the music, although I thought it was worse than noise. *There's no accounting for taste.*

**There will be the devil to pay.** There will be lots of trouble. □ *If you damage my car, there will be the devil to pay.* □ *Bill broke a window, and now there will be the devil to pay.*

**thick and fast** in large numbers or amounts and at a rapid rate. □ *The enemy soldiers came thick and fast.* □ *New problems seem to come thick and fast.*

**thick-skinned** not easily upset or hurt; insensitive to offense. (The opposite of thin-skinned.) □ *Tom won't worry about your insults. He's completely thick-skinned.* □ *Jane's so thick-skinned she didn't realize Fred was being rude to her.*

**think better of something** to reconsider something; to think again and decide not to do something. □ *Jack was going to escape, but he thought better of it.* □ *Jill had planned to resign but thought better of it.*

**think on one's feet** to think while one is talking. □ *If you want to be a successful teacher, you must be able to think on your feet.* □ *I have to write out everything I'm going to say, because I can't think on my feet very well.*

**think the world of someone or something** to be very fond of someone or something. □ *Mary thinks the world of her little sister.* □ *The old lady thinks the world of her cats.*

**thin on top** balding. (Informal.) □ *James is wearing a hat because he's getting thin on top.* □ *Father got a little thin on top as he got older.*

**thin-skinned** easily upset or hurt; sensitive. (The opposite of thick-skinned.) □ *You'll have to handle Mary's mother carefully. She's very thin-skinned.* □ *Jane weeps easily when people tease her. She's too thin-skinned.*

**thrash something out** to discuss something thoroughly and solve any problems. □ *The committee took hours to thrash the whole matter out.* Ⓣ *Fred and Ann thrashed out the reasons for their constant disagreements.*

**through thick and thin** through good times and bad times. (A cliché.) □ *We've been together through thick and thin, and we won't desert each other now.* □ *Over the years, we went through thick and thin and enjoyed every minute of it.*

**throw a monkey wrench in the works** to cause problems for someone's plans. □ *I don't want to throw a monkey wrench in the works, but have you checked your plans with a lawyer?* □ *When John refused to help us, he really threw a monkey wrench in the works.*

**throw caution to the wind** to become very careless. (A cliché.) □ *Jane, who is usually very cautious, threw caution to the wind and went surfing.* □ *I don't mind taking a little chance now and then, but I'm not the type of person who throws caution to the wind.*

**throw cold water on something** See pour cold water on something.

**throw down the gauntlet** to challenge (someone) to an argument or (figurative) combat. □ *When Bob challenged my conclusions, he threw down the gauntlet. I was ready for an argument.* □ *Frowning at Bob is the same as throwing down the gauntlet. He loves to get into a fight about anything.*

**throw good money after bad** to waste additional money after wasting money once. (A cliché.) □ *I bought a used car and then had to spend $300 on repairs. That was throwing good money after bad.* □ *The Browns are always throwing good money after bad. They bought an acre of land that turned out to be swamp, and then had to pay to have it filled in.*

**throw in the sponge** See throw in the towel.

**throw in the towel** AND **throw in the sponge** to quit (doing something). □ *When John could stand no more of Mary's bad temper, he threw in the towel and left.* □ *Don't give up now! It's too soon to throw in the sponge.*

**throw oneself at someone's feet** to bow down humbly at someone's feet. □ *Do I have to throw myself at your feet in order to convince you that I'm sorry?* □ *I love you sincerely, Jane. I'll throw myself at your feet and await your command. I'm your slave!*

**throw oneself at the mercy of the court** See throw oneself on the mercy of the court.

**throw oneself on the mercy of the court** AND **throw oneself at the mercy of the court** to plead for mercy from a judge in a courtroom. □ *Your Honor, please believe me, I didn't do it on purpose. I throw myself on the mercy of the court and beg for a light sentence.* □ *Jane threw herself at the mercy of the court and hoped for the best.*

**throw someone a curve** AND **pitch someone a curve 1.** to pitch a curve ball to someone in baseball. □ *The pitcher threw John a curve, and John swung wildly against thin air.* □ *During that game, the pitcher pitched everyone a curve at least once.* **2.** to confuse someone by doing something unexpected. □ *When you said "house," you threw me a curve. The password was supposed to be "home."* □ *John pitched me a curve when we were making our presentation, and I forgot my speech.*

**throw someone for a loop** AND **knock someone for a loop** to confuse or shock someone. □ *When Bill heard the news, it threw him for a loop.* □ *The manager knocked Bob for a loop by firing him right then.*

**throw someone to the wolves** to sacrifice someone to something or some fate. (A cliché.) □ *The press was demanding an explanation, so the mayor blamed the mess on John and threw him to the wolves.* □ *I wouldn't let them throw me to the wolves! I did nothing wrong, and I won't take the blame for their errors.*

**throw something into the bargain** to include something in a deal. □ *To encourage me to buy a new car, the car dealer threw a free radio into the bargain.* □ *If you purchase three pounds of chocolates, I'll throw one pound of salted nuts into the bargain.*

**thumb a ride** AND **hitch a ride** to get a ride from a passing motorist; to hitchhike; to make a sign with one's thumb that indicates to passing drivers that one is begging for a ride. □ *My car broke down on the highway, and I had to thumb a ride to get back to town.* □ *Sometimes it's dangerous to hitch a ride with a stranger.*

**thumb one's nose at someone or something** to (figuratively or literally) make a rude gesture of disgust with one's thumb and nose at someone or something. □ *The boy thumbed his nose at the lady and walked away.* □ *You can't just thumb your nose at people who give you trouble. You've got to learn to get along.*

**tickle someone's fancy** to interest someone; to make someone curious. □ *I have an interesting problem here that I think will tickle your fancy.* □ *This doesn't tickle my fancy at all. This is dull and boring.*

**tied to one's mother's apron strings** dominated by one's mother; dependent on one's mother. □ *Tom is still tied to his mother's apron strings.* □ *Isn't he a little old to be tied to his mother's apron strings?*

**tie someone in knots** to make someone anxious or upset. □ *John tied himself in knots worrying about his wife during the operation.* □ *This waiting and worrying really ties me in knots.*

**tie someone's hands** to prevent someone from doing something. (See also have one's hands tied.) □ *I'd like to help you, but my boss has tied my hands.* □ *Please don't tie my hands with unnecessary restrictions. I'd like the freedom to do whatever is necessary.*

**tie the knot** to get married. □ *Well, I hear that you and John are going to tie the knot.* □ *My parents tied the knot almost forty years ago.*

**tighten one's belt** to manage to spend less money. □ *Things are beginning to cost more and more. It looks like we'll all have to tighten our belts.* □ *Times are hard, and prices are high. I can tighten my belt for only so long.*

**tilt at windmills** to fight battles with imaginary enemies; to fight against unimportant enemies or issues. (As with the fictional character Don Quixote, who attacked windmills, imagining them to be enemies.) □ *Aren't you too smart to go around tilting at windmills?* □ *I'm not going to fight this issue. I've wasted too much of my life tilting at windmills.*

**time flies** time passes very quickly. (From the Latin *tempus fugit.*) □ *I didn't really think it was so late when the party ended. Doesn't time fly?* □ *Time simply flew when the old friends got together.*

**Time hangs heavy on someone's hands.** a phrase meaning that time seems to go slowly when one has nothing to do. □ *I don't like it when time hangs heavy on my hands.* □ *John looks so bored. Time hangs heavy on his hands.*

**Time is money.** a proverb meaning that time is valuable and shouldn't be wasted. □ *I can't afford to spend a lot of time standing here talking. Time is money, you know!* □ *People who keep saying time is money may be working too hard.*

**time was (when)** there was a time when; at a time in the past. □ *Time was when old people were taken care of at home.* □ *Time was when people didn't travel around so much.*

**tip the scales at something** to weigh some amount. □ *Tom tips the scales at nearly 200 pounds.* □ *I'll be glad when I tip the scales at a few pounds less.*

**toe the line** See toe the mark.

**toe the mark** AND **toe the line** to do what one is expected to do; to follow the rules. □ *You'll get ahead, Sally. Don't worry. Just toe the mark, and everything will be okay.* □ *John finally got fired. He just couldn't learn to toe the line.*

**tongue-in-cheek** insincere; joking. □ *Ann made a tongue-in-cheek remark to John, and he got mad because he thought she was serious.* □ *The play seemed very serious at first, but then everyone saw that it was tongue-in-cheek, and the audience began laughing.*

**too good to be true** almost unbelievable; so good as to be unbelievable. (A cliché.) □ *The news was too good to be true.* □ *When I finally got a big raise, it was too good to be true.*

**Too many cooks spoil the broth.** See Too many cooks spoil the stew.

**Too many cooks spoil the stew.** AND **Too many cooks spoil the broth.** a proverb meaning that too many people trying to manage something simply spoil it. □ *Let's decide who is in charge around here. Too many cooks spoil the stew.* □ *Everyone is giving orders, but no one is following them! Too many cooks spoil the broth.*

**to one's heart's content** as much as one wants. □ *John wanted a week's vacation so he could go to the lake and fish to his heart's content.* □ *I just sat there, eating chocolate to my heart's content.*

**toot one's own horn** AND **blow one's own horn** to boast or praise oneself. □ *Tom is always tooting his own horn. Is he really as good as he says he is?* □ *I find it hard to blow my own horn because I'm shy.*

**toss one's hat into the ring** to state that one is running for an elective office. □ *Jane wanted to run for treasurer, so she tossed her hat into the ring.* □ *The mayor never tossed his hat into the ring. Instead, he announced his retirement.*

**to the ends of the earth** everywhere possible, even to the remotest and most inaccessible points on the earth. □ *I'll pursue him to the ends of the earth.* □ *We've almost explored the whole world. We've traveled to the ends of the earth trying to learn about our world.*

**To the victor belong the spoils.** a proverb meaning that the winner achieves power over people and property. □ *The new mayor took office and immediately fired many workers and hired new ones. Everyone said, "To the victor belong the spoils."* □ *The office of president includes the* *right to live in the White House and at Camp David. To the victor belong the spoils.*

**touch someone for something** to ask someone for a loan of something, usually a sum of money. (Informal.) □ *Fred's always trying to touch people for money.* □ *Jack touched John for ten dollars.*

a **tough act to follow** a presentation or performance of such high quality that one will have difficulty maintaining the same standard of quality when one follows it with one's own presentation or performance. (A cliché.) □ *Bill's speech was excellent. It was a tough act to follow, but my speech was good also.* □ *Although I had a tough act to follow, I did my best.*

a **tough row to hoe** a difficult task to undertake. (A cliché.) □ *It was a tough row to hoe, but I finally got a college degree.* □ *Getting the contract signed is going to be a tough row to hoe, but I'm sure I can do it.*

a **tower of strength** a person who can always be depended on to provide support and encouragement, especially in times of trouble. □ *Mary was a tower of strength when Jean was in the hospital. She looked after her whole family.* □ *Jack was a tower of strength during the time that his father was unemployed.*

**tread on someone's toes** See step on someone's toes.

**trot something out** to mention something regularly or habitually, without giving it much thought. (Informal.) □ *When James disagreed with Mary, she simply trotted her same old political arguments out.* T *Jack always trots out the same excuses for being late.*

**true to one's word** keeping one's promise. □ *True to his word, Tom showed up at exactly eight o'clock.* □ *We'll soon know if Jane is true to her word. We'll see if she does what she promised.*

**try one's wings (out)** to try to do something one has recently become qualified to do. (As a young bird uses its wings to try to fly.) T *John just got his driver's license and wants to borrow the car to try out his wings.* □ *I learned to skin-dive, and I want to go to the seaside to try my wings.* □ *You've read about it enough. It's time to try your wings out.*

**try someone's patience** to do something annoying that may cause someone to lose patience; to cause someone to be annoyed. □ *Stop whistling. You're trying my patience. Very soon I'm going to lose my temper.* □ *Some students think it's fun to try the teacher's patience.*

**turn a blind eye to someone or something** to ignore something and pretend one does not see it. □ *The usher turned a blind eye to the little boy who sneaked into the theater.* □ *How can you turn a blind eye to all those starving children?*

**turn a deaf ear (to something)** to ignore what someone says; to ignore a cry for help. □ *How can you just turn a deaf ear to their cries for food and shelter?* □ *The government has turned a deaf ear.*

**turn on a dime** to turn in a very tight turn. □ *This car handles very well. It can turn on a dime.* □ *The speeding car turned on a dime and headed in the other direction.*

**turn one's nose up at someone or something** to sneer at someone or something; to reject someone or something. □ *John turned his nose up at Ann, and that hurt her feelings.* ⊤ *I never turn up my nose at dessert, no matter what it is.*

**turn over a new leaf** to start again with the intention of doing better; to begin again, ignoring past errors. (A cliché.) □ *Tom promised to turn over a new leaf and do better from then on.* □ *After a minor accident, Sally decided to turn over a new leaf and drive more carefully.*

**turn over in one's grave** [for a dead person] to be shocked or horrified. (A cliché.) □ *If Beethoven heard Mary play one of his sonatas, he'd turn over in his grave.* □ *If Aunt Jane knew what you were doing with her old china, she would turn over in her grave.*

**turn someone's head** to make someone conceited. □ *John's compliments really turned Sally's head.* □ *Victory in the competition is bound to turn Tom's head. He'll think he's too good for us.*

**turn someone's stomach** to make someone (figuratively or literally) ill. □ *This milk is spoiled. The smell of it turns my stomach.* □ *The play was so bad that it turned my stomach.*

**turn something to good account** to use something in such a way that it is to one's advantage; to make good use of a situation, experience, etc. □ *Pam turned her illness to good account and did a lot of reading.* □ *Many people turn their retirement to good account and take up interesting hobbies.*

**turn something to one's advantage** to make an advantage for oneself out of something that might otherwise be a disadvantage. □ *Sally* *found a way to turn the problem to her advantage.* □ *The ice-cream store manager was able to turn the hot weather to her advantage.*

**turn the other cheek** to choose not to respond to abuse or to an insult. (Biblical.) □ *When Bob got mad at Mary and yelled at her, she just turned the other cheek.* □ *Usually I turn the other cheek when someone is rude to me.*

**turn the tide** to cause a reversal in the direction of events; to cause a reversal in public opinion. □ *It looked as if the team would lose, but near the end of the game, our star player turned the tide.* □ *At first, people were opposed to our plan. After a lot of discussion, we were able to turn the tide.*

**twiddle one's thumbs** to fill up time by playing with one's fingers. □ *What am I supposed to do while waiting for you? Sit here and twiddle my thumbs?* □ *Don't sit around twiddling your thumbs. Get busy!*

**twist someone around one's little finger** to manipulate and control someone. (A cliché.) □ *Bob really fell for Jane. She can twist him around her little finger.* □ *Billy's mother has twisted him around her little finger. He's very dependent on her.*

**twist someone's arm** to force or persuade someone. □ *At first she refused, but after I twisted her arm a little, she agreed to help.* □ *I didn't want to run for mayor, but everyone twisted my arm.*

**two of a kind** people or things that are the same type or similar in character, attitude, etc. □ *Jack and Tom are two of a kind. They're both ambitious.* □ *The companies are two of a kind. They both pay their employees poorly.*

**Two's company(, three's a crowd).** a saying meaning that two people want to be alone and a third person would be in the way. □ *Two's company. I'm sure Tom and Jill won't want his sister to go to the cinema with them.* □ *John has been invited to join Jane and Peter on their picnic, but he says, "Two's company, three's a crowd."*

**under a cloud (of suspicion)** to be suspected of something. □ *Someone stole some money at work, and now everyone is under a cloud of suspicion.* □ *Even the manager is under a cloud.*

**under construction** in the process of being built or repaired. □ *We cannot travel on this road because it's under construction.* □ *Our new home has been under construction all summer. We hope to move in next month.*

**under fire** during an attack. □ *There was a scandal in city hall, and the mayor was forced to resign under fire.* □ *John is a good lawyer because he can think under fire.*

**under one's own steam** by one's own power or effort. □ *I missed my ride to class, so I had to get there under my own steam.* □ *John will need some help with this project. He can't do it under his own steam.*

**under someone's (very) nose** AND **right under someone's nose**
**1.** right in front of someone. □ *I thought I'd lost my purse, but it was sitting on the table under my very nose.* □ *How did Mary fail to see the book? It was right under her nose.* **2.** in someone's presence. □ *The thief stole Jim's wallet right under his nose.* □ *The jewels were stolen from under the very noses of the security guards.*

**under the counter** [for something to be bought or sold] secretly or illegally. □ *The drugstore owner was arrested for selling liquor under the counter.* □ *This owner was also selling dirty books under the counter.*

**under the table** in secret, as with the giving of a bribe; illegally. □ *The mayor had been paying money to the construction company under the table.* □ *Tom transferred the property to his wife under the table.*

**under the weather** ill. □ *I'm a bit under the weather today, so I can't go to the office.* □ *My head is aching, and I feel a little under the weather.*

**under the wire** just barely in time or on time. □ *I turned in my report just under the wire.* □ *Bill was the last person to get in the door. He got in under the wire.*

**up a blind alley** at a dead end; on a route that leads nowhere. □ *I have been trying to find out something about my ancestors, but I'm up a blind alley. I can't find anything.* □ *The police are up a blind alley in their investigation of the crime.*

**up in arms** rising up in anger, as if armed with weapons. □ *My father was really up in arms when he got his tax bill this year.* □ *The citizens were up in arms, pounding on the gates of the palace, demanding justice.*

**up in the air** undecided; uncertain. □ *I don't know what Sally plans to do. Things were sort of up in the air the last time we talked.* □ *Let's leave this question up in the air until next week.*

the **upper crust** the higher levels of society; the upper class. (Informal. From the top, as opposed to the bottom, crust of a pie.) □ *Jane speaks like that because she pretends to be from the upper crust, but her father was a miner.* □ *James is from the upper crust, but he is penniless.*

**upset the applecart** to ruin or make a mess of a situation. □ *Tom really upset the applecart by telling Mary the truth about Jane. Now their friendship is over.* □ *I always knew he'd upset the applecart somehow.*

**up to one's ears (in something)** See up to one's neck (in something).

**up to one's neck (in something)** AND **up to one's ears (in something)** very much involved in something. □ *I can't come to the meeting. I'm up to my neck in these reports.* □ *Mary is up to her ears in her work.*

**up to par** as good as the standard or average; up to the standard. □ *I'm just not feeling up to par today. I must be coming down with something.* □ *The manager said that the report was not up to par and gave it back to Mary to do over again.*

**use every trick in the book** to use every method possible. □ *I used every trick in the book, but I still couldn't manage to get a ticket to the game Saturday.* □ *Bob used every trick in the book, but he still failed.*

**vanish into thin air** to disappear without leaving a trace. □ *My money gets spent so fast. It seems to vanish into thin air.* □ *When I came back, my car was gone. I had locked it, but it had vanished into thin air!*

**Variety is the spice of life.** a proverb meaning that differences and changes make life interesting. □ *Mary reads all kinds of books. She says variety is the spice of life.* □ *The Franklins travel all over the world so they can learn how different people live. After all, variety is the spice of life.*

**vent one's spleen** to get rid of one's feelings of anger by attacking someone or something. □ *Jack vented his spleen at not getting the job by shouting at his wife.* □ *Peter kicked his car to vent his spleen after losing the race.*

the **very thing** the exact thing that is required. □ *The vacuum cleaner is the very thing for cleaning the stairs.* □ *I have the very thing to remove that stain.*

**villain of the piece** someone or something that is responsible for something bad or wrong. □ *I wonder who told the newspapers about the local scandal. I discovered that Joan was the villain of the piece.* □ *We couldn't think who had stolen the meat. The dog next door turned out to be the villain of the piece.*

**vote a straight ticket** to cast a ballot on which all the votes are for members of the same political party. □ *I'm not a member of any political party, so I never vote a straight ticket.* □ *I usually vote a straight ticket because I believe in the principles of one party and not in the other's.*

**vote of confidence 1.** a poll taken to discover whether or not a person, party, etc., still has the majority's support. □ *The government easily won the vote of confidence called for by the opposition.* □ *The president of the club resigned when one of the members called for a vote of confidence in his leadership.* **2.** an expression of confidence in someone or something; an expression of support for someone or something. □ *My boss said I was doing a great job, and I thanked him for the vote of confidence.* □ *The audience applauded, and that vote of confidence encouraged the lecturer.*

**vote of thanks** a speech expressing appreciation and thanks to a speaker, lecturer, organizer, etc., and inviting the audience to applaud. □ *John gave a vote of thanks to Professor Jones for his talk.* □ *Mary was given a vote of thanks for organizing the dance.*

**wait-and-see attitude** a skeptical attitude; an uncertain attitude where someone will wait to see what happens before reacting. □ *John thought that Mary couldn't do it, but he took a wait-and-see attitude.* □ *His wait-and-see attitude didn't influence me at all.*

**waiting in the wings** ready or prepared to do something, especially to take over someone else's job or position. (As an actor waits at the side of the stage to make an entrance.) □ *Mr. Smith retires as manager next year, and Mr. Jones is just waiting in the wings.* □ *Jane was waiting in the wings, hoping that a member of the hockey team would drop out and she would get a place on the team.*

**wait on someone hand and foot** to serve someone very well, attending to all personal needs. □ *I don't mind bringing you your coffee, but I don't intend to wait on you hand and foot.* □ *I don't want anyone to wait on me hand and foot. I can take care of myself.*

**walk a tightrope** to be in a situation where one must be very cautious. □ *I've been walking a tightrope all day. I need to relax.* □ *Our business is about to fail. We've been walking a tightrope for three months.*

**walk away with something** AND **walk off with something 1.** to steal something. □ *Did you see that kid walk away with that candy bar?* □ *A shoplifter just walked off with a $30 necktie.* **2.** to win something easily. □ *The other team walked away with the game.* □ *The home team walked off with the win.*

**walk off with something** See walk away with something.

**walk on air** to be very happy; to be euphoric. □ *Ann was walking on air when she got the job.* □ *On the last day of school, all the children are walking on air.*

**walk on eggs** to be very cautious. □ *The manager is very hard to deal with. You really have to walk on eggs.* □ *I've been walking on eggs ever since I started working here.*

**walk the floor** to pace nervously while waiting. □ *While Bill waited for news of the operation, he walked the floor for hours on end.* □ *Walking the floor won't help. You might as well sit down and relax.*

**Walls have ears.** We may be overheard. (A cliché.) □ *Let's not discuss this matter here. Walls have ears, you know.* □ *Shhh. Walls have ears. Someone may be listening.*

**want for nothing** to lack nothing; to have everything one needs or desires. □ *The Smiths don't have much money, but their children seem to want for nothing.* □ *Jean's husband spoils her. She wants for nothing.*

**warm the bench** [for a player] to remain out of play during a game— seated on a bench. □ *John spent the whole game warming the bench.* □ *Mary never warms the bench. She plays from the beginning to the end.*

**warm the cockles of someone's heart** to make someone warm and happy. (A cliché.) □ *It warms the cockles of my heart to hear you say that.* □ *Hearing that old song again warmed the cockles of her heart.*

**warts and all** including all faults and disadvantages. □ *Jim has many faults, but Jean loves him, warts and all.* □ *The place where we went on vacation had some very run-down parts, but we liked it warts and all.*

**wash one's dirty linen in public** to discuss one's personal problems in public. (See also air one's dirty linen in public.) □ *Jim is always telling us about his quarrels with his wife. I wish he wouldn't wash his dirty linen in public.* □ *Jean will talk to anyone about her financial problems. Why does she wash her dirty linen in public?*

**wash one's hands of someone or something** to end one's association with someone or something. □ *I washed my hands of Tom. I wanted no more to do with him.* □ *That car was a real headache. I washed my hands of it long ago.*

**Waste not, want not.** a saying meaning that if one never wastes anything, one will never be short of anything. □ *Bob always saves the used string from parcels. "Waste not, want not," he says.* □ *Mary always reuses envelopes. We think she's cheap, but she says that it's a case of waste not, want not.*

**waste one's breath** to waste one's time talking; to talk in vain. □ *Don't waste your breath talking to her. She won't listen.* □ *You can't persuade me. You're just wasting your breath.*

A **watched pot never boils.** a proverb meaning that if you are waiting for something to happen, concentrating on it will not make it happen any sooner. (Refers to the seemingly long time it takes water to boil when you are waiting for it. Said about a problem that a person is watching very closely.) □ *John was looking out the window, waiting eagerly for the mail to be delivered. Ann said, "Be patient. A watched pot never boils."* □ *Billy weighed himself four times a day while he was trying to lose weight. His mother said, "Relax. A watched pot never boils."*

**watch one's step** to act with care and caution so as not to make a mistake or offend someone. □ *John had better watch his step with the new boss. She won't put up with his lateness.* □ *Mary was told by her adviser to watch her step and stop missing classes, or she would be asked to leave the college.*

**watch someone like a hawk** to watch someone very carefully. □ *The teacher watched the pupils like a hawk to make sure they did not cheat on the exam.* □ *We had to watch our dog like a hawk in case he ran away.*

**water under the bridge** past and forgotten. (A cliché.) □ *Please don't worry about it anymore. It's all water under the bridge.* □ *I can't change the past. It's water under the bridge.*

**wear more than one hat** to have more than one set of responsibilities; to hold more than one office. □ *The mayor is also the police chief. She wears more than one hat.* □ *I have too much to do to wear more than one hat.*

**wear off** to become less; to stop gradually. □ *The effects of the painkiller wore off, and my tooth began to hurt.* □ *I was annoyed at first, but my anger wore off.*

**wear out one's welcome** to stay too long (at an event to which one has been invited); to visit somewhere too often. (A cliché.) □ *Tom visited the Smiths so often that he wore out his welcome.* □ *At about midnight, I decided that I had worn out my welcome, so I went home.*

**weed someone or something out** to remove someone or something unwanted or undesirable from a group or collection. □ *I'm going through my books to weed those out that I don't read anymore.* Ⓣ *The auditions were held to weed out the actors with least ability.*

**well-fixed** See well-heeled.

**well-heeled** AND **well-fixed; well-off** wealthy; having a sufficient amount of money. □ *My uncle can afford a new car. He's well-heeled.* □ *Everyone in his family is well-off.*

**well-off** See well-heeled.

**well-to-do** wealthy and of good social position. (Often with *quite*, as in the examples.) □ *The Jones family is quite well-to-do.* □ *There is a gentleman waiting for you at the door. He appears quite well-to-do.*

**wet behind the ears** young and inexperienced. □ *John's too young to take on a job like this! He's still wet behind the ears!* □ *He may be wet behind the ears, but he's well trained and totally competent.*

a **wet blanket** a dull or depressing person who spoils other people's enjoyment. □ *Jack is fun at parties, but his brother is a wet blanket.* □ *I was with Ann, and she was being a real wet blanket.*

**What about (doing) something?** Would you like to do something? □ *What about going on a picnic?* □ *What about a picnic?*

**What about (having) something?** Would you like to have something? □ *What about having another drink?* □ *What about another drink?*

**What is sauce for the goose is sauce for the gander.** a proverb meaning that what is appropriate for one is appropriate for the other. □ *If John gets a new coat, I should get one, too. After all, what is sauce for the goose is sauce for the gander.* □ *If I get punished for breaking the window, so should Mary. What is sauce for the goose is sauce for the gander.*

**what makes someone tick** that which motivates someone; that which makes someone behave in a certain way. □ *William is sort of strange. I don't know what makes him tick.* □ *When you get to know people, you find out what makes them tick.*

**When in Rome, do as the Romans do.** a proverb meaning that one should behave however the people around one are behaving. □ *I don't usually eat lamb, but I did when I went to Australia. When in Rome, do as the Romans do.* □ *I always carry an umbrella when I visit London. When in Rome, do as the Romans do.*

**When the cat's away, the mice will play.** a proverb meaning some people will get into mischief when they are not being watched. (A cliché.) □ *The students behaved very badly for the substitute teacher. When the cat's away, the mice will play.* □ *John had a wild party at his* house when his parents were out of town. *When the cat's away, the mice will play.*

**when the time is ripe** at exactly the right time. □ *I'll tell her the good news when the time is ripe.* □ *When the time is ripe, I'll bring up the subject again.*

**Where there's a will, there's a way.** a proverb meaning that one can do something if one really wants to. □ *Don't give up, Ann. You can do it. Where there's a will, there's a way.* □ *They told John he'd never walk again after his accident. He worked at it, and he was able to walk again! Where there's a will, there's a way.*

**Where there's smoke, there's fire.** a proverb meaning that some evidence of a problem probably indicates that there really is a problem. □ *There is a lot of noise coming from the classroom. There is probably something wrong. Where there's smoke, there's fire.* □ *I think there is something wrong at the house on the corner. The police are there again. Where there's smoke, there's fire.*

**whistle for something** to expect or look for something with no hope of getting it. (Informal.) □ *I'm afraid you'll have to whistle for it if you want to borrow money. I don't have any.* □ *Jane's father told her to whistle for it when she asked him to buy her a car.*

**white elephant** something that is useless and either is a nuisance or is expensive to keep up. (From the gift of a white elephant by the kings of Siam to courtiers who displeased them. The kings knew the cost of the upkeep would ruin the courtiers.) □ *Bob's father-in-law has given him an old Rolls Royce, but it's a real white elephant. He has no place to park it and can't afford the gas for it.* □ *Those antique vases Aunt Mary gave me are white elephants. They're ugly and take ages to clean.*

**whole shooting match** the entire affair or organization. □ *John's not a good manager. Instead of delegating jobs to others, he runs the whole shooting match himself.* □ *There's not a hard worker in that whole shooting match.*

**whoop it up** to enjoy oneself in a lively and noisy manner. (Informal.) □ *John's friends really whooped it up at his bachelor party.* □ *Jean wants to have a party and whoop it up to celebrate her promotion.*

**the whys and wherefores of something** the reasons or causes relating to something. □ *I refuse to discuss the whys and wherefores of my decision. It's final.* □ *Bob doesn't know the whys and wherefores of his con-*

tract. *He just knows that it means he will get a lot of money when he finishes the work.*

**wide of the mark 1.** far from the target. □ *Tom's shot was wide of the mark.* □ *The pitch was quite fast but wide of the mark.* **2.** inadequate; far from what is required or expected. □ *Jane's efforts were sincere but wide of the mark.* □ *He failed the course because everything he did was wide of the mark.*

**wild-goose chase** a worthless hunt or chase; a futile pursuit. □ *I wasted all afternoon on a wild-goose chase.* □ *John was angry because he was sent out on a wild-goose chase.*

**win by a nose** to win by the slightest amount of difference. (As in a horse race where one horse wins with only its nose ahead of the horse that comes in second.) □ *I ran the fastest race I could, but I only won by a nose.* □ *Sally won the race, but she only won by a nose.*

**window-shopping** the habit or practice of looking at goods in shop windows or stores without actually buying anything. □ *The women do a lot of window-shopping during their lunch hour, looking for things to buy when they get paid.* □ *Joan said she was just window-shopping, but she bought a new coat.*

**win someone over** to succeed in gaining the support and sympathy of someone. □ *Jane's parents disapproved of her engagement at first, but she won them over.* □ *I'm trying to win the boss over and get him to give us the day off.*

**wishful thinking** believing that something is true or that something will happen just because one wishes that it were true or would happen. □ *Hoping for a car as a birthday present is just wishful thinking. Your parents can't afford it.* □ *Mary thinks that she is going to get a big raise, but that's wishful thinking. Her boss is so mean.*

**with all one's heart and soul** very sincerely. (A cliché.) □ *Oh, Bill, I love you with all my heart and soul, and I always will!* □ *She thanked us with all her heart and soul for the gift.*

**with a will** with determination and enthusiasm. □ *The children worked with a will to finish the project on time.* □ *The workers set about manufacturing the new products with a will.*

**with both hands tied behind one's back** See with one hand tied behind one's back.

**wither on the vine** AND **die on the vine** [for something] to decline or fade away at an early stage of development. □ *You have a great plan, Tom. Let's keep it alive. Don't let it wither on the vine.* □ *The whole project died on the vine when the director lost interest.*

**with every (other) breath** [saying something] repeatedly or continually. □ *Bob was out in the yard, raking leaves and cursing with every other breath.* □ *The child was so grateful that she was thanking me with every breath.*

**with flying colors** easily and excellently. □ *John passed his geometry test with flying colors.* □ *Sally qualified for the race with flying colors.*

**within an inch of one's life** very close to taking one's life; almost to death. (A cliché.) □ *The accident frightened me within an inch of my life.* □ *When Mary was seriously ill in the hospital, she came within an inch of her life.*

**with it** (Informal.) **1.** up-to-date; fashionable. □ *Bob thinks he's with it, but he's wearing clothes from the 1960s.* □ *Mary's mother embarrasses her by trying to be with it. She wears clothes that are too young for her.* **2.** able to think clearly; able to understand things. □ *Jean's mother is not really with it anymore. She's becoming senile.* □ *Peter's not with it yet. He's only just woken up from the anesthetic.*

**with no strings attached** AND **without any strings attached** unconditionally; with no obligations. □ *My parents gave me a computer without any strings attached.* □ *I want this only if there are no strings attached.*

**with one hand tied behind one's back** AND **with both hands tied behind one's back** under a handicap; easily. (A cliché.) □ *I could put an end to this argument with one hand tied behind my back.* □ *John could do this job with both hands tied behind his back.*

**without any strings attached** See with no strings attached.

**without batting an eye** without showing alarm or response; without blinking an eye. (A cliché.) □ *I knew I had insulted her, but I was surprised when, without batting an eye, she turned to me and asked me to leave.* □ *Right in the middle of the speech—without batting an eye—the speaker walked off the stage.*

**without further ado** without further talk. (A cliché. An overworked phrase usually heard in public announcements.) □ *And without further* *ado, I would like to introduce Mr. Bill Franklin!* □ *The time has come to leave, so without further ado, good evening and good-bye.*

**with the best will in the world** however much one wishes to do something; however hard one tries to do something. □ *With the best will in the world, Jack won't be able to help Mary get the job.* □ *With the best will in the world, they won't finish the job in time.*

**with the naked eye** with the human eye, unassisted by such optics as a telescope, microscope, or eyeglasses. □ *I can't see the bird's markings with the naked eye.* □ *The scientist could see nothing in the liquid with the naked eye, but with the aid of a microscope, she identified the bacteria.*

**woe betide someone** someone will regret something very much. (Literary.) □ *Woe betide John if he's late. Mary will be angry.* □ *Woe betide the students if they don't work harder. They will be asked to leave college.*

**Woe is me!** I am unfortunate; I am unhappy. (Usually humorous.) □ *Woe is me! I have to work when the rest of the family are on vacation.* □ *Woe is me! I have the flu, and my friends have gone to a party.*

**wolf in sheep's clothing** something threatening disguised as something harmless. (A cliché.) □ *Beware of the police chief. He seems polite, but he's a wolf in sheep's clothing.* □ *This proposal seems harmless enough, but I think it's a wolf in sheep's clothing.*

**woman-to-woman** See man-to-man.

**woolgathering** daydreaming. (From the practice of wandering along, collecting tufts of sheep's wool from hedges.) □ *John never listens to the teacher. He's always woolgathering.* □ *I wish my new secretary would get on with the work and stop woolgathering.*

**work like a horse** to work very hard. (A cliché.) □ *I've been working like a horse all day, and I'm tired.* □ *I'm too old to work like a horse. I'd prefer to relax more.*

**work one's fingers to the bone** to work very hard. (A cliché.) □ *I worked my fingers to the bone so you children could have everything you needed. Now look at the way you treat me!* □ *I spent the day working my fingers to the bone, and now I want to relax.*

**work out for the best** to end up in the best possible way. □ *Don't worry. Things will work out for the best.* □ *It seems bad now, but it'll work out for the best.*

**work something off** to get rid of something by taking physical exercise. □ *Bob put on weight while on vacation and is trying to work it off by swimming regularly.* □ *Jane tried to work off her depression by playing a game of tennis.*

**worth one's or its weight in gold** very valuable. (A cliché.) □ *This book is worth its weight in gold.* □ *Oh, Bill. You're wonderful. You're worth your weight in gold.*

**worth one's salt** worth one's salary. (A cliché.) □ *Tom doesn't work very hard, and he's just barely worth his salt, but he's very easy to get along with.* □ *I think he's more than worth his salt. He's a good worker.*

**worth someone's while** worth one's time and trouble. □ *The job pays so badly it's not worth your while even going for an interview.* □ *It's not worth Mary's while going all that way just for a one-hour meeting.*

**worthy of the name** deserving or good enough to be called something. □ *There was not an actor worthy of the name in that play.* □ *Any art critic worthy of the name would know that painting is a fake.*

**X marks the spot.** This is the exact spot. (A cliché.) □ *This is where the rock struck my car—X marks the spot.* □ *Now, please move that table over here. Yes, right here—X marks the spot.*

**year in, year out** year after year; all year long. □ *I seem to have hay fever year in, year out. I never get over it.* □ *John wears the same old suit, year in, year out.*

**You can say that again!** AND **You said it!** That is certainly true!; You are correct. (The word *that* is emphasized.) □ *MARY: It sure is hot today. JANE: You can say that again!* □ *BILL: This cake is yummy! BOB: You said it!*

**You can't take it with you.** a proverb meaning that one should enjoy one's money and possessions now, because they are of no use when one is dead. (A cliché.) □ *My uncle is a wealthy miser. I keep telling him, "You can't take it with you."* □ *If you have money, you should use it. You can't take it with you, you know!*

**You can't teach an old dog new tricks.** a proverb meaning that old people cannot learn anything new. □ *"Of course I can learn," bellowed Uncle John. "Who says you can't teach an old dog new tricks?"* □ *I'm sorry. I can't seem to learn to do it right. Oh, well. You can't teach an old dog new tricks.*

**Your guess is as good as mine.** Your answer is as likely to be correct as mine is. □ *I don't know where the scissors are. Your guess is as good as mine.* □ *Your guess is as good as mine as to when the train will arrive.*

**You said it!** See You can say that again!

# Z

**zero in on something** to aim or focus directly on something. □ *"Now," said Mr. Smith, "I would like to zero in on another important point." □ Mary is very good about zeroing in on the most important and helpful ideas.*

# Phrase-Finder Index

All of the major words of the phrases in this dictionary have been indexed in the following list. Use this index to find the form of a phrase that you want to look up in the dictionary. First, pick out any major word in the phrase you are seeking. Second, look that word up in this index to find the form of the phrase used in the dictionary. Third, look up the phrase in the main body of the dictionary.

**ABCs** know one's ABCs
**able** not able to see the forest for the trees
**abode** take up one's abode somewhere
**about** at sea (about something)
**about** be halfhearted (about someone or something)
**about** beat about the bush
**about** get second thoughts about someone or something
**about** get worked up about something
**about** go about one's business
**about** go into one's song and dance about something
**about** have mixed feelings (about someone or something)
**about** make cracks (about someone or something)
**about** man about town
**about** millstone about one's neck
**about** much ado about nothing
**about** no (ifs, ands, or) buts about it
**about** out and about
**about** see eye to eye (about something)
**about** send one about one's business
**about** What about (doing) something?
**about** What about (having) something?
**above** get above oneself

**above** get one's head above water
**above** head and shoulders above someone or something
**above** keep one's head above water
**absence** conspicuous by one's absence
**according** according to Hoyle
**account** cook the accounts
**account** give a good account of oneself
**account** turn something to good account
**accounting** There's no accounting for taste.
**Achilles** Achilles' heel
**acid** acid test
**act** act high-and-mighty
**act** act of God
**act** act one's age
**act** read someone the riot act
**act** tough act to follow a
**action** Actions speak louder than words.
**active** on active duty
**Adam** not know someone from Adam
**add** add fuel to the fire
**add** add fuel to the flame
**add** add insult to injury
**ado** much ado about nothing
**ado** without further ado
**advantage** turn something to one's advantage

**advocate** play (the) devil's advocate

**afraid** afraid of one's own shadow

**after** morning after (the night before)

**after** throw good money after bad

**again** go and never darken one's door again

**again** You can say that again!

**against** against the clock

**against** bang one's head against a brick wall

**against** beat one's head against the wall

**against** get two strikes against one

**against** go against the grain

**against** hope against all hope

**against** odds are against one

**against** play both ends (against the middle)

**against** smear campaign (against someone)

**against** swim against the current

**against** swim against the tide

**age** act one's age

**age** come of age

**age** ripe old age

**ahead** ahead of one's time

**ahead** come out ahead

**ahead** full steam ahead

**air** air one's dirty linen in public

**air** build castles in the air

**air** give oneself airs

**air** in the air

**air** off the air

**air** on the air

**air** out of thin air

**air** pull something out of thin air

**air** put on airs

**air** up in the air

**air** vanish into thin air

**air** walk on air

**all** all in a day's work

**all** all joking aside

**all** all over but the shouting

**all** All roads lead to Rome.

**all** all skin and bones

**all** All that glitters is not gold.

**all** all thumbs

**all** all walks of life

**all** All work and no play makes Jack a dull boy.

**all** All's well that ends well.

**all** as bad as all that

**all** blow something out of (all) proportion

**all** firing on all cylinders

**all** first of all

**all** free-for-all

**all** get (all) dolled up

**all** hope against all hope

**all** jack-of-all-trades

**all** know (all) the tricks of the trade

**all** Money is the root of all evil.

**all** of all the nerve

**all** on all fours

**all** out of (all) proportion

**all** pull out all the stops

**all** put all one's eggs in one basket

**all** warts and all

**all** with all one's heart and soul

**alley** up a blind alley

**along** get along (on a shoestring)

**along** go along for the ride

**along** play along with someone or something

**along** tag along

**and** cross one's heart (and hope to die)

**and** eye for an eye (and a tooth for a tooth)

**and** no (ifs, ands, or) buts about it

**and** pitch in (and help)

**angel** Fools rush in (where angels fear to tread).

**another** dance to another tune

**another** horse of another color

**another** One good turn deserves another.

**another** One man's meat is another man's poison.

**any** any port in a storm

**any** without any strings attached

**apart** be poles apart

**apart** come apart at the seams

**apple** apple of someone's eye

**apple** as easy as (apple) pie

**applecart** upset the applecart

**apron** tied to one's mother's apron strings

as When in Rome, do as the Romans do.
as Your guess is as good as mine.
aside all joking aside
aside as an aside
ask ask for the moon
ask ask for trouble
asleep asleep at the switch
at asleep at the switch
at at a premium
at at a snail's pace
at at a stretch
at at death's door
at at half-mast
at at loggerheads
at at loose ends
at at one fell swoop
at at one's wit's end
at at sea (about something)
at at sixes and sevens
at at someone's doorstep
at at the bottom of the ladder
at at the drop of a hat
at at the eleventh hour
at at the end of one's rope
at at the end of one's tether
at at the last minute
at at the outside
at at the top of one's lungs
at at the top of one's voice
at at this stage (of the game)
at burn someone at the stake
at burn the candle at both ends
at burst at the seams
at champ at the bit
at Charity begins at home.
at close at hand
at come apart at the seams
at foam at the mouth
at go at it hammer and tongs
at go at it tooth and nail
at have something at hand
at have something at one's fingertips
at look daggers at someone
at love at first sight
at make oneself at home
at point the finger at someone
at poke fun (at someone)
at see the light (at the end of the tunnel)
at sit at someone's feet

at take someone or something at face value
at throw oneself at someone's feet
at throw oneself at the mercy of the court
at thumb one's nose at someone or something
at tilt at windmills
at tip the scales at something
at turn one's nose up at someone or something
attached with no strings attached
attached without any strings attached
attitude wait-and-see attitude
auction Dutch auction
average on the average
away away from one's desk
away come away empty-handed
away Fire away!
away give the bride away
away go away empty-handed
away stone's throw (away)
away take someone's breath away
away walk away with something
away When the cat's away, the mice will play.
ax have an ax to grind
babe babe in the woods
baby as soft as a baby's bottom
baby leave someone holding the baby
back back in circulation
back back to the drawing board
back back to the salt mines
back back-to-back
back break one's back (to do something)
back date back (to something)
back get one's back up
back give someone the shirt off one's back
back go back on one's word
back have eyes in the back of one's head
back have one's back to the wall
back know someone or something like the back of one's hand
back like water off a duck's back
back one's back is to the wall
back put something on the back burner

**bear** bear the brunt (of something)
**bear** bear watching
**bear** grin and bear it
**beard** beard the lion in his den
**beat** beat a dead horse
**beat** beat a path to someone's door
**beat** beat about the bush
**beat** beat around the bush
**beat** beat one's head against the wall
**beat** beat the gun
**beat** pound a beat
**beauty** Beauty is only skin deep.
**beaver** as busy as a beaver
**beaver** eager beaver
**bed** Early to bed, early to rise(, makes a man healthy, wealthy, and wise).
**bed** get out of the wrong side of the bed
**bed** get up on the wrong side of the bed
**bed** put someone or something to bed
**bed** should have stood in bed
**bee** as busy as a bee
**bee** birds and the bees
**bee** have a bee in one's bonnet
**bee** put a bee in someone's bonnet
**beeline** make a beeline for someone or something
**been** been through the mill
**before** before you can say Jack Robinson
**before** cast (one's) pearls before swine
**before** count one's chickens before they hatch
**before** cross a bridge before one comes to it
**before** cry before one is hurt
**before** morning after (the night before)
**before** put the cart before the horse
**beggar** beggar description
**beggar** Beggars can't be choosers.
**begin** begin to see daylight
**begin** begin to see the light

**begin** Charity begins at home.
**behind** burn one's bridges (behind one)
**behind** dry behind the ears
**behind** wet behind the ears
**behind** with both hands tied behind one's back
**behind** with one hand tied behind one's back
**belfry** have bats in one's belfry
**believe** believe it or not
**bell** saved by the bell
**belong** To the victor belong the spoils.
**belt** get something under one's belt
**belt** tighten one's belt
**bench** on the bench
**bench** warm the bench
**bend** bend someone's ear
**bend** go (a)round the bend
**benefit** get the benefit of the doubt
**benefit** give someone the benefit of the doubt
**berth** give someone or something a wide berth
**best** come off second best
**best** He laughs best who laughs last.
**best** in someone's (own) (best) interest(s)
**best** put one's best foot forward
**best** with the best will in the world
**best** work out for the best
**betide** woe betide someone
**better** Half a loaf is better than none.
**better** know better
**better** one's better half
**better** think better of something
**between** between a rock and a hard place
**between** between the devil and the deep blue sea
**between** draw a line between something and something else
**between** fall between two stools
**between** have one's tail between one's legs

**between** hit someone (right) between the eyes
**between** one's tail is between one's legs
**between** read between the lines
**between** strike a balance (between two things)
**beyond** beyond one's depth
**beyond** beyond one's means
**beyond** beyond the pale
**beyond** can't see beyond the end of one's nose
**beyond** live beyond one's means
**big** big frog in a small pond
**big** have a big mouth
**bigger** have eyes bigger than one's stomach
**bigger** one's eyes are bigger than one's stomach
**bill** fill the bill
**bill** foot the bill
**bill** get a clean bill of health
**bill** give someone a clean bill of health
**bill** pad the bill
**bill** sell someone a bill of goods
**bird** as free as a bird
**bird** bird in the hand is worth two in the bush
**bird** bird's-eye view
**bird** birds and the bees
**bird** Birds of a feather flock together.
**bird** early bird
**bird** eat like a bird
**bird** kill two birds with one stone
**bird** little bird told me
**birthday** in one's birthday suit
**bit** champ at the bit
**bit** hair of the dog (that bit one)
**bite** bite off more than one can chew
**bite** bite one's nails
**bite** bite one's tongue
**bite** bite the dust
**bite** bite the hand that feeds one
**bite** One's bark is worse than one's bite.
**bitter** take the bitter with the sweet
**black** black and blue
**black** black sheep of the family

**black** get a black eye
**black** give someone a black eye
**black** in black and white
**black** in the black
**black** pot calling the kettle black
**blanche** carte blanche
**blank** blank check
**blank** draw a blank
**blanket** wet blanket
**blessing** thankful for small blessings
**blind** as blind as a bat
**blind** blind leading the blind
**blind** turn a blind eye to someone or something
**blind** up a blind alley
**block** chip off the old block
**block** on the block
**block** stumbling block
**blood** blue blood
**blood** draw blood
**blood** flesh and blood
**blood** fresh blood
**blood** in one's blood
**blood** in the blood
**blood** make someone's blood boil
**blood** make someone's blood run cold
**blood** new blood
**bloody** cry bloody murder
**bloody** scream bloody murder
**blow** blow off steam
**blow** blow one's own horn
**blow** blow someone's cover
**blow** blow something out of (all) proportion
**blow** blow the whistle (on someone)
**blue** between the devil and the deep blue sea
**blue** black and blue
**blue** blue blood
**blue** burn with a low blue flame
**blue** like a bolt out of the blue
**blue** once in a blue moon
**blue** out of a clear blue sky
**blue** out of the blue
**blue** talk a blue streak
**blue** talk until one is blue in the face
**blues** get the blues
**board** back to the drawing board

**boat** in the same boat
**boat** rock the boat
**body** keep body and soul together
**boggle** boggle someone's mind
**boil** have a low boiling point
**boil** make someone's blood boil
**boil** watched pot never boils
**bolt** like a bolt out of the blue
**bolt** nuts and bolts (of something)
**bone** all skin and bones
**bone** bone of contention
**bone** chilled to the bone
**bone** cut someone or something to the bone
**bone** feel something in one's bones
**bone** have a bone to pick (with someone)
**bone** know something in one's bones
**bone** nothing but skin and bones
**bone** work one's fingers to the bone
**bonnet** have a bee in one's bonnet
**bonnet** put a bee in someone's bonnet
**book** have one's nose in a book
**book** know someone or something like a book
**book** open book
**book** read someone like a book
**book** take a leaf out of someone's book
**book** use every trick in the book
**boom** lower the boom on someone
**boot** quake in one's boots
**boot** shake in one's boots
**bootstrap** pull oneself up (by one's own bootstraps)
**boredom** die of boredom
**born** born with a silver spoon in one's mouth
**born** not born yesterday
**both** burn the candle at both ends
**both** cut both ways
**both** have a foot in both camps
**both** play both ends (against the middle)
**both** with both hands tied behind one's back

**bottom** as soft as a baby's bottom
**bottom** at the bottom of the ladder
**bottom** from the bottom of one's heart
**bottom** from top to bottom
**bottom** get to the bottom of something
**bottom** hit bottom
**bottom** learn something from the bottom up
**bottom** scrape the bottom of the barrel
**bound** bound hand and foot
**bound** by leaps and bounds
**bow** bow and scrape
**box** open Pandora's box
**box** stuff the ballot box
**boy** All work and no play makes Jack a dull boy.
**boy** separate the men from the boys
**brain** rack one's brain(s)
**branch** hold out the olive branch
**brass** get down to brass tacks
**brave** put on a brave face
**brave** put up a (brave) front
**bread** bread and butter
**bread** know which side one's bread is buttered on
**breadth** by a hair's breadth
**break** break (out) into tears
**break** break camp
**break** break new ground
**break** break one's back (to do something)
**break** break one's neck (to do something)
**break** break one's word
**break** break out in a cold sweat
**break** break someone's fall
**break** break someone's heart
**break** break the bank
**break** break the ice
**break** break the news (to someone)
**breast** make a clean breast of something
**breath** Don't hold your breath.
**breath** get time to catch one's breath
**breath** in the same breath

**but** nothing but
**butter** bread and butter
**butter** know which side one's bread is buttered on
**butter** look as if butter wouldn't melt in one's mouth
**button** button one's lip
**button** on the button
**buy** buy a pig in a poke
**buy** buy something
**buzz** give someone a buzz
**by** by a hair's breadth
**by** by a show of hands
**by** by a whisker
**by** by leaps and bounds
**by** by return mail
**by** by the nape of the neck
**by** by the same token
**by** by the seat of one's pants
**by** by the skin of one's teeth
**by** by the sweat of one's brow
**by** by virtue of something
**by** by word of mouth
**by** come by something
**by** conspicuous by one's absence
**by** do something by hand
**by** hang by a hair
**by** hang by a thread
**by** inch by inch
**by** know someone by sight
**by** let something slide by
**by** let something slip by
**by** let the chance slip by
**by** little by little
**by** live by one's wits
**by** miss (something) by a mile
**by** play by ear
**by** play something by ear
**by** pull oneself up (by one's own bootstraps)
**by** saved by the bell
**by** set great store by someone or something
**by** squeak by
**by** take someone or something by storm
**by** take the bull by the horns
**by** win by a nose
**bye** kiss something good-bye
**bygones** Let bygones be bygones.
**cake** eat one's cake and have it too

**cake** have one's cake and eat it too
**cake** slice of the cake
**calf** kill the fatted calf
**call** call a spade a spade
**call** call it a day
**call** call it quits
**call** call of nature
**call** call someone on the carpet
**call** call the dogs off
**call** have a close call
**call** pot calling the kettle black
**camel** That's the straw that broke the camel's back.
**camp** break camp
**camp** have a foot in both camps
**campaign** smear campaign (against someone)
**can** before you can say Jack Robinson
**can** bite off more than one can chew
**can** open a can of worms
**can** You can say that again!
**can't** Beggars can't be choosers.
**can't** can't carry a tune
**can't** can't hold a candle to someone
**can't** can't make heads or tails (out) of someone or something
**can't** can't see beyond the end of one's nose
**can't** can't see one's hand in front of one's face
**can't** You can't take it with you.
**can't** You can't teach an old dog new tricks.
**canary** look like the cat that swallowed the canary
**candle** burn the candle at both ends
**candle** can't hold a candle to someone
**canoe** paddle one's own canoe
**cap** feather in one's cap
**cap** put on one's thinking cap
**card** in the cards
**card** lay one's cards on the table
**card** play one's cards close to one's vest
**card** play one's cards close to the vest

**card** put one's cards on the table
**care** That takes care of that.
**carpet** brush something under the carpet
**carpet** call someone on the carpet
**carpet** get the red-carpet treatment
**carpet** give someone the red-carpet treatment
**carpet** roll out the red carpet for someone
**carpet** sweep something under the carpet
**carry** as fast as one's feet would carry one
**carry** can't carry a tune
**carry** carry a torch (for someone)
**carry** carry coals to Newcastle
**carry** carry one's cross
**carry** carry the ball
**carry** carry the torch
**carry** carry the weight of the world on one's shoulders
**carry** carry weight (with someone)
**carry** cash-and-carry
**cart** put the cart before the horse
**carte** carte blanche
**case** case in point
**case** open-and-shut case
**cash** cash in (on something)
**cash** cash-and-carry
**cast** cast (one's) pearls before swine
**cast** cast in the same mold
**cast** cast the first stone
**castle** build castles in Spain
**castle** build castles in the air
**cat** Curiosity killed the cat.
**cat** let the cat out of the bag
**cat** look like the cat that swallowed the canary
**cat** play cat and mouse (with someone)
**cat** rain cats and dogs
**cat** There's more than one way to skin a cat.
**cat** When the cat's away, the mice will play.
**catch** catch cold
**catch** catch one's death (of cold)
**catch** catch someone napping
**catch** catch someone off balance

**catch** catch someone's eye
**catch** get time to catch one's breath
**caught** caught in the cross fire
**caught** caught short
**cause** cause (some) eyebrows to raise
**cause** cause (some) tongues to wag
**caution** throw caution to the wind
**cent** put in one's two cents(' worth)
**central** as busy as Grand Central Station
**champ** champ at the bit
**chance** fat chance
**chance** fighting chance
**chance** let the chance slip by
**chance** on the off chance
**chance** sporting chance
**change** change horses in midstream
**change** change of pace
**change** change the subject
**channel** go through channels
**chapter** recite something chapter and verse
**charity** Charity begins at home.
**chase** lead someone on a merry chase
**chase** wild-goose chase
**cheap** dirt cheap
**check** blank check
**check** honor someone's check
**check** tongue-in-cheek
**cheek** turn the other cheek
**chest** get something off one's chest
**chew** bite off more than one can chew
**chicken** count one's chickens before they hatch
**chicken** no spring chicken
**chicken** run around like a chicken with its head cut off
**child** be child's play
**child** expecting (a child)
**childhood** in one's second childhood
**chill** chilled to the bone
**chin** take something on the chin
**china** bull in a china shop

chip  chip off the old block

chip  have a chip on one's shoulder

choice  Hobson's choice

choose  pick and choose

chooser  Beggars can't be choosers.

chord  strike a chord (with someone)

church  as poor as a church mouse

circle  come full circle

circle  go (a)round in circles

circle  in a vicious circle

circle  run (around) in circles

circle  talk in circles

circulation  back in circulation

circulation  out of circulation

circus  like a three-ring circus

civil  keep a civil tongue (in one's head)

clam  as happy as a clam

class  cut class

clay  have feet of clay

clean  get a clean bill of health

clean  give someone a clean bill of health

clean  have clean hands

clean  make a clean breast of something

clean  start (off) with a clean slate

clear  as clear as mud

clear  clear the table

clear  coast is clear

clear  out of a clear blue sky

climb  climb on the bandwagon

clip  clip someone's wings

cloak  cloak-and-dagger

clock  against the clock

clockwork  as regular as clockwork

clockwork  go like clockwork

close  close at hand

close  close ranks

close  have a close call

close  have a close shave

close  play one's cards close to one's vest

close  play one's cards close to the vest

closet  come out of the closet

closet  skeleton in the closet

cloth  make something up out of whole cloth

clothing  wolf in sheep's clothing

cloud  Every cloud has a silver lining.

cloud  have one's head in the clouds

cloud  on cloud nine

cloud  under a cloud (of suspicion)

club  Join the club!

coal  carry coals to Newcastle

coal  haul someone over the coals

coal  rake someone over the coals

coast  coast is clear

coast  coast-to-coast

cock  cock of the walk

cock  cock-and-bull story

cockles  warm the cockles of someone's heart

coffin  nail in someone's or something's coffin

cold  break out in a cold sweat

cold  catch cold

cold  catch one's death (of cold)

cold  cold comfort

cold  dash cold water on something

cold  get cold feet

cold  knock someone cold

cold  make someone's blood run cold

cold  out cold

cold  pour cold water on something

cold  take cold

cold  take one's death (of cold)

cold  throw cold water on something

collar  hot under the collar

color  horse of a different color

color  horse of another color

color  off-color

color  show one's (true) colors

color  with flying colors

comb  go over something with a fine-tooth comb

comb  search something with a fine-tooth comb

come  come a cropper

come  come apart at the seams

come  come away empty-handed

come  come by something

come  come down in the world

come come full circle
come come home (to roost)
come come in out of the rain
come come into one's or its own
come come of age
come come off second best
come come out ahead
come come out in the wash
come come out of the closet
come come to a bad end
come come to a dead end
come come to a head
come come to a standstill
come come to an end
come come to an untimely end
come come to grief
come come to grips with
   something
come come to light
come come to one's senses
come come to pass
come come to the point
come come to think of it
come come true
come come up in the world
come come what may
come cross a bridge before one
   comes to it
come cross a bridge when one
   comes to it
come dream come true
come easy come, easy go
come first come, first served
come if worst comes to worst
come Johnny-come-lately
come not know enough to come
   in out of the rain
comfort cold comfort
comfortable as comfortable as an
   old shoe
commission out of commission
company Two's company(, three's
   a crowd).
compliment fish for a compliment
condition in good condition
condition in mint condition
condition in the pink (of
   condition)
confidence vote of confidence
conspicuous conspicuous by one's
   absence
construction under construction

contempt Familiarity breeds
   contempt.
content to one's heart's content
contention bone of contention
contradiction contradiction in
   terms
contrary on the contrary
control control the purse strings
cook cook someone's goose
cook cook the accounts
cook Too many cooks spoil the
   broth.
cook Too many cooks spoil the
   stew.
cool as cool as a cucumber
cool cool one's heels
copycat be a copycat
corner out of the corner of one's
   eye
correct stand corrected
cost cost a pretty penny
cost cost an arm and a leg
could so quiet you could hear a
   pin drop
could so still you could hear a pin
   drop
count count heads
count count noses
count count one's chickens before
   they hatch
count every minute counts
count every moment counts
count stand up and be counted
counter under the counter
courage Dutch courage
courage screw up one's courage
court laugh something out of
   court
court throw oneself at the mercy
   of the court
court throw oneself on the mercy
   of the court
cover blow someone's cover
cover cover a lot of ground
cover cover for someone
cow sacred cow
crack crack a joke
crack crack a smile
crack make cracks (about
   someone or something)
cradle rob the cradle
cramp cramp someone's style

**crazy** as crazy as a loon
**cream** cream of the crop
**creation** in creation
**credit** give credit where credit is due
**crime** Crime doesn't pay.
**crisp** burn someone or something to a crisp
**crocodile** shed crocodile tears
**crop** cream of the crop
**cropper** come a cropper
**cross** bear one's cross
**cross** carry one's cross
**cross** caught in the cross fire
**cross** cross a bridge before one comes to it
**cross** cross a bridge when one comes to it
**cross** cross one's heart (and hope to die)
**cross** cross swords (with someone)
**cross** cross-examine someone
**crow** as the crow flies
**crowd** Two's company(, three's a crowd).
**crust** upper crust
**crutch** as funny as a crutch
**crux** crux of the matter
**cry** cry before one is hurt
**cry** cry bloody murder
**cry** cry one's eyes out
**cry** cry over spilled milk
**cry** cry wolf
**cry** hue and cry
**cucumber** as cool as a cucumber
**cue** take one's cue from someone
**cuff** put something on the cuff
**cup** not someone's cup of tea
**cure** ounce of prevention is worth a pound of cure
**curiosity** Curiosity killed the cat.
**curl** curl someone's hair
**curl** curl up and die
**current** swim against the current
**curtain** bring down the curtain (on something)
**curtain** ring down the curtain (on something)
**curve** pitch someone a curve
**curve** throw someone a curve
**cut** cut both ways

**cut** cut class
**cut** cut off one's nose to spite one's face
**cut** cut one's (own) throat
**cut** cut one's losses
**cut** cut someone or something (off) short
**cut** cut someone or something to the bone
**cut** cut someone to the quick
**cut** cut something (too) fine
**cut** cut the ground out from under someone
**cut** fish or cut bait
**cut** run around like a chicken with its head cut off
**cylinder** firing on all cylinders
**dab** smack-dab in the middle
**dagger** cloak-and-dagger
**dagger** look daggers at someone
**daily** daily dozen
**damn** damn someone or something with faint praise
**dance** dance to another tune
**dance** go into one's song and dance about something
**dander** get one's dander up
**dangerous** little knowledge is a dangerous thing
**dark** dark horse
**darken** go and never darken one's door again
**dash** dash cold water on something
**date** date back (to something)
**Davy** Davy Jones's locker
**Davy** go to Davy Jones's locker
**day** all in a day's work
**day** as different as night and day
**day** as plain as day
**day** call it a day
**day** Every dog has his day.
**day** Every dog has its day.
**day** have had its day
**day** late in the day
**day** nine days' wonder
**day** one's days are numbered
**day** order of the day
**day** Rome wasn't built in a day.
**day** save something for a rainy day
**day** save the day
**day** see the light (of day)

**daylight** begin to see daylight
**daylight** daylight robbery
**daylight** in broad daylight
**dead** as dead as a dodo
**dead** as dead as a doornail
**dead** beat a dead horse
**dead** come to a dead end
**dead** dead and buried
**dead** dead to the world
**dead** have someone dead to rights
**dead** in a dead heat
**dead** leave someone for dead
**deaf** turn a deaf ear (to something)
**deal** square deal
**death** at death's door
**death** catch one's death (of cold)
**death** death on someone or something
**death** kiss of death
**death** matter of life and death
**death** sign one's own death warrant
**death** take one's death (of cold)
**debt** pay one's debt (to society)
**deep** Beauty is only skin deep.
**deep** between the devil and the deep blue sea
**deep** go off the deep end
**deep** in deep water
**deep** jump off the deep end
**deep** Still waters run deep.
**deliver** signed, sealed, and delivered
**den** beard the lion in his den
**depth** beyond one's depth
**description** beggar description
**desert** desert a sinking ship
**deserts** get one's just deserts
**deserve** One good turn deserves another.
**desk** away from one's desk
**devil** between the devil and the deep blue sea
**devil** for the devil of it
**devil** give the devil her due
**devil** give the devil his due
**devil** play (the) devil's advocate
**devil** speak of the devil
**devil** There will be the devil to pay.
**diamond** diamond in the rough

**dibs** have dibs on something
**dibs** put one's dibs on something
**Dick** as tight as Dick's hatband
**Dick** every Tom, Dick, and Harry
**die** cross one's heart (and hope to die)
**die** curl up and die
**die** die of a broken heart
**die** die of boredom
**die** die on the vine
**difference** split the difference
**different** as different as night and day
**different** horse of a different color
**different** march to a different drummer
**dig** dig in one's heels
**dig** dig one's own grave
**dig** dig up some dirt on someone
**dilemma** on the horns of a dilemma
**dime** turn on a dime
**dirt** dig up some dirt on someone
**dirt** dirt cheap
**dirty** air one's dirty linen in public
**dirty** dirty one's hands
**dirty** dirty work
**dirty** get one's hands dirty
**dirty** wash one's dirty linen in public
**disease** have foot-in-mouth disease
**dish** do the dishes
**distance** go the distance
**do** break one's back (to do something)
**do** break one's neck (to do something)
**do** Crime doesn't pay.
**do** do a land-office business
**do** do someone a good turn
**do** do someone's heart good
**do** do something by hand
**do** do the dishes
**do** do the honors
**do** Easy does it.
**do** find it in one's heart (to do something)
**do** get up enough nerve (to do something)
**do** have the presence of mind to do something

**do** in no mood to do something
**do** move heaven and earth to do something
**do** Pretty is as pretty does.
**do** risk one's neck (to do something)
**do** well-to-do
**do** What about (doing) something?
**do** When in Rome, do as the Romans do.
**doctor** just what the doctor ordered
**dodo** as dead as a dodo
**doesn't** Crime doesn't pay.
**dog** as sick as a dog
**dog** call the dogs off
**dog** dog eat dog
**dog** dog in the manger
**dog** Every dog has his day.
**dog** Every dog has its day.
**dog** go to the dogs
**dog** hair of the dog (that bit one)
**dog** lead a dog's life
**dog** Let sleeping dogs lie.
**dog** live a dog's life
**dog** rain cats and dogs
**dog** shaggy-dog story
**dog** tail wagging the dog
**dog** You can't teach an old dog new tricks.
**doghouse** in the doghouse
**doldrums** in the doldrums
**doll** get (all) dolled up
**dollar** dollar for dollar
**dollar** feel like a million (dollars)
**dollar** look like a million dollars
**don't** Don't hold your breath.
**don't** Don't let someone or something get you down.
**don't** Don't look a gift horse in the mouth.
**done** as good as done
**door** at death's door
**door** beat a path to someone's door
**door** get one's foot in the door
**door** go and never darken one's door again
**door** keep the wolf from the door
**doornail** as dead as a doornail
**doorstep** at someone's doorstep
**doorstep** on someone's doorstep

**dose** dose of one's own medicine
**dot** on the dot
**dot** sign on the dotted line
**double** see double
**doubt** doubting Thomas
**doubt** get the benefit of the doubt
**doubt** give someone the benefit of the doubt
**down** breathe down someone's neck
**down** bring down the curtain (on something)
**down** bring down the house
**down** come down in the world
**down** Don't let someone or something get you down.
**down** down and out
**down** down in the dumps
**down** down in the mouth
**down** down the drain
**down** down the tube(s)
**down** down to the wire
**down** down-to-earth
**down** dressing-down
**down** fall down on the job
**down** get down to brass tacks
**down** get down to business
**down** get down to work
**down** go down in history
**down** hands down
**down** lay down the law
**down** lead someone down the garden path
**down** let one's hair down
**down** pour money down the drain
**down** ring down the curtain (on something)
**down** take something lying down
**down** throw down the gauntlet
**dozen** daily dozen
**dozen** six of one and half a dozen of the other
**drab** dribs and drabs
**drag** drag one's feet
**drain** down the drain
**drain** pour money down the drain
**draw** back to the drawing board
**draw** draw a blank
**draw** draw a line between something and something else
**draw** draw blood
**draw** quick on the draw

**dream** dream come true
**dream** pipe dream
**dressing** dressing-down
**drib** dribs and drabs
**drink** drink to excess
**drive** drive a hard bargain
**drive** drive someone to the wall
**driven** as white as the driven snow
**drop** at the drop of a hat
**drop** drop in one's tracks
**drop** drop someone a few lines
**drop** drop someone a line
**drop** drop someone's name
**drop** drop the ball
**drop** drop the name of someone
**drop** name-dropping
**drop** so quiet you could hear a pin drop
**drop** so still you could hear a pin drop
**drown** drown one's sorrows
**drown** drown one's troubles
**drug** drug on the market
**drum** drum someone out of something
**drum** drum something into someone('s head)
**drum** drum up some business
**drummer** march to a different drummer
**dry** dry behind the ears
**dry** dry run
**dry** dry someone out
**dry** dry up
**dry** leave someone high and dry
**duck** as a duck takes to water
**duck** as easy as duck soup
**duck** get one's ducks in a row
**duck** like a sitting duck
**duck** like sitting ducks
**duck** like water off a duck's back
**duck** lovely weather for ducks
**due** give credit where credit is due
**due** give the devil her due
**due** give the devil his due
**dues** pay one's dues
**dull** All work and no play makes Jack a dull boy.
**dumps** down in the dumps
**dust** bite the dust
**Dutch** Dutch auction

**Dutch** Dutch courage
**Dutch** Dutch treat
**Dutch** Dutch uncle
**Dutch** go Dutch
**duty** in the line of duty
**duty** off duty
**duty** on active duty
**duty** on duty
**eager** eager beaver
**eagle** eagle eye
**ear** bend someone's ear
**ear** dry behind the ears
**ear** get someone's ear
**ear** go in one ear and out the other
**ear** have one's ear to the ground
**ear** in one ear and out the other
**ear** keep one's ear to the ground
**ear** lend an ear (to someone)
**ear** make a silk purse out of a sow's ear
**ear** play by ear
**ear** play something by ear
**ear** prick up one's ears
**ear** turn a deaf ear (to something)
**ear** up to one's ears (in something)
**ear** Walls have ears.
**ear** wet behind the ears
**early** early bird
**early** Early to bed, early to rise(, makes a man healthy, wealthy, and wise).
**earn** earn one's keep
**earn** penny saved is a penny earned
**earth** down-to-earth
**earth** like nothing on earth
**earth** move heaven and earth to do something
**earth** on earth
**earth** run someone or something to earth
**earth** salt of the earth
**earth** to the ends of the earth
**easy** as easy as (apple) pie
**easy** as easy as duck soup
**easy** easy come, easy go
**easy** Easy does it.
**easy** free and easy
**eat** dog eat dog
**eat** eat humble pie

247

**eat** eat like a bird
**eat** eat like a horse
**eat** eat one's cake and have it too
**eat** eat one's hat
**eat** eat one's heart out
**eat** eat one's words
**eat** eat out of someone's hand(s)
**eat** eat someone out of house and home
**eat** have one's cake and eat it too
**edge** set someone's teeth on edge
**edgeways** get a word in edgeways
**edgewise** get a word in edgewise
**eel** as slippery as an eel
**effigy** hang someone in effigy
**egg** have egg on one's face
**egg** kill the goose that laid the golden egg
**egg** lay an egg
**egg** put all one's eggs in one basket
**egg** teach one's grandmother to suck eggs
**egg** walk on eggs
**elbow** rub elbows with someone
**element** out of one's element
**elephant** white elephant
**eleventh** at the eleventh hour
**else** draw a line between something and something else
**empty** come away empty-handed
**empty** go away empty-handed
**end** All's well that ends well.
**end** at loose ends
**end** at one's wit's end
**end** at the end of one's rope
**end** at the end of one's tether
**end** burn the candle at both ends
**end** business end of something
**end** can't see beyond the end of one's nose
**end** come to a bad end
**end** come to a dead end
**end** come to an end
**end** come to an untimely end
**end** end in itself
**end** end of the line
**end** end of the road
**end** end up with the short end of the stick
**end** get the short end of the stick
**end** go off the deep end

**end** hold up one's end (of the bargain)
**end** jump off the deep end
**end** make someone's hair stand on end
**end** meet one's end
**end** not see further than the end of one's nose
**end** play both ends (against the middle)
**end** see the light (at the end of the tunnel)
**end** to the ends of the earth
**enough** Enough is enough.
**enough** get up enough nerve (to do something)
**enough** not know enough to come in out of the rain
**enter** enter one's mind
**envy** green with envy
**errand** on a fool's errand
**even** keep on an even keel
**even** keep something on an even keel
**every** Every cloud has a silver lining.
**every** Every dog has his day.
**every** Every dog has its day.
**every** every inch a something
**every** every inch the something
**every** every living soul
**every** every minute counts
**every** every moment counts
**every** every Tom, Dick, and Harry
**every** hang on someone's every word
**every** use every trick in the book
**every** with every (other) breath
**everything** everything but the kitchen sink
**everything** everything from A to Z
**everything** everything from soup to nuts
**evil** Money is the root of all evil.
**examine** cross-examine someone
**excess** drink to excess
**expecting** expecting (a child)
**expedition** go on a fishing expedition
**eye** apple of someone's eye
**eye** bird's-eye view
**eye** catch someone's eye

**fast** thick and fast
**fat** fat chance
**fat** fat is in the fire
**fat** kill the fatted calf
**fat** live off the fat of the land
**fate** leave one to one's fate
**fear** Fools rush in (where angels fear to tread).
**fear** for fear of something
**feast** feast one's eyes (on someone or something)
**feather** as light as a feather
**feather** Birds of a feather flock together.
**feather** feather in one's cap
**feather** feather one's (own) nest
**feather** in fine feather
**feather** make the feathers fly
**feather** ruffle someone's feathers
**feed** bite the hand that feeds one
**feed** feed the kitty
**feed** spoon-feed someone
**feel** feel like a million (dollars)
**feel** feel like a new person
**feel** feel out of place
**feel** feel something in one's bones
**feel** feel the pinch
**feelings** have mixed feelings (about someone or something)
**feet** as fast as one's feet would carry one
**feet** drag one's feet
**feet** find one's feet
**feet** get a load off one's feet
**feet** get cold feet
**feet** get one's feet on the ground
**feet** get one's feet wet
**feet** get to one's feet
**feet** have feet of clay
**feet** keep one's feet on the ground
**feet** let grass grow under one's feet
**feet** on one's feet
**feet** sit at someone's feet
**feet** stand on one's own two feet
**feet** take a load off one's feet
**feet** think on one's feet
**feet** throw oneself at someone's feet
**fell** at one fell swoop
**fell** in one fell swoop
**fellow** hail-fellow-well-met

**fence** mend (one's) fences
**fence** sit on the fence
**fever** run a fever
**few** drop someone a few lines
**few** precious few
**fiddle** as fit as a fiddle
**fiddle** fiddle while Rome burns
**fiddle** play second fiddle (to someone)
**field** out in left field
**field** play the field
**fight** fight someone or something hammer and tongs
**fight** fight someone or something tooth and nail
**fight** fighting chance
**figure** in round figures
**fill** fill someone's shoes
**fill** fill the bill
**fill** get one's fill of someone or something
**final** final fling
**final** get the final word
**find** find it in one's heart (to do something)
**find** find one's feet
**find** find one's or its way somewhere
**find** find one's own level
**finder** Finders keepers(, losers weepers).
**fine** cut something (too) fine
**fine** fine kettle of fish
**fine** go over something with a fine-tooth comb
**fine** in fine feather
**fine** search something with a fine-tooth comb
**finger** get one's fingers burned
**finger** have one's finger in the pie
**finger** lay a finger on someone or something
**finger** point the finger at someone
**finger** slip through someone's fingers
**finger** twist someone around one's little finger
**finger** work one's fingers to the bone
**fingertip** have something at one's fingertips
**finish** from start to finish

fire add fuel to the fire
fire caught in the cross fire
fire fat is in the fire
fire Fire away!
fire firing on all cylinders
fire hang fire
fire have too many irons in the fire
fire keep the home fires burning
fire out of the frying pan into the fire
fire play with fire
fire set the world on fire
fire under fire
fire Where there's smoke, there's fire.
first cast the first stone
first first and foremost
first first come, first served
first first of all
first first thing (in the morning)
first First things first.
first get to first base (with someone or something)
first love at first sight
first of the first water
first reach first base (with someone or something)
fish fine kettle of fish
fish fish for a compliment
fish fish in troubled waters
fish fish or cut bait
fish go on a fishing expedition
fish have other fish to fry
fish like a fish out of water
fish neither fish nor fowl
fish There are plenty of other fish in the sea.
fist hand over fist
fit as fit as a fiddle
fit fit for a king
fit fit like a glove
fit fit someone to a T
fit If the shoe fits, wear it.
fix fix someone's wagon
fix well-fixed
flame add fuel to the flame
flame burn with a low blue flame
flame fan the flames (of something)
flame go up in flames
flash flash in the pan

flash in a flash
flat as flat as a pancake
flat fall flat (on one's or its face)
flat flat broke
flat in nothing flat
flesh flesh and blood
flesh in the flesh
flight flight of fancy
fling final fling
float float a loan
flock Birds of a feather flock together.
floor walk the floor
fly as the crow flies
fly fly in the face of someone or something
fly fly in the ointment
fly fly in the teeth of someone or something
fly fly off the handle
fly get off to a flying start
fly make the feathers fly
fly make the fur fly
fly time flies
fly with flying colors
foam foam at the mouth
follow follow one's heart
follow tough act to follow
food food for thought
fool fool and his money are soon parted
fool fool's paradise
fool Fools rush in (where angels fear to tread).
fool nobody's fool
fool on a fool's errand
fool play the fool
foolish penny-wise and pound-foolish
foot bound hand and foot
foot foot the bill
foot get one's foot in the door
foot have a foot in both camps
foot have foot-in-mouth disease
foot not set foot somewhere
foot put one's best foot forward
foot put one's foot in it
foot put one's foot in one's mouth
foot set foot somewhere
foot shoe is on the other foot
foot stick one's foot in one's mouth

**foot** wait on someone hand and foot
**footloose** footloose and fancy free
**for** ask for the moon
**for** ask for trouble
**for** buy something for a song
**for** carry a torch (for someone)
**for** cover for someone
**for** dollar for dollar
**for** eye for an eye (and a tooth for a tooth)
**for** fish for a compliment
**for** fit for a king
**for** food for thought
**for** for fear of something
**for** for the devil of it
**for** for the heck of it
**for** for the hell of it
**for** for the record
**for** fork money out (for something)
**for** free-for-all
**for** give one's right arm (for someone or something)
**for** give someone tit for tat
**for** give someone what for
**for** glutton for punishment
**for** go along for the ride
**for** go to bat for someone
**for** gun for someone
**for** have a lot going (for one)
**for** have a soft spot in one's heart for someone or something
**for** have a weakness for someone or something
**for** hold out for something
**for** hunt high and low for someone or something
**for** jockey for position
**for** keep an eye out (for someone or something)
**for** knock someone for a loop
**for** leave someone for dead
**for** like looking for a needle in a haystack
**for** lovely weather for ducks
**for** make a beeline for someone or something
**for** make a run for it
**for** make life miserable for someone
**for** make someone the scapegoat for something

**for** make up for lost time
**for** none the worse for wear
**for** not able to see the forest for the trees
**for** not long for this world
**for** pay an arm and a leg (for something)
**for** pay through the nose (for something)
**for** penny for your thoughts
**for** put in a good word (for someone)
**for** riding for a fall
**for** roll out the red carpet for someone
**for** run for it
**for** run for one's life
**for** save something for a rainy day
**for** search high and low for someone or something
**for** speak for themselves
**for** speaks for itself
**for** take someone or something for granted
**for** thankful for small blessings
**for** There's no accounting for taste.
**for** throw someone for a loop
**for** touch someone for something
**for** want for nothing
**for** What is sauce for the goose is sauce for the gander.
**for** whistle for something
**for** work out for the best
**forbidden** forbidden fruit
**force** force someone to the wall
**force** force someone's hand
**foremost** first and foremost
**forest** not able to see the forest for the trees
**forget** forgive and forget
**forgive** forgive and forget
**fork** fork money out (for something)
**forked** speak with a forked tongue
**form** form an opinion
**fort** hold the fort
**forty** take forty winks
**forward** put one's best foot forward
**foul** fall foul of someone or something
**foul** foul one's own nest

**gander** What is sauce for the goose is sauce for the gander.

**garden** lead someone down the garden path

**gas** out of gas

**gas** run out of gas

**gas** step on the gas

**gather** rolling stone gathers no moss

**gather** woolgathering

**gauntlet** throw down the gauntlet

**get** Don't let someone or something get you down.

**get** early bird gets the worm

**get** get (all) dolled up

**get** get (someone) off the hook

**get** get a black eye

**get** get a clean bill of health

**get** get a load off one's feet

**get** get a load off one's mind

**get** get a lump in one's throat

**get** get a word in edgeways

**get** get a word in edgewise

**get** get above oneself

**get** get along (on a shoestring)

**get** get cold feet

**get** get down to brass tacks

**get** get down to business

**get** get down to work

**get** get fresh (with someone)

**get** get goose bumps

**get** get goose pimples

**get** get in someone's hair

**get** get into the swing of things

**get** get off scot-free

**get** get off to a flying start

**get** get on someone's nerves

**get** get on the bandwagon

**get** get one's back up

**get** get one's dander up

**get** get one's ducks in a row

**get** get one's feet on the ground

**get** get one's feet wet

**get** get one's fill of someone or something

**get** get one's fingers burned

**get** get one's foot in the door

**get** get one's hackles up

**get** get one's hands dirty

**get** get one's head above water

**get** get one's Irish up

**get** get one's just deserts

**get** get one's second wind

**get** get one's teeth into something

**get** get out of the wrong side of the bed

**get** get second thoughts about someone or something

**get** get someone over a barrel

**get** get someone under one's thumb

**get** get someone's ear

**get** get someone's eye

**get** get something into someone's thick head

**get** get something off (the ground)

**get** get something off one's chest

**get** get something sewed up

**get** get something straight

**get** get something through someone's thick skull

**get** get something under one's belt

**get** get something under way

**get** get something wrapped up

**get** get stars in one's eyes

**get** get the benefit of the doubt

**get** get the blues

**get** get the final word

**get** get the hang of something

**get** get the inside track

**get** get the jump on someone

**get** get the last laugh

**get** get the last word

**get** get the message

**get** get the nod

**get** get the red-carpet treatment

**get** get the runaround

**get** get the shock of one's life

**get** get the short end of the stick

**get** get the upper hand (on someone)

**get** get the word

**get** get time to catch one's breath

**get** get to first base (with someone or something)

**get** get to one's feet

**get** get to the bottom of something

**get** get to the heart of the matter

**get** get to the point

**get** get two strikes against one

**get** get under someone's skin

**get** get up enough nerve (to do something)

**go** go to wrack and ruin
**go** go up in flames
**go** go up in smoke
**go** have a lot going (for one)
**go** make a go of it
**go** on the go
**go** rarin' to go
**goat** separate the sheep from the goats
**God** act of God
**gold** All that glitters is not gold.
**gold** as good as gold
**gold** have a heart of gold
**gold** worth one's or its weight in gold
**golden** kill the goose that laid the golden egg
**good** as good as done
**good** as good as gold
**good** do someone a good turn
**good** do someone's heart good
**good** give a good account of oneself
**good** give as good as one gets
**good** have a good head on one's shoulders
**good** in good condition
**good** in good shape
**good** kiss something good-bye
**good** make good money
**good** One good turn deserves another.
**good** put in a good word (for someone)
**good** throw good money after bad
**good** too good to be true
**good** turn something to good account
**good** Your guess is as good as mine.
**goods** sell someone a bill of goods
**goose** cook someone's goose
**goose** get goose bumps
**goose** get goose pimples
**goose** kill the goose that laid the golden egg
**goose** What is sauce for the goose is sauce for the gander.
**goose** wild-goose chase
**gotten** ill-gotten gains
**grace** fall from grace
**grade** make the grade

**grain** go against the grain
**grain** take something with a grain of salt
**grand** as busy as Grand Central Station
**grandmother** teach one's grandmother to suck eggs
**granted** take someone or something for granted
**grass** let grass grow under one's feet
**grave** dig one's own grave
**grave** turn over in one's grave
**gravy** ride the gravy train
**gray** gray area
**gray** gray matter
**great** make a great show of something
**great** set great store by someone or something
**green** green with envy
**green** have a green thumb
**grief** come to grief
**grin** grin and bear it
**grind** grind to a halt
**grind** have an ax to grind
**grindstone** keep one's nose to the grindstone
**grindstone** put one's nose to the grindstone
**grip** come to grips with something
**grip** lose one's grip
**grit** grit one's teeth
**ground** break new ground
**ground** cover a lot of ground
**ground** cut the ground out from under someone
**ground** from the ground up
**ground** gain ground
**ground** get one's feet on the ground
**ground** get something off (the ground)
**ground** have one's ear to the ground
**ground** hold one's ground
**ground** keep one's ear to the ground
**ground** keep one's feet on the ground
**ground** stand one's ground

**grow** let grass grow under one's feet

**guess** Your guess is as good as mine.

**guinea** serve as a guinea pig

**gun** beat the gun

**gun** gun for someone

**gun** jump the gun

**gun** stick to one's guns

**guts** hate someone's guts

**gutter** in the gutter

**hackles** get one's hackles up

**had** have had its day

**hail** hail-fellow-well-met

**hair** by a hair's breadth

**hair** curl someone's hair

**hair** get in someone's hair

**hair** hair of the dog (that bit one)

**hair** hang by a hair

**hair** let one's hair down

**hair** make someone's hair stand on end

**hair** neither hide nor hair

**hair** part someone's hair

**hair** tear one's hair (out)

**hale** hale and hearty

**half** at half-mast

**half** Half a loaf is better than none.

**half** one's better half

**half** six of one and half a dozen of the other

**halfhearted** be halfhearted (about someone or something)

**halfway** meet someone halfway

**halt** grind to a halt

**hammer** fight someone or something hammer and tongs

**hammer** go at it hammer and tongs

**hammer** hammer something home (to someone)

**hand** be putty in someone's hands

**hand** bird in the hand is worth two in the bush

**hand** bite the hand that feeds one

**hand** bound hand and foot

**hand** by a show of hands

**hand** can't see one's hand in front of one's face

**hand** close at hand

**hand** come away empty-handed

**hand** dirty one's hands

**hand** do something by hand

**hand** eat out of someone's hand(s)

**hand** force someone's hand

**hand** from hand to hand

**hand** get one's hands dirty

**hand** get the upper hand (on someone)

**hand** go away empty-handed

**hand** hand in glove (with someone)

**hand** hand over fist

**hand** hand over hand

**hand** hands down

**hand** have clean hands

**hand** have one's hand in the till

**hand** have one's hands full (with someone or something)

**hand** have one's hands tied

**hand** have someone or something in one's hands

**hand** have something at hand

**hand** know someone or something like the back of one's hand

**hand** know someone or something like the palm of one's hand

**hand** live from hand to mouth

**hand** one's hands are tied

**hand** out of hand

**hand** put one's hand to the plow

**hand** show one's hand

**hand** sit on its hands

**hand** sit on one's hands

**hand** soil one's hands

**hand** take the law into one's own hands

**hand** tie someone's hands

**hand** Time hangs heavy on someone's hands.

**hand** wait on someone hand and foot

**hand** wash one's hands of someone or something

**hand** with both hands tied behind one's back

**hand** with one hand tied behind one's back

**handle** fly off the handle

**handle** handle someone with kid gloves

**handwriting** see the (hand)writing on the wall
**hang** get the hang of something
**hang** hang by a hair
**hang** hang by a thread
**hang** hang fire
**hang** hang in the balance
**hang** hang on someone's every word
**hang** Hang on to your hat!
**hang** Hang on!
**hang** hang one's hat up somewhere
**hang** hang someone in effigy
**hang** have something hanging over one's head
**hang** keep someone or something hanging in midair
**hang** leave someone or something hanging in midair
**hang** Time hangs heavy on someone's hands.
**happy** as happy as a clam
**happy** as happy as a lark
**happy** hit a happy medium
**happy** strike a happy medium
**hard** as hard as nails
**hard** between a rock and a hard place
**hard** drive a hard bargain
**hard** hard on someone's heels
**hard** hard-and-fast rule
**hardly** hardly have time to breathe
**hare** as mad as a March hare
**Harry** every Tom, Dick, and Harry
**has** Every cloud has a silver lining.
**has** Every dog has his day.
**has** Every dog has its day.
**haste** Haste makes waste.
**hat** at the drop of a hat
**hat** be old hat
**hat** eat one's hat
**hat** Hang on to your hat!
**hat** hang one's hat up somewhere
**hat** Hold on to your hat!
**hat** keep something under one's hat
**hat** pass the hat
**hat** pull something out of a hat
**hat** talk through one's hat
**hat** toss one's hat into the ring

**hat** wear more than one hat
**hatband** as tight as Dick's hatband
**hatch** count one's chickens before they hatch
**hatchet** bury the hatchet
**hate** hate someone's guts
**hatter** as mad as a hatter
**haul** haul someone over the coals
**haul** over the long haul
**haul** over the short haul
**have** as luck would have it
**have** eat one's cake and have it too
**have** hardly have time to breathe
**have** have a bee in one's bonnet
**have** have a big mouth
**have** have a bone to pick (with someone)
**have** have a brush with something
**have** have a chip on one's shoulder
**have** have a close call
**have** have a close shave
**have** have a familiar ring
**have** have a foot in both camps
**have** have a frog in one's throat
**have** have a good head on one's shoulders
**have** have a green thumb
**have** have a heart
**have** have a lot going (for one)
**have** have a low boiling point
**have** have a one-track mind
**have** have a price on one's head
**have** have a scrape (with someone or something)
**have** have a soft spot in one's heart for someone or something
**have** have a sweet tooth
**have** have a vested interest in something
**have** have a weakness for someone or something
**have** have an ax to grind
**have** have an in (with someone)
**have** have an itching palm
**have** have an itchy palm
**have** have bats in one's belfry
**have** have clean hands
**have** have dibs on something
**have** have egg on one's face

**have** have eyes bigger than one's stomach
**have** have eyes in the back of one's head
**have** have feet of clay
**have** have foot-in-mouth disease
**have** have had its day
**have** have mixed feelings (about someone or something)
**have** have money to burn
**have** have one's back to the wall
**have** have one's cake and eat it too
**have** have one's ear to the ground
**have** have one's finger in the pie
**have** have one's hand in the till
**have** have one's hands full (with someone or something)
**have** have one's hands tied
**have** have one's head in the clouds
**have** have one's heart in one's mouth
**have** have one's heart set on something
**have** have one's nose in a book
**have** have one's tail between one's legs
**have** have one's words stick in one's throat
**have** have other fish to fry
**have** have someone dead to rights
**have** have someone in one's pocket
**have** have someone or something in one's hands
**have** have someone's eye
**have** have something at hand
**have** have something at one's fingertips
**have** have something hanging over one's head
**have** have something in stock
**have** have something to spare
**have** have the Midas touch
**have** have the presence of mind to do something
**have** have the right-of-way
**have** have the time of one's life
**have** have too many irons in the fire
**have** not have a leg to stand on

**have** should have stood in bed
**have** Walls have ears.
**have** What about (having) something?
**haw** hem and haw
**hawk** watch someone like a hawk
**hay** Make hay while the sun is shining.
**haystack** like looking for a needle in a haystack
**he** He laughs best who laughs last.
**he** He who laughs last, laughs longest.
**head** bang one's head against a brick wall
**head** beat one's head against the wall
**head** bring something to a head
**head** bury one's head in the sand
**head** can't make heads or tails (out) of someone or something
**head** come to a head
**head** count heads
**head** drum something into someone('s head)
**head** get one's head above water
**head** get something into someone's thick head
**head** go over someone's head
**head** go to someone's head
**head** have a good head on one's shoulders
**head** have a price on one's head
**head** have eyes in the back of one's head
**head** have one's head in the clouds
**head** have something hanging over one's head
**head** head and shoulders above someone or something
**head** heads will roll
**head** hide one's head in the sand
**head** hit the nail (right) on the head
**head** hold one's head up
**head** in over one's head
**head** keep a civil tongue (in one's head)
**head** keep one's head above water
**head** make someone's head spin
**head** make someone's head swim

259

**head** off the top of one's head
**head** on someone's head
**head** out of one's head
**head** over someone's head
**head** rear its ugly head
**head** run around like a chicken with its head cut off
**head** turn someone's head
**health** get a clean bill of health
**health** give someone a clean bill of health
**healthy** Early to bed, early to rise(, makes a man healthy, wealthy, and wise).
**hear** so quiet you could hear a pin drop
**hear** so still you could hear a pin drop
**heart** break someone's heart
**heart** cross one's heart (and hope to die)
**heart** die of a broken heart
**heart** do someone's heart good
**heart** eat one's heart out
**heart** find it in one's heart (to do something)
**heart** follow one's heart
**heart** from the bottom of one's heart
**heart** get to the heart of the matter
**heart** have a heart
**heart** have a soft spot in one's heart for someone or something
**heart** have one's heart in one's mouth
**heart** have one's heart set on something
**heart** lose heart
**heart** one's heart is in one's mouth
**heart** one's heart is set on something
**heart** open one's heart (to someone)
**heart** set one's heart on something
**heart** to one's heart's content
**heart** warm the cockles of someone's heart
**heart** with all one's heart and soul
**hearty** hale and hearty

**heat** in a dead heat
**heat** in heat
**heaven** in seventh heaven
**heaven** manna from heaven
**heaven** move heaven and earth to do something
**heavy** Time hangs heavy on someone's hands.
**heck** for the heck of it
**heel** Achilles' heel
**heel** cool one's heels
**heel** dig in one's heels
**heel** hard on someone's heels
**heel** kick up one's heels
**heel** on the heels of something
**heel** set one back on one's heels
**heel** take to one's heels
**heel** well-heeled
**hell** for the hell of it
**hell** like a bat out of hell
**help** pitch in (and help)
**hem** hem and haw
**hen** as mad as a wet hen
**hens** as scarce as hens' teeth
**hens** scarcer than hens' teeth
**her** give the devil her due
**here** Here's to someone or something.
**hide** hide one's head in the sand
**hide** hide one's light under a bushel
**hide** neither hide nor hair
**high** act high-and-mighty
**high** as high as a kite
**high** as high as the sky
**high** high man on the totem pole
**high** hunt high and low for someone or something
**high** leave someone high and dry
**high** run high
**high** search high and low for someone or something
**hill** over the hill
**hip** shoot from the hip
**his** beard the lion in his den
**his** Every dog has his day.
**his** fool and his money are soon parted
**his** give the devil his due
**history** go down in history
**hit** hit (someone) like a ton of bricks

hungry as hungry as a bear
hunt hunt high and low for someone or something
hurt cry before one is hurt
hush hush money
ice break the ice
ice on thin ice
ice put something on ice
ice skate on thin ice
if If the shoe fits, wear it.
if if worst comes to worst
if If you give one an inch, one will take a mile.
if look as if butter wouldn't melt in one's mouth
if no (ifs, ands, or) buts about it
ill ill-gotten gains
image be the spit and image of someone
image be the spitting image of someone
in air one's dirty linen in public
in all in a day's work
in any port in a storm
in arm-in-arm
in as snug as a bug in a rug
in babe in the woods
in back in circulation
in be a thorn in someone's side
in be putty in someone's hands
in bear someone or something in mind
in beard the lion in his den
in big frog in a small pond
in bird in the hand is worth two in the bush
in born with a silver spoon in one's mouth
in break out in a cold sweat
in build castles in Spain
in build castles in the air
in bull in a china shop
in bury one's head in the sand
in buy a pig in a poke
in can't see one's hand in front of one's face
in case in point
in cash in (on something)
in cast in the same mold
in caught in the cross fire
in change horses in midstream
in come down in the world

in come in out of the rain
in come out in the wash
in come up in the world
in contradiction in terms
in diamond in the rough
in dig in one's heels
in dog in the manger
in Don't look a gift horse in the mouth.
in down in the dumps
in down in the mouth
in drop in one's tracks
in end in itself
in fat is in the fire
in feather in one's cap
in feel something in one's bones
in find it in one's heart (to do something)
in first thing (in the morning)
in fish in troubled waters
in flash in the pan
in fly in the face of someone or something
in fly in the ointment
in fly in the teeth of someone or something
in Fools rush in (where angels fear to tread).
in friend in need is a friend indeed
in get a lump in one's throat
in get a word in edgeways
in get a word in edgewise
in get in someone's hair
in get one's ducks in a row
in get one's foot in the door
in get stars in one's eyes
in go (a)round in circles
in go down in history
in go in one ear and out the other
in go up in flames
in go up in smoke
in hand in glove (with someone)
in hang in the balance
in hang someone in effigy
in have a bee in one's bonnet
in have a foot in both camps
in have a frog in one's throat
in have a soft spot in one's heart for someone or something
in have a vested interest in something
in have an in (with someone)

in    have bats in one's belfry
in    have eyes in the back of one's
      head
in    have foot-in-mouth disease
in    have one's finger in the pie
in    have one's hand in the till
in    have one's head in the clouds
in    have one's heart in one's mouth
in    have one's nose in a book
in    have one's words stick in one's
      throat
in    have someone in one's pocket
in    have someone or something in
      one's hands
in    have something in stock
in    have too many irons in the fire
in    hide one's head in the sand
in    hole in one
in    horn in (on someone)
in    in a (tight) spot
in    in a dead heat
in    in a flash
in    in a huff
in    in a mad rush
in    in a pinch
in    in a vicious circle
in    in a world of one's own
in    in bad faith
in    in bad sorts
in    in bad taste
in    in black and white
in    in broad daylight
in    in creation
in    in deep water
in    in fine feather
in    in full swing
in    in good condition
in    in good shape
in    in heat
in    in less than no time
in    in mint condition
in    in name only
in    in no mood to do something
in    in nothing flat
in    in one ear and out the other
in    in one fell swoop
in    in one's birthday suit
in    in one's blood
in    in one's mind's eye
in    in one's or its prime
in    in one's right mind
in    in one's second childhood

in    in one's spare time
in    in over one's head
in    in poor taste
in    in print
in    in rags
in    in round figures
in    in round numbers
in    in season
in    in seventh heaven
in    in short order
in    in short supply
in    in someone's (own) (best)
      interest(s)
in    in stock
in    in the air
in    in the bargain
in    in the black
in    in the blood
in    in the bullpen
in    in the cards
in    in the doghouse
in    in the doldrums
in    in the flesh
in    in the gutter
in    in the hole
in    in the interest(s) of something
in    in the know
in    in the lap of luxury
in    in the limelight
in    in the line of duty
in    in the long run
in    in the money
in    in the nick of time
in    in the pink (of condition)
in    in the prime of life
in    in the public eye
in    in the red
in    in the right
in    in the same boat
in    in the same breath
in    in the spotlight
in    in the twinkling of an eye
in    in the wind
in    in the world
in    in the wrong
in    in two shakes of a lamb's tail
in    ins and outs of something
in    keep a civil tongue (in one's
      head)
in    keep someone in stitches
in    keep someone or something
      hanging in midair

in keep someone or something in mind
in know something in one's bones
in late in the day
in leave a bad taste in someone's mouth
in leave someone in peace
in leave someone in the lurch
in leave someone or something hanging in midair
in like looking for a needle in a haystack
in live in an ivory tower
in look as if butter wouldn't melt in one's mouth
in lose oneself in something
in lost in thought
in man in the street
in melt in one's mouth
in mention something in passing
in milestone in someone's life
in Money burns a hole in someone's pocket.
in move up (in the world)
in nail in someone's or something's coffin
in nip something in the bud
in not know enough to come in out of the rain
in once in a blue moon
in one in a hundred
in one in a million
in one in a thousand
in one's heart is in one's mouth
in one's words stick in one's throat
in out in left field
in packed (in) like sardines
in pie in the sky
in pitch in (and help)
in put a bee in someone's bonnet
in put all one's eggs in one basket
in put in a good word (for someone)
in put in one's oar
in put in one's two cents(' worth)
in put one's foot in it
in put one's foot in one's mouth
in quake in one's boots
in ring in the new year
in roll in
in rolling in something
in Rome wasn't built in a day.

in rub salt in a wound
in rub someone's nose in something
in run (around) in circles
in run in the family
in shake in one's boots
in ships that pass in the night
in shot in the arm
in should have stood in bed
in skeleton in the closet
in slap in the face
in sleep in
in smack-dab in the middle
in square peg in a round hole
in stab someone in the back
in stare someone in the face
in stew in one's own juice
in stick one's foot in one's mouth
in take something in stride
in talk in circles
in talk until one is blue in the face
in tempest in a teapot
in There are plenty of other fish in the sea.
in throw a monkey wrench in the works
in throw in the sponge
in throw in the towel
in tie someone in knots
in tongue-in-cheek
in turn over in one's grave
in up in arms
in up in the air
in up to one's ears (in something)
in up to one's neck (in something)
in use every trick in the book
in waiting in the wings
in wash one's dirty linen in public
in When in Rome, do as the Romans do.
in with the best will in the world
in wolf in sheep's clothing
in worth one's or its weight in gold
in year in, year out
in zero in on something
inch every inch a something
inch every inch the something
inch Give one an inch, and one will take a mile.
inch If you give one an inch, one will take a mile.

it come to think of it
it cross a bridge before one comes to it
it cross a bridge when one comes to it
it Easy does it.
it eat one's cake and have it too
it find it in one's heart (to do something)
it for the devil of it
it for the heck of it
it for the hell of it
it go at it hammer and tongs
it go at it tooth and nail
it grin and bear it
it have one's cake and eat it too
it If the shoe fits, wear it.
it It never rains but it pours.
it lay it on thick
it lord it over someone
it make a go of it
it make a run for it
it no (ifs, ands, or) buts about it
it play it safe
it pour it on thick
it put one's foot in it
it rough it
it run for it
it spread it on thick
it step on it
it strike it rich
it take it or leave it
it whoop it up
it with it
it You can't take it with you.
it You said it!
itch have an itching palm
itchy have an itchy palm
its come into one's or its own
its Every dog has its day.
its falls flat on one's or its face
its find one's or its way somewhere
its have had its day
its in one's or its prime
its on one's or its last legs
its put something through its paces
its rear its ugly head
its run around like a chicken with its head cut off
its sit on its hands

its tell its own story
its tell its own tale
its worth one's or its weight in gold
itself end in itself
itself lend oneself or itself to something
itself speaks for itself
ivory live in an ivory tower
Jack All work and no play makes Jack a dull boy.
Jack before you can say Jack Robinson
jack jack-of-all-trades
job fall down on the job
job job lot
jockey jockey for position
Johnny Johnny-come-lately
Johnny Johnny-on-the-spot
join Join the club!
joint put someone's nose out of joint
joke all joking aside
joke crack a joke
joke no joke
joke standing joke
Jones Davy Jones's locker
Jones go to Davy Jones's locker
Jones keep up (with the Joneses)
joy burst with joy
judge as sober as a judge
juice stew in one's own juice
jump get the jump on someone
jump jump off the deep end
jump jump on the bandwagon
jump jump out of one's skin
jump jump the gun
jump jump the track
jump jumping-off point
just get one's just deserts
just just so
just just what the doctor ordered
just stop (just) short (of something)
justice miscarriage of justice
justice poetic justice
keel keep on an even keel
keel keep something on an even keel
keep earn one's keep
keep keep a civil tongue (in one's head)

**ladder** at the bottom of the ladder
**lady** ladies' man
**lady** lady-killer
**laid** kill the goose that laid the golden egg
**lamb** as innocent as a lamb
**lamb** in two shakes of a lamb's tail
**lamb** like a lamb to the slaughter
**lamb** like lambs to the slaughter
**land** do a land-office business
**land** land of Nod
**land** land someone with someone or something
**land** land up somehow or somewhere
**land** live off the fat of the land
**landslide** landslide victory
**language** speak the same language
**lap** in the lap of luxury
**large** loom large
**lark** as happy as a lark
**last** at the last minute
**last** breathe one's last
**last** get the last laugh
**last** get the last word
**last** He laughs best who laughs last.
**last** He who laughs last, laughs longest.
**last** last but not least
**last** on one's or its last legs
**last** That's the last straw.
**late** keep late hours
**late** late in the day
**lately** Johnny-come-lately
**laugh** get the last laugh
**laugh** He laughs best who laughs last.
**laugh** He who laughs last, laughs longest.
**laugh** laugh out of the other side of one's mouth
**laugh** laugh something out of court
**laugh** laugh up one's sleeve
**laugh** no laughing matter
**laurels** look to one's laurels
**law** law unto oneself
**law** lay down the law

**law** take the law into one's own hands
**lay** lay a finger on someone or something
**lay** lay an egg
**lay** lay down the law
**lay** lay it on thick
**lay** lay one's cards on the table
**lay** lay something on the line
**lay** lay something to waste
**lay** lay waste to something
**lead** All roads lead to Rome.
**lead** blind leading the blind
**lead** lead a dog's life
**lead** lead someone down the garden path
**lead** lead someone on a merry chase
**lead** lead the life of Riley
**lead** lead up to something
**leaf** take a leaf out of someone's book
**leaf** turn over a new leaf
**leap** by leaps and bounds
**learn** learn something from the bottom up
**lease** new lease on life
**least** last but not least
**least** line of least resistance
**least** path of least resistance
**leave** leave a bad taste in someone's mouth
**leave** leave a sinking ship
**leave** leave no stone unturned
**leave** leave one to one's fate
**leave** leave someone for dead
**leave** leave someone high and dry
**leave** leave someone holding the baby
**leave** leave someone holding the bag
**leave** leave someone in peace
**leave** leave someone in the lurch
**leave** leave someone or something hanging in midair
**leave** take it or leave it
**left** out in left field
**leg** cost an arm and a leg
**leg** have one's tail between one's legs
**leg** not have a leg to stand on
**leg** on one's or its last legs

**leg** one's tail is between one's legs
**leg** pay an arm and a leg (for something)
**leg** pull someone's leg
**leg** stretch one's legs
**lend** lend an ear (to someone)
**lend** lend oneself or itself to something
**less** in less than no time
**let** Don't let someone or something get you down.
**let** Let bygones be bygones.
**let** let grass grow under one's feet
**let** let off steam
**let** let one's hair down
**let** Let sleeping dogs lie.
**let** let someone off (the hook)
**let** let something slide
**let** let something slip by
**let** let the cat out of the bag
**let** let the chance slip by
**let** live and let live
**level** (strictly) on the level
**level** find one's own level
**level** on the level
**liberties** take liberties with someone or something
**lick** give something a lick and a promise
**lick** lick one's lips
**lie** Let sleeping dogs lie.
**lie** lie through one's teeth
**lie** take something lying down
**life** all walks of life
**life** get the shock of one's life
**life** have the time of one's life
**life** in the prime of life
**life** lead a dog's life
**life** lead the life of Riley
**life** life of the party
**life** live a dog's life
**life** live the life of Riley
**life** make life miserable for someone
**life** matter of life and death
**life** milestone in someone's life
**life** new lease on life
**life** run for one's life
**life** seamy side of life
**life** Variety is the spice of life.
**life** within an inch of one's life

**light** as light as a feather
**light** begin to see the light
**light** bring something to light
**light** come to light
**light** hide one's light under a bushel
**light** make light of something
**light** out like a light
**light** see the light (at the end of the tunnel)
**light** see the light (of day)
**like** eat like a bird
**like** eat like a horse
**like** feel like a million (dollars)
**like** feel like a new person
**like** fit like a glove
**like** go like clockwork
**like** hit (someone) like a ton of bricks
**like** know someone or something like a book
**like** know someone or something like the back of one's hand
**like** know someone or something like the palm of one's hand
**like** like a bat out of hell
**like** like a bolt out of the blue
**like** like a bump on a log
**like** like a fish out of water
**like** like a lamb to the slaughter
**like** like a sitting duck
**like** like a three-ring circus
**like** like lambs to the slaughter
**like** like looking for a needle in a haystack
**like** like nothing on earth
**like** like sitting ducks
**like** like water off a duck's back
**like** look like a million dollars
**like** look like the cat that swallowed the canary
**like** out like a light
**like** packed (in) like sardines
**like** read someone like a book
**like** run around like a chicken with its head cut off
**like** sell like hotcakes
**like** sleep like a log
**like** spread like wildfire
**like** watch someone like a hawk
**like** work like a horse
**likely** as likely as not

**lily** gild the lily
**limb** out on a limb
**limelight** in the limelight
**limit** go the limit
**limit** sky's the limit
**line** draw a line between something and something else
**line** drop someone a few lines
**line** drop someone a line
**line** end of the line
**line** in the line of duty
**line** lay something on the line
**line** line of least resistance
**line** party line
**line** put something on the line
**line** read between the lines
**line** sign on the dotted line
**line** step out of line
**line** toe the line
**linen** air one's dirty linen in public
**linen** wash one's dirty linen in public
**lining** Every cloud has a silver lining.
**lion** beard the lion in his den
**lion** lion's share (of something)
**lip** button one's lip
**lip** keep a stiff upper lip
**lip** lick one's lips
**list** on a waiting list
**little** little bird told me
**little** little by little
**little** little knowledge is a dangerous thing
**little** precious little
**little** twist someone around one's little finger
**live** every living soul
**live** live a dog's life
**live** live and let live
**live** live beyond one's means
**live** live by one's wits
**live** live from hand to mouth
**live** live in an ivory tower
**live** live off the fat of the land
**live** live out of a suitcase
**live** live the life of Riley
**live** live within one's means
**load** get a load off one's feet
**load** get a load off one's mind
**load** take a load off one's feet

**loaf** Half a loaf is better than none.
**loan** float a loan
**lock** lock horns (with someone)
**lock** lock, stock, and barrel
**locker** Davy Jones's locker
**locker** go to Davy Jones's locker
**log** like a bump on a log
**log** sleep like a log
**loggerheads** at loggerheads
**loins** gird (up) one's loins
**long** in the long run
**long** Long time no see.
**long** make a long story short
**long** not long for this world
**long** over the long haul
**longest** He who laughs last, laughs longest.
**look** Don't look a gift horse in the mouth.
**look** like looking for a needle in a haystack
**look** look as if butter wouldn't melt in one's mouth
**look** look daggers at someone
**look** look like a million dollars
**look** look like the cat that swallowed the canary
**look** look the other way
**look** look to one's laurels
**loom** loom large
**loon** as crazy as a loon
**loop** knock someone for a loop
**loop** throw someone for a loop
**loose** at loose ends
**loose** play fast and loose (with someone or something)
**lord** lord it over someone
**lose** lose face
**lose** lose heart
**lose** lose one's grip
**lose** lose one's temper
**lose** lose one's train of thought
**lose** lose oneself in something
**loser** Finders keepers(, losers weepers).
**loss** cut one's losses
**lost** lost in thought
**lost** lost on someone
**lost** make up for lost time
**lot** cover a lot of ground
**lot** have a lot going (for one)

**make** make something worth someone's while
**make** make the feathers fly
**make** make the fur fly
**make** make the grade
**make** make up for lost time
**make** what makes someone tick
**man** be a marked man
**man** Early to bed, early to rise(, makes a man healthy, wealthy, and wise).
**man** high man on the totem pole
**man** ladies' man
**man** low man on the totem pole
**man** man about town
**man** man in the street
**man** man-to-man
**man** odd man out
**man** One man's meat is another man's poison.
**man** separate the men from the boys
**manger** dog in the manger
**manna** manna from heaven
**many** have too many irons in the fire
**many** Too many cooks spoil the broth.
**many** Too many cooks spoil the stew.
**March** as mad as a March hare
**march** march to a different drummer
**march** steal a march (on someone)
**mark** be a marked man
**mark** toe the mark
**mark** wide of the mark
**mark** X marks the spot.
**market** drug on the market
**market** on the market
**mast** at half-mast
**match** meet one's match
**match** strike a match
**match** whole shooting match
**matter** crux of the matter
**matter** get to the heart of the matter
**matter** gray matter
**matter** matter of life and death
**matter** matter of opinion
**matter** no laughing matter

**may** come what may
**me** little bird told me
**me** Woe is me!
**meal** square meal
**mealy** mealy-mouthed
**means** beyond one's means
**means** live beyond one's means
**means** live within one's means
**measure** made to measure
**meat** One man's meat is another man's poison.
**medicine** dose of one's own medicine
**medicine** take one's medicine
**medium** hit a happy medium
**medium** strike a happy medium
**meet** meet one's end
**meet** meet one's match
**meet** meet someone halfway
**melt** look as if butter wouldn't melt in one's mouth
**melt** melt in one's mouth
**memory** know something from memory
**men** separate the men from the boys
**mend** mend (one's) fences
**mend** mend one's ways
**mend** on the mend
**mention** mention something in passing
**mercy** throw oneself at the mercy of the court
**mercy** throw oneself on the mercy of the court
**merry** lead someone on a merry chase
**merry** make merry
**message** get the message
**met** hail-fellow-well-met
**mice** When the cat's away, the mice will play.
**midair** keep someone or something hanging in midair
**midair** leave someone or something hanging in midair
**Midas** have the Midas touch
**middle** middle-of-the-road
**middle** play both ends (against the middle)
**middle** smack-dab in the middle
**midnight** burn the midnight oil

**midstream** change horses in midstream

**mighty** act high-and-mighty

**mile** Give one an inch, and one will take a mile.

**mile** If you give one an inch, one will take a mile.

**mile** miss (something) by a mile

**mile** stand out a mile

**mile** stick out a mile

**milestone** milestone in someone's life

**milk** cry over spilled milk

**milk** milk of human kindness

**mill** been through the mill

**million** feel like a million (dollars)

**million** look like a million dollars

**million** one in a million

**millstone** millstone about one's neck

**mincemeat** make mincemeat of someone

**mind** bear someone or something in mind

**mind** boggle someone's mind

**mind** enter one's mind

**mind** get a load off one's mind

**mind** give someone a piece of one's mind

**mind** have a one-track mind

**mind** have the presence of mind to do something

**mind** in one's mind's eye

**mind** in one's right mind

**mind** keep someone or something in mind

**mind** mind one's own business

**mind** mind one's p's and q's

**mind** mind you

**mind** on one's mind

**mind** out of one's mind

**mind** Out of sight, out of mind.

**mind** slip one's mind

**mine** back to the salt mines

**mine** mine of information

**mine** Your guess is as good as mine.

**mint** in mint condition

**minute** at the last minute

**minute** every minute counts

**miscarriage** miscarriage of justice

**mischief** make mischief

**miserable** make life miserable for someone

**miss** miss (something) by a mile

**miss** miss the point

**Missouri** be from Missouri

**mixed** have mixed feelings (about someone or something)

**mixed** mixed bag

**mold** cast in the same mold

**molehill** make a mountain out of a molehill

**moment** every moment counts

**moment** moment of truth

**moment** on the spur of the moment

**money** fool and his money are soon parted

**money** fork money out (for something)

**money** have money to burn

**money** hush money

**money** in the money

**money** make good money

**money** Money burns a hole in someone's pocket.

**money** Money is no object.

**money** Money is the root of all evil.

**money** Money talks.

**money** pour money down the drain

**money** Put your money where your mouth is!

**money** throw good money after bad

**money** Time is money.

**monkey** monkey business

**monkey** throw a monkey wrench in the works

**mood** in no mood to do something

**moon** ask for the moon

**moon** once in a blue moon

**moon** promise someone the moon

**moon** promise the moon (to someone)

**more** bite off more than one can chew

**more** There's more than one way to skin a cat.

**more** wear more than one hat

**morning** first thing (in the morning)

**morning** morning after (the night before)

**moss** rolling stone gathers no moss

**mother** tied to one's mother's apron strings

**motion** go through the motions

**mountain** make a mountain out of a molehill

**mouse** as poor as a church mouse

**mouse** as quiet as a mouse

**mouse** play cat and mouse (with someone)

**mouse** When the cat's away, the mice will play.

**mouth** born with a silver spoon in one's mouth

**mouth** by word of mouth

**mouth** Don't look a gift horse in the mouth.

**mouth** down in the mouth

**mouth** foam at the mouth

**mouth** have a big mouth

**mouth** have foot-in-mouth disease

**mouth** have one's heart in one's mouth

**mouth** laugh out of the other side of one's mouth

**mouth** leave a bad taste in someone's mouth

**mouth** live from hand to mouth

**mouth** look as if butter wouldn't melt in one's mouth

**mouth** make someone's mouth water

**mouth** mealy-mouthed

**mouth** melt in one's mouth

**mouth** not open one's mouth

**mouth** one's heart is in one's mouth

**mouth** put one's foot in one's mouth

**mouth** put words into someone's mouth

**mouth** Put your money where your mouth is!

**mouth** stick one's foot in one's mouth

**mouth** straight from the horse's mouth

**mouth** take the words (right) out of one's mouth

**move** move heaven and earth to do something

**move** move up (in the world)

**move** on the move

**mover** prime mover

**much** much ado about nothing

**mud** as clear as mud

**mule** as stubborn as a mule

**murder** cry bloody murder

**murder** scream bloody murder

**music** face the music

**nail** as hard as nails

**nail** bite one's nails

**nail** fight someone or something tooth and nail

**nail** go at it tooth and nail

**nail** hit the nail (right) on the head

**nail** nail in someone's or something's coffin

**naked** with the naked eye

**name** drop someone's name

**name** drop the name of someone

**name** in name only

**name** name-dropping

**name** worthy of the name

**nap** catch someone napping

**nape** by the nape of the neck

**nature** call of nature

**nature** second nature to someone

**near** nowhere near

**neck** break one's neck (to do something)

**neck** breathe down someone's neck

**neck** by the nape of the neck

**neck** millstone about one's neck

**neck** neck and neck

**neck** risk one's neck (to do something)

**neck** stick one's neck out

**neck** up to one's neck (in something)

**need** friend in need is a friend indeed

**needle** like looking for a needle in a haystack

**needle** on pins and needles

**needle** pins and needles

**neither** neither fish nor fowl

**not** not able to see the forest for the trees
**not** not born yesterday
**not** not have a leg to stand on
**not** not hold water
**not** not know enough to come in out of the rain
**not** not know someone from Adam
**not** not long for this world
**not** not open one's mouth
**not** not see further than the end of one's nose
**not** not set foot somewhere
**not** not sleep a wink
**not** not someone's cup of tea
**not** not up to scratch
**not** not up to snuff
**not** not utter a word
**not** Waste not, want not.
**note** hit a sour note
**note** strike a sour note
**nothing** in nothing flat
**nothing** like nothing on earth
**nothing** much ado about nothing
**nothing** next to nothing
**nothing** nothing but
**nothing** nothing short of something
**nothing** Nothing ventured, nothing gained.
**nothing** sweet nothings
**nothing** want for nothing
**notice** sit up and take notice
**nowhere** nowhere near
**nuisance** make a nuisance of oneself
**number** in round numbers
**number** one's days are numbered
**number** one's number is up
**nut** everything from soup to nuts
**nut** nuts and bolts (of something)
**oar** put in one's oar
**oat** sow one's wild oats
**object** Money is no object.
**odd** odd man out
**odds** odds are against one
**odor** odor of sanctity
**of** act of God
**of** afraid of one's own shadow
**of** ahead of one's time
**of** all walks of life

**of** apple of someone's eye
**of** at the bottom of the ladder
**of** at the drop of a hat
**of** at the end of one's rope
**of** at the end of one's tether
**of** at the top of one's lungs
**of** at the top of one's voice
**of** at this stage (of the game)
**of** bag of tricks
**of** be a fan of someone
**of** be the spit and image of someone
**of** be the spitting image of someone
**of** bear the brunt (of something)
**of** Birds of a feather flock together.
**of** black sheep of the family
**of** blow something out of (all) proportion
**of** bone of contention
**of** business end of something
**of** by a show of hands
**of** by the nape of the neck
**of** by the seat of one's pants
**of** by the skin of one's teeth
**of** by the sweat of one's brow
**of** by virtue of something
**of** by word of mouth
**of** call of nature
**of** can't make heads or tails (out) of someone or something
**of** can't see beyond the end of one's nose
**of** can't see one's hand in front of one's face
**of** carry the weight of the world on one's shoulders
**of** catch one's death (of cold)
**of** change of pace
**of** cock of the walk
**of** come in out of the rain
**of** come of age
**of** come out of the closet
**of** come to think of it
**of** cover a lot of ground
**of** cream of the crop
**of** crux of the matter
**of** die of a broken heart
**of** die of boredom
**of** dose of one's own medicine
**of** drop the name of someone

of lull someone into a false sense of security
of make a clean breast of something
of make a go of it
of make a great show of something
of make a mountain out of a molehill
of make a nuisance of oneself
of make a silk purse out of a sow's ear
of make fast work of someone or something
of make light of something
of make mincemeat of someone
of make short work of someone or something
of make something up out of whole cloth
of matter of life and death
of matter of opinion
of middle-of-the-road
of milk of human kindness
of mine of information
of miscarriage of justice
of moment of truth
of Money is the root of all evil.
of not know enough to come in out of the rain
of not see further than the end of one's nose
of not someone's cup of tea
of nothing short of something
of nuts and bolts (of something)
of odor of sanctity
of of all the nerve
of of the first water
of off the top of one's head
of on the heels of something
of on the horns of a dilemma
of on the spur of the moment
of on the tip of one's tongue
of on top of the world
of open a can of worms
of order of the day
of other side of the tracks
of ounce of prevention is worth a pound of cure
of out of (all) proportion
of out of a clear blue sky
of out of circulation

of out of commission
of out of gas
of out of hand
of out of luck
of out of one's element
of out of one's head
of out of one's mind
of out of one's senses
of out of order
of out of practice
of out of print
of out of season
of out of service
of Out of sight, out of mind.
of out of sorts
of out of the blue
of out of the corner of one's eye
of out of the frying pan into the fire
of out of the hole
of out of the question
of out of the red
of out of the running
of out of the woods
of out of thin air
of out of this world
of out of tune (with someone or something)
of out of turn
of part and parcel of something
of path of least resistance
of piece of the pie
of pull out (of something)
of pull something out of a hat
of pull something out of thin air
of put someone's nose out of joint
of rule of thumb
of run out of gas
of salt of the earth
of scrape the bottom of the barrel
of seamy side of life
of see the light (at the end of the tunnel)
of see the light (of day)
of sell someone a bill of goods
of shades of someone or something
of six of one and half a dozen of the other
of slice of the cake
of slip of the tongue

**on** (strictly) on the level
**on** as plain as the nose on one's face
**on** bank on something
**on** blow the whistle (on someone)
**on** bring down the curtain (on something)
**on** call someone on the carpet
**on** carry the weight of the world on one's shoulders
**on** cash in (on something)
**on** climb on the bandwagon
**on** dash cold water on something
**on** death on someone or something
**on** die on the vine
**on** dig up some dirt on someone
**on** drug on the market
**on** fall down on the job
**on** fall flat (on one's or its face)
**on** feast one's eyes (on someone or something)
**on** firing on all cylinders
**on** get along (on a shoestring)
**on** get on someone's nerves
**on** get on the bandwagon
**on** get one's feet on the ground
**on** get the jump on someone
**on** get the upper hand (on someone)
**on** get up on the wrong side of the bed
**on** go (out) on strike
**on** go back on one's word
**on** go off on a tangent
**on** go on a fishing expedition
**on** hang on someone's every word
**on** Hang on to your hat!
**on** Hang on!
**on** hard on someone's heels
**on** have a chip on one's shoulder
**on** have a good head on one's shoulders
**on** have a price on one's head
**on** have dibs on something
**on** have egg on one's face
**on** have one's heart set on something
**on** high man on the totem pole
**on** hit the nail (right) on the head
**on** Hold on to your hat!
**on** horn in (on someone)

**on** hot on something
**on** Johnny-on-the-spot
**on** jump on the bandwagon
**on** keep on an even keel
**on** keep one's eye on the ball
**on** keep one's feet on the ground
**on** keep someone on tenterhooks
**on** keep something on an even keel
**on** knock on wood
**on** know which side one's bread is buttered on
**on** lay a finger on someone or something
**on** lay it on thick
**on** lay one's cards on the table
**on** lay something on the line
**on** lead someone on a merry chase
**on** like a bump on a log
**on** like nothing on earth
**on** lost on someone
**on** low man on the totem pole
**on** lower the boom on someone
**on** make someone's hair stand on end
**on** new lease on life
**on** new one on someone
**on** not have a leg to stand on
**on** on a fool's errand
**on** on a waiting list
**on** on active duty
**on** on all fours
**on** on cloud nine
**on** on duty
**on** on earth
**on** on one's feet
**on** on one's honor
**on** on one's mind
**on** on one's or its last legs
**on** on one's toes
**on** on pins and needles
**on** on second thought
**on** on someone's doorstep
**on** on someone's head
**on** on someone's say-so
**on** on someone's shoulders
**on** on target
**on** on the air
**on** on the average
**on** on the bench
**on** on the block

**oneself** pull oneself up (by one's own bootstraps)
**oneself** spread oneself too thin
**oneself** suit oneself
**oneself** throw oneself at someone's feet
**oneself** throw oneself at the mercy of the court
**oneself** throw oneself on the mercy of the court
**only** Beauty is only skin deep.
**only** in name only
**open** keep one's weather eye open
**open** not open one's mouth
**open** open a can of worms
**open** open book
**open** open one's heart (to someone)
**open** open Pandora's box
**open** open secret
**open** open-and-shut case
**opinion** form an opinion
**opinion** matter of opinion
**or** believe it or not
**or** can't make heads or tails (out) of someone or something
**or** fish or cut bait
**or** no (ifs, ands, or) buts about it
**or** rain or shine
**or** shape up or ship out
**or** sink or swim
**or** take it or leave it
**order** in short order
**order** just what the doctor ordered
**order** order of the day
**order** out of order
**other** go in one ear and out the other
**other** have other fish to fry
**other** in one ear and out the other
**other** laugh out of the other side of one's mouth
**other** look the other way
**other** none other than
**other** other side of the tracks
**other** shoe is on the other foot
**other** six of one and half a dozen of the other
**other** There are plenty of other fish in the sea.

**other** turn the other cheek
**other** with every (other) breath
**ounce** ounce of prevention is worth a pound of cure
**out** blow something out of (all) proportion
**out** break (out) into tears
**out** break out in a cold sweat
**out** can't make heads or tails (out) of someone or something
**out** come in out of the rain
**out** come out ahead
**out** come out in the wash
**out** come out of the closet
**out** cry one's eyes out
**out** cut the ground out from under someone
**out** down and out
**out** drum someone out of something
**out** dry someone out
**out** eat one's heart out
**out** eat out of someone's hand(s)
**out** eat someone out of house and home
**out** farm someone or something out
**out** feel out of place
**out** fork money out (for something)
**out** get out of the wrong side of the bed
**out** go (out) on strike
**out** go in one ear and out the other
**out** hold out for something
**out** hold out the olive branch
**out** in one ear and out the other
**out** ins and outs of something
**out** jump out of one's skin
**out** keep an eye out (for someone or something)
**out** know something inside out
**out** laugh out of the other side of one's mouth
**out** laugh something out of court
**out** let the cat out of the bag
**out** like a bat out of hell
**out** like a bolt out of the blue
**out** like a fish out of water
**out** live out of a suitcase

**over** over the long haul
**over** over the short haul
**over** over the top
**over** party's over
**over** pull the wool over someone's eyes
**over** rake someone over the coals
**over** ride roughshod over someone or something
**over** turn over a new leaf
**over** turn over in one's grave
**over** win someone over
**overboard** go overboard
**owl** as wise as an owl
**owl** night owl
**own** afraid of one's own shadow
**own** blow one's own horn
**own** come into one's or its own
**own** cut one's (own) throat
**own** dig one's own grave
**own** dose of one's own medicine
**own** feather one's (own) nest
**own** find one's own level
**own** foul one's own nest
**own** hoist with one's own petard
**own** hold one's own
**own** in a world of one's own
**own** in someone's (own) (best) interest(s)
**own** mind one's own business
**own** paddle one's own canoe
**own** pull oneself up (by one's own bootstraps)
**own** sign one's own death warrant
**own** stand on one's own two feet
**own** stew in one's own juice
**own** take the law into one's own hands
**own** tell its own story
**own** tell its own tale
**own** toot one's own horn
**own** under one's own steam
**ox** as strong as an ox
**P** mind one's p's and q's
**pace** at a snail's pace
**pace** change of pace
**pace** put one through one's paces
**pace** put something through its paces
**pack** packed (in) like sardines
**pack** send someone packing
**pad** pad the bill

**paddle** paddle one's own canoe
**paint** paint the town red
**pale** beyond the pale
**palm** have an itching palm
**palm** have an itchy palm
**palm** know someone or something like the palm of one's hand
**pan** flash in the pan
**pan** out of the frying pan into the fire
**pancake** as flat as a pancake
**Pandora** open Pandora's box
**pants** by the seat of one's pants
**paper** put something on paper
**par** up to par
**paradise** fool's paradise
**parcel** part and parcel of something
**part** fool and his money are soon parted
**part** part and parcel of something
**part** part someone's hair
**party** life of the party
**party** party line
**party** party's over
**pass** come to pass
**pass** mention something in passing
**pass** pass the buck
**pass** pass the hat
**pass** ships that pass in the night
**pasture** put someone or something out to pasture
**path** beat a path to someone's door
**path** lead someone down the garden path
**path** path of least resistance
**patience** try someone's patience
**Paul** rob Peter to pay Paul
**pavement** pound the pavement
**pay** Crime doesn't pay.
**pay** pay an arm and a leg (for something)
**pay** pay one's debt (to society)
**pay** pay one's dues
**pay** pay the piper
**pay** pay through the nose (for something)
**pay** rob Peter to pay Paul
**pay** There will be the devil to pay.
**pea** as thick as pea soup

**point** miss the point
**point** point the finger at someone
**poison** One man's meat is another man's poison.
**poke** buy a pig in a poke
**poke** poke fun (at someone)
**poke** poke one's nose in(to something)
**pole** be poles apart
**pole** high man on the totem pole
**pole** low man on the totem pole
**pond** big frog in a small pond
**poor** as poor as a church mouse
**poor** in poor taste
**pop** pop the question
**port** any port in a storm
**position** jockey for position
**possible** as soon as possible
**post** from pillar to post
**post** keep someone posted
**pot** go to pot
**pot** pot calling the kettle black
**pot** watched pot never boils
**pound** ounce of prevention is worth a pound of cure
**pound** penny-wise and pound-foolish
**pound** pound a beat
**pound** pound the pavement
**pour** It never rains but it pours.
**pour** pour cold water on something
**pour** pour it on thick
**pour** pour money down the drain
**pour** pour oil on troubled water
**powder** sitting on a powder keg
**power** powers that be
**practice** out of practice
**practice** practice what you preach
**praise** damn someone or something with faint praise
**praise** sing someone's praises
**preach** practice what you preach
**precious** precious few
**precious** precious little
**premium** at a premium
**presence** have the presence of mind to do something
**press** press one's luck
**press** press someone to the wall

**pretty** as pretty as a picture
**pretty** cost a pretty penny
**pretty** Pretty is as pretty does.
**prevention** ounce of prevention is worth a pound of cure
**price** have a price on one's head
**prick** prick up one's ears
**prime** in one's or its prime
**prime** in the prime of life
**prime** prime mover
**print** in print
**print** out of print
**print** small print
**promise** give something a lick and a promise
**promise** promise someone the moon
**promise** promise the moon (to someone)
**proportion** blow something out of (all) proportion
**proportion** out of (all) proportion
**proud** as proud as a peacock
**public** air one's dirty linen in public
**public** in the public eye
**public** wash one's dirty linen in public
**pull** pull oneself up (by one's own bootstraps)
**pull** pull out (of something)
**pull** pull out all the stops
**pull** pull someone's leg
**pull** pull someone's or something's teeth
**pull** pull something out of a hat
**pull** pull something out of thin air
**pull** pull the rug out (from under someone)
**pull** pull the wool over someone's eyes
**pull** pull up stakes
**punishment** glutton for punishment
**purse** control the purse strings
**purse** make a silk purse out of a sow's ear
**push** push off
**push** push one's luck
**push** push someone to the wall
**put** put a bee in someone's bonnet

**put** put all one's eggs in one basket

**put** put in a good word (for someone)

**put** put in one's oar

**put** put in one's two cents(' worth)

**put** put on a brave face

**put** put on airs

**put** put on one's thinking cap

**put** put one through one's paces

**put** put one's best foot forward

**put** put one's cards on the table

**put** put one's dibs on something

**put** put one's foot in it

**put** put one's foot in one's mouth

**put** put one's hand to the plow

**put** put one's nose to the grindstone

**put** put one's shoulder to the wheel

**put** put someone or something out to pasture

**put** put someone or something to bed

**put** put someone or something to sleep

**put** put someone through the wringer

**put** put someone to shame

**put** put someone to the test

**put** put someone's nose out of joint

**put** put something on ice

**put** put something on paper

**put** put something on the back burner

**put** put something on the cuff

**put** put something on the line

**put** put something through its paces

**put** put the cart before the horse

**put** put two and two together

**put** put up a (brave) front

**put** put upon someone

**put** put words into someone's mouth

**put** Put your money where your mouth is!

**put** stay put

**putty** be putty in someone's hands

**Q** mind one's p's and q's

**QT** on the QT

**quake** quake in one's boots

**question** out of the question

**question** pop the question

**quick** as quick as a wink

**quick** cut someone to the quick

**quick** quick on the draw

**quick** quick on the trigger

**quick** quick on the uptake

**quiet** as quiet as a mouse

**quiet** so quiet you could hear a pin drop

**quit** call it quits

**quite** quite something

**race** rat race

**race** Slow and steady wins the race.

**rack** go to rack and ruin

**rack** rack one's brain(s)

**ragged** run someone ragged

**rags** from rags to riches

**rags** in rags

**rain** come in out of the rain

**rain** It never rains but it pours.

**rain** not know enough to come in out of the rain

**rain** rain cats and dogs

**rain** rain or shine

**rainy** save something for a rainy day

**raise** cause (some) eyebrows to raise

**raise** raise one's sights

**raise** raise some eyebrows

**rake** rake someone over the coals

**rake** rake something up

**rally** rally (a)round someone or something

**rank** close ranks

**rant** rant and rave

**raring** rarin' to go

**rat** rat race

**rate** second-rate

**rave** rant and rave

**reach** reach first base (with someone or something)

**read** read between the lines

**read** read someone like a book

**read** read someone the riot act

**rear** bring up the rear

**rear** rear its ugly head

**recite** recite something chapter and verse
**record** for the record
**record** off the record
**red** get the red-carpet treatment
**red** give someone the red-carpet treatment
**red** in the red
**red** out of the red
**red** paint the town red
**red** red tape
**red** roll out the red carpet for someone
**regular** as regular as clockwork
**resistance** line of least resistance
**resistance** path of least resistance
**return** by return mail
**rich** strike it rich
**riches** from rags to riches
**ride** go along for the ride
**ride** hitch a ride
**ride** ride roughshod over someone or something
**ride** ride the gravy train
**ride** riding for a fall
**ride** thumb a ride
**right** give one's right arm (for someone or something)
**right** have someone dead to rights
**right** have the right-of-way
**right** hit someone (right) between the eyes
**right** hit the nail (right) on the head
**right** in one's right mind
**right** in the right
**right** right off the bat
**right** right under someone's nose
**right** serve someone right
**right** take the words (right) out of one's mouth
**Riley** lead the life of Riley
**Riley** live the life of Riley
**ring** give someone a ring
**ring** have a familiar ring
**ring** like a three-ring circus
**ring** ring down the curtain (on something)
**ring** ring in the new year
**ring** ring true
**ring** toss one's hat into the ring

**riot** read someone the riot act
**ripe** ripe old age
**ripe** when the time is ripe
**rise** Early to bed, early to rise(, makes a man healthy, wealthy, and wise).
**rise** rise and shine
**risk** risk one's neck (to do something)
**road** All roads lead to Rome.
**road** end of the road
**road** middle-of-the-road
**road** road hog
**rob** rob Peter to pay Paul
**rob** rob the cradle
**robbery** daylight robbery
**Robinson** before you can say Jack Robinson
**rock** between a rock and a hard place
**rock** rock the boat
**roll** heads will roll
**roll** roll in
**roll** roll out the red carpet for someone
**roll** rolling in something
**roll** rolling stone gathers no moss
**Roman** When in Rome, do as the Romans do.
**Rome** All roads lead to Rome.
**Rome** fiddle while Rome burns
**Rome** Rome wasn't built in a day.
**Rome** When in Rome, do as the Romans do.
**roof** go through the roof
**roost** come home (to roost)
**roost** rule the roost
**root** Money is the root of all evil.
**root** root something out
**root** rooted to the spot
**rope** at the end of one's rope
**rope** know the ropes
**rope** show someone the ropes
**rough** diamond in the rough
**rough** rough it
**roughshod** ride roughshod over someone or something
**round** go (a)round in circles
**round** go (a)round the bend
**round** in round figures
**round** in round numbers

**score** know the score
**scot-free** get off scot-free
**scot-free** go scot-free
**scrape** bow and scrape
**scrape** have a scrape (with someone or something)
**scrape** scrape the bottom of the barrel
**scratch** make something from scratch
**scratch** not up to scratch
**scratch** scratch the surface
**scratch** start from scratch
**scream** scream bloody murder
**screw** screw up one's courage
**scrimp** scrimp and save
**sea** at sea (about something)
**sea** between the devil and the deep blue sea
**sea** There are plenty of other fish in the sea.
**seal** signed, sealed, and delivered
**seam** burst at the seams
**seam** come apart at the seams
**seamy** seamy side of life
**search** search high and low for someone or something
**search** search something with a fine-tooth comb
**season** in season
**season** out of season
**season** silly season
**seat** by the seat of one's pants
**seat** take a back seat (to someone)
**second** come off second best
**second** get one's second wind
**second** get second thoughts about someone or something
**second** in one's second childhood
**second** on second thought
**second** play second fiddle (to someone)
**second** second nature to someone
**second** second-rate
**secret** open secret
**security** lull someone into a false sense of security
**see** begin to see daylight
**see** begin to see the light

**see** can't see beyond the end of one's nose
**see** can't see one's hand in front of one's face
**see** Long time no see.
**see** not able to see the forest for the trees
**see** not see further than the end of one's nose
**see** see double
**see** see eye to eye (about something)
**see** see eye to eye on something
**see** see stars
**see** see the (hand)writing on the wall
**see** see the light (at the end of the tunnel)
**see** see the light (of day)
**see** see things
**see** seeing that
**see** wait-and-see attitude
**seed** go to seed
**seed** run to seed
**sell** sell like hotcakes
**sell** sell someone a bill of goods
**sell** sell someone or something short
**send** send one about one's business
**send** send someone packing
**send** send someone to the showers
**sense** come to one's senses
**sense** horse sense
**sense** lull someone into a false sense of security
**sense** out of one's senses
**sense** sixth sense
**separate** separate the men from the boys
**separate** separate the sheep from the goats
**serve** first come, first served
**serve** serve as a guinea pig
**serve** serve someone right
**service** out of service
**set** have one's heart set on something
**set** not set foot somewhere
**set** one's heart is set on something
**set** set foot somewhere

**sick** as sick as a dog
**side** be a thorn in someone's side
**side** get out of the wrong side of the bed
**side** get up on the wrong side of the bed
**side** know which side one's bread is buttered on
**side** laugh out of the other side of one's mouth
**side** other side of the tracks
**side** seamy side of life
**sight** buy something sight unseen
**sight** know someone by sight
**sight** love at first sight
**sight** lower one's sights
**sight** Out of sight, out of mind.
**sight** raise one's sights
**sight** set one's sights on something
**sign** sign on the dotted line
**sign** sign one's own death warrant
**sign** signed, sealed, and delivered
**silk** make a silk purse out of a sow's ear
**silly** silly season
**silver** born with a silver spoon in one's mouth
**silver** Every cloud has a silver lining.
**sing** sing someone's praises
**sink** desert a sinking ship
**sink** everything but the kitchen sink
**sink** leave a sinking ship
**sink** sink one's teeth into something
**sink** sink or swim
**sit** like a sitting duck
**sit** like sitting ducks
**sit** sit at someone's feet
**sit** sit on its hands
**sit** sit on one's hands
**sit** sit on the fence
**sit** sit tight
**sit** sit up and take notice
**sit** sitting on a powder keg
**sit** sitting target
**six** at sixes and sevens
**six** six of one and half a dozen of the other
**sixth** sixth sense

**skate** skate on thin ice
**skeleton** skeleton in the closet
**skin** all skin and bones
**skin** Beauty is only skin deep.
**skin** by the skin of one's teeth
**skin** get under someone's skin
**skin** jump out of one's skin
**skin** no skin off someone's nose
**skin** no skin off someone's teeth
**skin** nothing but skin and bones
**skin** There's more than one way to skin a cat.
**skin** thick-skinned
**skin** thin-skinned
**skull** get something through someone's thick skull
**sky** as high as the sky
**sky** out of a clear blue sky
**sky** pie in the sky
**sky** sky's the limit
**slap** slap in the face
**slate** start (off) with a clean slate
**slaughter** like a lamb to the slaughter
**slaughter** like lambs to the slaughter
**sleep** Let sleeping dogs lie.
**sleep** not sleep a wink
**sleep** put someone or something to sleep
**sleep** sleep in
**sleep** sleep like a log
**sleep** sleep on something
**sleeve** laugh up one's sleeve
**slice** slice of the cake
**slide** let something slide
**slip** let something slip by
**slip** let the chance slip by
**slip** slip of the tongue
**slip** slip one's mind
**slip** slip through someone's fingers
**slippery** as slippery as an eel
**slow** Slow and steady wins the race.
**slow** slow on the uptake
**smack** smack-dab in the middle
**small** big frog in a small pond
**small** small fry
**small** small print
**small** small-time
**small** thankful for small blessings
**smart** as smart as a fox

**spot** have a soft spot in one's heart for someone or something
**spot** hit the spot
**spot** in a (tight) spot
**spot** Johnny-on-the-spot
**spot** on the spot
**spot** rooted to the spot
**spot** X marks the spot.
**spotlight** in the spotlight
**spotlight** steal the spotlight
**spread** spread it on thick
**spread** spread like wildfire
**spread** spread oneself too thin
**spring** no spring chicken
**spur** on the spur of the moment
**square** square deal
**square** square meal
**square** square peg in a round hole
**square** square up to someone or something
**square** square up with someone
**squeak** squeak by
**stab** stab someone in the back
**stag** go stag
**stage** at this stage (of the game)
**stake** burn someone at the stake
**stake** pull up stakes
**stand** make someone's hair stand on end
**stand** not have a leg to stand on
**stand** stand corrected
**stand** stand on one's own two feet
**stand** stand one's ground
**stand** stand out a mile
**stand** stand up and be counted
**stand** standing joke
**stand** take the stand
**standstill** come to a standstill
**star** get stars in one's eyes
**star** see stars
**star** thank one's lucky stars
**stare** stare someone in the face
**start** from start to finish
**start** get off to a flying start
**start** off to a running start
**start** start (off) with a clean slate
**start** start from scratch
**station** as busy as Grand Central Station
**stay** stay put
**steady** Slow and steady wins the race.

**steal** steal a base
**steal** steal a march (on someone)
**steal** steal someone's thunder
**steal** steal the show
**steal** steal the spotlight
**steam** blow off steam
**steam** full steam ahead
**steam** let off steam
**steam** under one's own steam
**stem** from stem to stern
**step** step on it
**step** step on someone's toes
**step** step on the gas
**step** step out of line
**step** watch one's step
**stern** from stem to stern
**stew** stew in one's own juice
**stew** Too many cooks spoil the stew.
**stick** end up with the short end of the stick
**stick** get the short end of the stick
**stick** have one's words stick in one's throat
**stick** one's words stick in one's throat
**stick** stick one's foot in one's mouth
**stick** stick one's neck out
**stick** stick one's nose in(to something)
**stick** stick out a mile
**stick** stick to one's guns
**stiff** keep a stiff upper lip
**still** so still you could hear a pin drop
**still** Still waters run deep.
**stir** stir up a hornet's nest
**stitches** keep someone in stitches
**stock** have something in stock
**stock** in stock
**stock** lock, stock, and barrel
**stomach** have eyes bigger than one's stomach
**stomach** one's eyes are bigger than one's stomach
**stomach** turn someone's stomach
**stone** cast the first stone
**stone** have a heart of stone
**stone** kill two birds with one stone
**stone** leave no stone unturned

**tab** pick up the tab
**table** clear the table
**table** lay one's cards on the table
**table** put one's cards on the table
**table** under the table
**tack** get down to brass tacks
**tag** tag along
**tail** can't make heads or tails (out) of someone or something
**tail** have one's tail between one's legs
**tail** in two shakes of a lamb's tail
**tail** one's tail is between one's legs
**tail** tail wagging the dog
**tailspin** go into a tailspin
**take** as a duck takes to water
**take** Give one an inch, and one will take a mile.
**take** If you give one an inch, one will take a mile.
**take** sit up and take notice
**take** take a back seat (to someone)
**take** take a leaf out of someone's book
**take** take a load off one's feet
**take** take a nosedive
**take** take cold
**take** take forty winks
**take** take it or leave it
**take** take liberties with someone or something
**take** take one's cue from someone
**take** take one's death (of cold)
**take** take one's medicine
**take** take someone or something at face value
**take** take someone or something by storm
**take** take someone or something for granted
**take** take someone under one's wing
**take** take someone's breath away
**take** take something in stride
**take** take something lying down
**take** take something on faith
**take** take something on the chin
**take** take something with a grain of salt
**take** take something with a pinch of salt

**take** take the bitter with the sweet
**take** take the bull by the horns
**take** take the law into one's own hands
**take** take the stand
**take** take the words (right) out of one's mouth
**take** take to one's heels
**take** take up one's abode somewhere
**take** That takes care of that.
**take** You can't take it with you.
**tale** tall tale
**tale** tell its own tale
**tale** tell tales out of school
**talk** Money talks.
**talk** talk a blue streak
**talk** talk in circles
**talk** talk of the town
**talk** talk shop
**talk** talk through one's hat
**talk** talk until one is blue in the face
**tall** tall story
**tall** tall tale
**tangent** go off on a tangent
**tape** red tape
**tar** tarred with the same brush
**target** on target
**target** sitting target
**taste** in bad taste
**taste** in poor taste
**taste** leave a bad taste in someone's mouth
**taste** There's no accounting for taste.
**tat** give someone tit for tat
**taut** run a taut ship
**tea** not someone's cup of tea
**teach** teach one's grandmother to suck eggs
**teach** You can't teach an old dog new tricks.
**teacher** be the teacher's pet
**teapot** tempest in a teapot
**tear** break (out) into tears
**tear** shed crocodile tears
**tear** tear one's hair (out)
**teeth** armed to the teeth
**teeth** as scarce as hens' teeth
**teeth** by the skin of one's teeth

teeth  fly in the teeth of someone or something

teeth  get one's teeth into something

teeth  grit one's teeth

teeth  lie through one's teeth

teeth  no skin off someone's teeth

teeth  pull someone's or something's teeth

teeth  scarcer than hens' teeth

teeth  set someone's teeth on edge

teeth  sink one's teeth into something

teething  teething troubles

tell  tell its own story

tell  tell its own tale

tell  tell one to one's face

tell  tell tales out of school

temper  hold one's temper

temper  keep one's temper

temper  lose one's temper

temperature  run a temperature

tempest  tempest in a teapot

tenterhooks  keep someone on tenterhooks

term  contradiction in terms

test  acid test

test  put someone to the test

tether  at the end of one's tether

than  Actions speak louder than words.

than  bite off more than one can chew

than  Half a loaf is better than none.

than  have eyes bigger than one's stomach

than  holier-than-thou

than  in less than no time

than  none other than

than  not see further than the end of one's nose

than  One's bark is worse than one's bite.

than  one's eyes are bigger than one's stomach

than  scarcer than hens' teeth

than  There's more than one way to skin a cat.

than  wear more than one hat

thank  thank one's lucky stars

thankful  thankful for small blessings

thanks  vote of thanks

that  All that glitters is not gold.

that  All's well that ends well.

that  as bad as all that

that  bite the hand that feeds one

that  hair of the dog (that bit one)

that  kill the goose that laid the golden egg

that  look like the cat that swallowed the canary

that  powers that be

that  seeing that

that  ships that pass in the night

that  That takes care of that.

that  That's the last straw.

that  That's the straw that broke the camel's back.

that  That's the ticket.

that  You can say that again!

themselves  speak for themselves

there  There are plenty of other fish in the sea.

there  There will be the devil to pay.

there  There's more than one way to skin a cat.

there  There's no accounting for taste.

there  Where there's a will, there's a way.

there  Where there's smoke, there's fire.

they  count one's chickens before they hatch

thick  as thick as pea soup

thick  as thick as thieves

thick  get something into someone's thick head

thick  get something through someone's thick skull

thick  lay it on thick

thick  pour it on thick

thick  spread it on thick

thick  thick and fast

thick  thick-skinned

thick  through thick and thin

thicken  plot thickens

thief  as thick as thieves

thin  on thin ice

thin  out of thin air

**thin** pull something out of thin air
**thin** skate on thin ice
**thin** spread oneself too thin
**thin** thin on top
**thin** thin-skinned
**thin** through thick and thin
**thin** vanish into thin air
**thing** first thing (in the morning)
**thing** First things first.
**thing** get into the swing of things
**thing** little knowledge is a dangerous thing
**thing** see things
**thing** strike a balance (between two things)
**thing** very thing
**think** come to think of it
**think** put on one's thinking cap
**think** think better of something
**think** think on one's feet
**think** think the world of someone or something
**think** wishful thinking
**this** at this stage (of the game)
**this** not long for this world
**this** out of this world
**Thomas** doubting Thomas
**thorn** be a thorn in someone's side
**thou** holier-than-thou
**thought** food for thought
**thought** get second thoughts about someone or something
**thought** lose one's train of thought
**thought** lost in thought
**thought** on second thought
**thought** penny for your thoughts
**thought** Perish the thought.
**thousand** one in a thousand
**thrash** thrash something out
**thread** hang by a thread
**three** like a three-ring circus
**three** Two's company(, three's a crowd).
**throat** cut one's (own) throat
**throat** get a lump in one's throat
**throat** have a frog in one's throat
**throat** have one's words stick in one's throat
**throat** one's words stick in one's throat

**through** been through the mill
**through** get something through someone's thick skull
**through** go through channels
**through** go through the motions
**through** go through the roof
**through** lie through one's teeth
**through** pay through the nose (for something)
**through** put one through one's paces
**through** put someone through the wringer
**through** put something through its paces
**through** slip through someone's fingers
**through** talk through one's hat
**through** through thick and thin
**throw** stone's throw (away)
**throw** throw a monkey wrench in the works
**throw** throw caution to the wind
**throw** throw cold water on something
**throw** throw down the gauntlet
**throw** throw good money after bad
**throw** throw in the sponge
**throw** throw in the towel
**throw** throw oneself at someone's feet
**throw** throw oneself at the mercy of the court
**throw** throw oneself on the mercy of the court
**throw** throw someone a curve
**throw** throw someone for a loop
**throw** throw someone to the wolves
**throw** throw something into the bargain
**thumb** all thumbs
**thumb** get someone under one's thumb
**thumb** have a green thumb
**thumb** rule of thumb
**thumb** thumb a ride
**thumb** thumb one's nose at someone or something
**thumb** twiddle one's thumbs

**to** cut off one's nose to spite one's face

**to** cut someone or something to the bone

**to** cut someone to the quick

**to** dance to another tune

**to** date back (to something)

**to** dead to the world

**to** down to the wire

**to** down-to-earth

**to** drink to excess

**to** drive someone to the wall

**to** Early to bed, early to rise(, makes a man healthy, wealthy, and wise).

**to** everything from A to Z

**to** everything from soup to nuts

**to** eyeball-to-eyeball

**to** find it in one's heart (to do something)

**to** fit someone to a T

**to** Fools rush in (where angels fear to tread).

**to** force someone to the wall

**to** from hand to hand

**to** from pillar to post

**to** from rags to riches

**to** from start to finish

**to** from stem to stern

**to** from top to bottom

**to** get down to brass tacks

**to** get down to business

**to** get down to work

**to** get off to a flying start

**to** get time to catch one's breath

**to** get to first base (with someone or something)

**to** get to one's feet

**to** get to the bottom of something

**to** get to the heart of the matter

**to** get to the point

**to** get up enough nerve (to do something)

**to** go to bat for someone

**to** go to Davy Jones's locker

**to** go to pot

**to** go to rack and ruin

**to** go to seed

**to** go to someone's head

**to** go to the dogs

**to** go to the wall

**to** go to town

**to** go to wrack and ruin

**to** grind to a halt

**to** hammer something home (to someone)

**to** Hang on to your hat!

**to** hardly have time to breathe

**to** have a bone to pick (with someone)

**to** have an ax to grind

**to** have money to burn

**to** have one's back to the wall

**to** have one's ear to the ground

**to** have other fish to fry

**to** have someone dead to rights

**to** have something to spare

**to** have the presence of mind to do something

**to** Here's to someone or something.

**to** Hold on to your hat!

**to** if worst comes to worst

**to** in no mood to do something

**to** keep one's ear to the ground

**to** keep one's nose to the grindstone

**to** keep something to oneself

**to** keep to oneself

**to** lay something to waste

**to** lay waste to something

**to** lead up to something

**to** leave one to one's fate

**to** lend an ear (to someone)

**to** lend oneself or itself to something

**to** like a lamb to the slaughter

**to** like lambs to the slaughter

**to** live from hand to mouth

**to** look to one's laurels

**to** made to measure

**to** man-to-man

**to** march to a different drummer

**to** move heaven and earth to do something

**to** next to nothing

**to** not able to see the forest for the trees

**to** not have a leg to stand on

**to** not know enough to come in out of the rain

**to** not up to scratch

**to** not up to snuff

**to** off to a running start

**tongue** tongue-in-cheek
**too** cut something (too) fine
**too** eat one's cake and have it too
**too** have one's cake and eat it too
**too** have too many irons in the fire
**too** none too
**too** spread oneself too thin
**too** too good to be true
**too** Too many cooks spoil the broth.
**too** Too many cooks spoil the stew.
**toot** toot one's own horn
**tooth** eye for an eye (and a tooth for a tooth)
**tooth** fight someone or something tooth and nail
**tooth** go at it tooth and nail
**tooth** go over something with a fine-tooth comb
**tooth** have a sweet tooth
**tooth** search something with a fine-tooth comb
**top** at the top of one's lungs
**top** at the top of one's voice
**top** from top to bottom
**top** off the top of one's head
**top** on top
**top** over the top
**top** thin on top
**torch** carry a torch (for someone)
**torch** carry the torch
**toss** toss one's hat into the ring
**totem** high man on the totem pole
**totem** low man on the totem pole
**touch** have the Midas touch
**touch** touch someone for something
**tough** tough act to follow
**tough** tough row to hoe
**towel** throw in the towel
**tower** live in an ivory tower
**tower** tower of strength
**town** go to town
**town** man about town
**town** out on the town
**town** paint the town red
**town** talk of the town
**track** drop in one's tracks
**track** get the inside track
**track** have a one-track mind

**track** jump the track
**track** on the wrong track
**track** other side of the tracks
**trade** jack-of-all-trades
**trade** know (all) the tricks of the trade
**train** lose one's train of thought
**train** ride the gravy train
**tread** Fools rush in (where angels fear to tread).
**tread** tread on someone's toes
**treat** Dutch treat
**treatment** get the red-carpet treatment
**treatment** give someone the red-carpet treatment
**tree** bark up the wrong tree
**tree** not able to see the forest for the trees
**trial** on trial
**trick** bag of tricks
**trick** know (all) the tricks of the trade
**trick** use every trick in the book
**trick** You can't teach an old dog new tricks.
**trigger** quick on the trigger
**trot** trot something out
**trouble** ask for trouble
**trouble** drown one's troubles
**trouble** fish in troubled waters
**trouble** pour oil on troubled water
**trouble** teething troubles
**true** come true
**true** dream come true
**true** hold true
**true** ring true
**true** show one's (true) colors
**true** too good to be true
**true** true to one's word
**truth** moment of truth
**try** try one's wings (out)
**try** try someone's patience
**tube** down the tube(s)
**tuck** nip and tuck
**tune** can't carry a tune
**tune** dance to another tune
**tune** out of tune (with someone or something)
**tunnel** see the light (at the end of the tunnel)
**turn** do someone a good turn

**up** get one's Irish up
**up** get something sewed up
**up** get something wrapped up
**up** get up enough nerve (to do something)
**up** get up on the wrong side of the bed
**up** get worked up (over something)
**up** get worked up about something
**up** gird (up) one's loins
**up** give up the ghost
**up** go up in flames
**up** go up in smoke
**up** hang one's hat up somewhere
**up** hold one's head up
**up** hold up one's end (of the bargain)
**up** keep up (with the Joneses)
**up** keep up (with the times)
**up** kick up a fuss
**up** kick up a row
**up** kick up a storm
**up** kick up one's heels
**up** kiss and make up
**up** land up somehow or somewhere
**up** laugh up one's sleeve
**up** lead up to something
**up** learn something from the bottom up
**up** make something up out of whole cloth
**up** make up for lost time
**up** move up (in the world)
**up** not up to scratch
**up** not up to snuff
**up** one's number is up
**up** pick up the tab
**up** prick up one's ears
**up** pull oneself up (by one's own bootstraps)
**up** pull up stakes
**up** put up a (brave) front
**up** rake something up
**up** run something up
**up** screw up one's courage
**up** settle up with someone
**up** shape up or ship out
**up** sit up and take notice
**up** square up to someone or something

**up** square up with someone
**up** stand up and be counted
**up** stir up a hornet's nest
**up** strike up a friendship
**up** take up one's abode somewhere
**up** turn one's nose up at someone or something
**up** up a blind alley
**up** up in arms
**up** up in the air
**up** up to one's ears (in something)
**up** up to one's neck (in something)
**up** up to par
**up** whoop it up
**upon** put upon someone
**upper** get the upper hand (on someone)
**upper** keep a stiff upper lip
**upper** upper crust
**upset** upset the applecart
**uptake** quick on the uptake
**uptake** slow on the uptake
**use** use every trick in the book
**utter** not utter a word
**vacation** on vacation
**value** take someone or something at face value
**vanish** vanish into thin air
**variety** Variety is the spice of life.
**vent** vent one's spleen
**venture** Nothing ventured, nothing gained.
**verse** recite something chapter and verse
**very** under someone's (very) nose
**very** very thing
**vest** play one's cards close to one's vest
**vest** play one's cards close to the vest
**vested** have a vested interest in something
**vicious** in a vicious circle
**victor** To the victor belong the spoils.
**victory** landslide victory
**view** bird's-eye view
**villain** villain of the piece
**vine** die on the vine
**vine** wither on the vine
**virtue** by virtue of something

voice at the top of one's voice
voice lower one's voice
vote vote a straight ticket
vote vote of confidence
vote vote of thanks
voyage maiden voyage
wag cause (some) tongues to wag
wag tail wagging the dog
wagon fix someone's wagon
wagon on the wagon
wait on a waiting list
wait wait on someone hand and foot
wait wait-and-see attitude
wait waiting in the wings
walk all walks of life
walk cock of the walk
walk walk a tightrope
walk walk away with something
walk walk off with something
walk walk on air
walk walk on eggs
walk walk the floor
wall bang one's head against a brick wall
wall beat one's head against the wall
wall drive someone to the wall
wall force someone to the wall
wall go to the wall
wall have one's back to the wall
wall one's back is to the wall
wall press someone to the wall
wall push someone to the wall
wall run into a stone wall
wall see the (hand)writing on the wall
wall Walls have ears.
want want for nothing
want Waste not, want not.
warm warm the bench
warm warm the cockles of someone's heart
warrant sign one's own death warrant
wart warts and all
was time was (when)
wash come out in the wash
wash wash one's dirty linen in public
wash wash one's hands of someone or something

wasn't Rome wasn't built in a day.
waste Haste makes waste.
waste lay something to waste
waste lay waste to something
waste Waste not, want not.
waste waste one's breath
watch bear watching
watch watch one's step
watch watch someone like a hawk
watch watched pot never boils
water as a duck takes to water
water dash cold water on something
water fish in troubled waters
water get one's head above water
water hold water
water in deep water
water keep one's head above water
water like a fish out of water
water like water off a duck's back
water make someone's mouth water
water not hold water
water of the first water
water pour cold water on something
water pour oil on troubled water
water Still waters run deep.
water throw cold water on something
water water under the bridge
way cut both ways
way find one's or its way somewhere
way get something under way
way have the right-of-way
way look the other way
way mend one's ways
way rub someone the wrong way
way rub someone's fur the wrong way
way There's more than one way to skin a cat.
way Where there's a will, there's a way.
weak as weak as a kitten
weakness have a weakness for someone or something
wealthy Early to bed, early to rise(, makes a man healthy, wealthy, and wise).

305

**wear** If the shoe fits, wear it.
**wear** none the worse for wear
**wear** wear more than one hat
**wear** wear off
**wear** wear out one's welcome
**weather** fair-weather friend
**weather** keep one's weather eye open
**weather** lovely weather for ducks
**weather** under the weather
**wedding** shotgun wedding
**weed** weed someone or something out
**weeper** Finders keepers(, losers weepers).
**weight** carry the weight of the world on one's shoulders
**weight** carry weight (with someone)
**weight** worth one's or its weight in gold
**welcome** wear out one's welcome
**well** All's well that ends well.
**well** hail-fellow-well-met
**well** well-fixed
**well** well-heeled
**well** well-off
**well** well-to-do
**were** as it were
**wet** as mad as a wet hen
**wet** get one's feet wet
**wet** wet behind the ears
**wet** wet blanket
**what** come what may
**what** give someone what for
**what** just what the doctor ordered
**what** know what's what
**what** practice what you preach
**what** What about (doing) something?
**what** What about (having) something?
**what** What is sauce for the goose is sauce for the gander.
**what** what makes someone tick
**wheel** put one's shoulder to the wheel
**when** cross a bridge when one comes to it
**when** time was (when)

**when** When in Rome, do as the Romans do.
**when** When the cat's away, the mice will play.
**when** when the time is ripe
**where** Fools rush in (where angels fear to tread).
**where** give credit where credit is due
**where** Put your money where your mouth is!
**where** Where there's a will, there's a way.
**where** Where there's smoke, there's fire.
**wherefore** whys and wherefores of something
**which** know which side one's bread is buttered on
**while** fiddle while Rome burns
**while** Make hay while the sun is shining.
**while** make something worth someone's while
**while** strike while the iron is hot
**while** worth someone's while
**whisker** by a whisker
**whistle** blow the whistle (on someone)
**whistle** whistle for something
**white** as white as the driven snow
**white** in black and white
**white** white elephant
**who** He laughs best who laughs last.
**who** He who laughs last, laughs longest.
**whole** make something up out of whole cloth
**whole** whole shooting match
**whoop** whoop it up
**why** whys and wherefores of something
**wide** give someone or something a wide berth
**wide** wide of the mark
**wild** sow one's wild oats
**wild** wild-goose chase
**wildfire** spread like wildfire
**will** Give one an inch, and one will take a mile.
**will** heads will roll

**with** start (off) with a clean slate
**with** strike a chord (with someone)
**with** take liberties with someone or something
**with** take something with a grain of salt
**with** take something with a pinch of salt
**with** take the bitter with the sweet
**with** tarred with the same brush
**with** walk away with something
**with** walk off with something
**with** with a will
**with** with all one's heart and soul
**with** with both hands tied behind one's back
**with** with every (other) breath
**with** with flying colors
**with** with it
**with** with no strings attached
**with** with one hand tied behind one's back
**with** with the best will in the world
**with** with the naked eye
**with** You can't take it with you.
**wither** wither on the vine
**within** live within one's means
**within** within an inch of one's life
**without** without any strings attached
**without** without batting an eye
**without** without further ado
**woe** woe betide someone
**woe** Woe is me!
**wolf** cry wolf
**wolf** keep the wolf from the door
**wolf** throw someone to the wolves
**wolf** wolf in sheep's clothing
**woman** woman-to-woman
**wonder** nine days' wonder
**wood** knock on wood
**woods** babe in the woods
**woods** out of the woods
**wool** pull the wool over someone's eyes
**wool** woolgathering
**word** Actions speak louder than words.

**word** break one's word
**word** by word of mouth
**word** eat one's words
**word** from the word go
**word** get a word in edgeways
**word** get a word in edgewise
**word** get the final word
**word** get the last word
**word** get the word
**word** go back on one's word
**word** hang on someone's every word
**word** have one's words stick in one's throat
**word** keep one's word
**word** not utter a word
**word** one's words stick in one's throat
**word** put in a good word (for someone)
**word** put words into someone's mouth
**word** take the words (right) out of one's mouth
**word** true to one's word
**work** all in a day's work
**work** All work and no play makes Jack a dull boy.
**work** dirty work
**work** get down to work
**work** get worked up (over something)
**work** get worked up about something
**work** make fast work of someone or something
**work** make short work of someone or something
**work** work like a horse
**work** work one's fingers to the bone
**work** work out for the best
**work** work something off
**works** throw a monkey wrench in the works
**world** carry the weight of the world on one's shoulders
**world** come down in the world
**world** come up in the world
**world** dead to the world
**world** in a world of one's own